In the Hour of Fate and

THE AZRIELI SERIES OF HOLOCAUST SURVIVOR MEMOIRS: PUBLISHED TITLES

ENGLISH TITLES

In the Hour of Fate and Danger

Ferenc Andai

TRANSLATED FROM HUNGARIAN
BY MARIETTA MORRY AND LYNDA MUIR

THE AZRIELI FOUNDATION · www.azrielifoundation.org

First published in Hungarian as *Mint tanu szólni: Bori történet* (To Bear Witness: A Story of Bor), by Ab Ovo, 2003. Translated by Marietta Morry and Lynda Muir, 2017. For all credits and permissions, see pages 237 to 239.

Cover design by Endpaper Studio
with photograph by James A. Guilliam · Photolibrary · Getty Images
Book design by Mark Goldstein
Map on page xxvii by François Blanc
Endpaper maps by Martin Gilbert

LIBRARY AND ARCHIVES CANADA CATALOGUING IN PUBLICATION

In the Hour of Fate and Danger / Ferenc Andai; translated from the Hungarian by Marietta Morry and Lynda Muir. Other titles: Mint tanu szólni. English

Andai, Ferenc, 1925–2013 author. Azrieli Foundation, publisher.
Azrieli series of Holocaust survivor memoirs. Series XII
Translation of: Mint tanu szólni: bori történet.
Canadiana 20200198610 · ISBN 9781988065564 (softcover) · 8 7 6 5 4 3 2 1

LCSH: Andai, Ferenc, 1925–2013 · LCSH: Holocaust, Jewish (1939–1945) — Personal narratives. LCSH: Concentration camps — Serbia — Bor. LCSH: Bor (Concentration camp) · LCSH: Jews, Hungarian — Serbia — Bor — Biography. LCGFT: Autobiographies.

LCC DS135.S353 A5313 2020 · DDC 940.53/18092 — DC23

The Azrieli Foundation's Holocaust Survivor Memoirs Program

Naomi Azrieli, Publisher

Jody Spiegel, Program Director
Arielle Berger, Managing Editor
Matt Carrington, Editor
Devora Levin, Editor and Special Projects Coordinator
Elizabeth Lasserre, Senior Editor, French-Language Editions
Elin Beaumont, Community and Education Initiatives
Catherine Person, Education and Academic Initiatives/French Editor
Stephanie Corazza, Academic and Education Initiatives
Marc-Olivier Cloutier, School and Education Initiatives
Elizabeth Banks, Digital Asset Curator and Archivist
Catherine Quintal, Digital Communications Assistant

Mark Goldstein, Art Director
François Blanc, Cartographer
Bruno Paradis, Layout, French-Language Editions

Contents

Series Preface:
In their own words...

In telling these stories, the writers have liberated themselves. For so many years we did not speak about it, even when we became free people living in a free society. Now, when at last we are writing about what happened to us in this dark period of history, knowing that our stories will be read and live on, it is possible for us to feel truly free. These unique historical documents put a face on what was lost, and allow readers to grasp the enormity of what happened to six million Jews — one story at a time.

David J. Azrieli, C.M., C.Q., M.Arch
Holocaust survivor and founder, The Azrieli Foundation

Since the end of World War II, approximately 40,000 Jewish Holocaust survivors have immigrated to Canada. Who they are, where they came from, what they experienced and how they built new lives for themselves and their families are important parts of our Canadian heritage. The Azrieli Foundation's Holocaust Survivor Memoirs Program was established in 2005 to preserve and share the memoirs written by those who survived the twentieth-century Nazi genocide of the Jews of Europe and later made their way to Canada. The memoirs encourage readers to engage thoughtfully and critically with the complexities of the Holocaust and to create meaningful connections with the lives of survivors.

Millions of individual stories are lost to us forever. By preserving the stories written by survivors and making them widely available to a broad audience, the Azrieli Foundation's Holocaust Survivor Memoirs Program seeks to sustain the memory of all those who perished at the hands of hatred, abetted by indifference and apathy. The personal accounts of those who survived against all odds are as different as the people who wrote them, but all demonstrate the courage, strength, wit and luck that it took to prevail and survive in such terrible adversity. The memoirs are also moving tributes to people — strangers and friends — who risked their lives to help others, and who, through acts of kindness and decency in the darkest of moments, frequently helped the persecuted maintain faith in humanity and courage to endure. These accounts offer inspiration to all, as does the survivors' desire to share their experiences so that new generations can learn from them.

The Holocaust Survivor Memoirs Program collects, archives and publishes select survivor memoirs and makes the print editions available free of charge to educational institutions and Holocaust-education programs across Canada. They are also available for sale online to the general public. All revenues to the Azrieli Foundation from the sales of the Azrieli Series of Holocaust Survivor Memoirs go toward the publishing and educational work of the memoirs program.

⌒

The Azrieli Foundation would like to express appreciation to the following people for their invaluable efforts in producing this book: Doris Bergen, Dr. András Bleyer, Mark Duffus (Maracle Inc), Mirjana Jovicic, Tilman Lewis, Marietta Morry, Lynda Muir, Susan Roitman, Irina Sadovina, Stephen Ullstrom, and Margie Wolfe & Emma Rodgers of Second Story Press.

About the Footnotes and Glossary

The following memoir contains a number of terms, concepts and historical references that may be unfamiliar to the reader. English translations of foreign-language words and terms have been added, as have parentheses for the names of present-day towns, cities or streets. Footnotes have been included for clarification, information relevant to the memoir and dates of Miklós Radnóti's poems. For general information on major organizations; significant historical events and people; geographical locations; religious and cultural terms; and foreign-language words and expressions that will help give context and background to the events described in the text, please see the glossary beginning on page 195.

Introduction

Ferenc Andai's memoir is an important addition to our understanding of the forced labour camp complex at Bor in Serbia, where some 6,000 Hungarian, mostly Jewish, men were imprisoned. Andai supplies not only many details about the difficult labour the men carried out and the deprivations they suffered, he also illustrates important aspects of the group dynamics between the prisoners and their urge to maintain whatever normalcy they could in the extreme situation in which they found themselves. Among the youngest of the prisoners in Bor, Andai was befriended by a number of somewhat older men, including the poet Miklós Radnóti, who looms large in Andai's memoir. Andai's references to Radnóti also add important fragments of information to this chapter of the poet's life in the few months before his death.

At the centre of Andai's story is the Hungarian forced labour service, into which Andai is conscripted in May 1944 and which has a long history preceding the events in this memoir. In 1939, Hungary began to reorganize its military in preparation for the likely upcoming war. As a result, the immediate roots of the Hungarian forced labour service as it developed during World War II may be found in Law no. 11 issued on March 11, 1939. This law created a framework for

---

Note: This introduction is in part based on the introduction I wrote for the book of testimonies from Bor. Adina Drechsler, ed., *Bor, Sipuro Shel Machane Leavodot Kfia 1943–1944, Mivchar Aduyot* (Jerusalem: Yad Vashem, 2015) [Hebrew].

military service for those in Hungary who were considered unworthy of carrying arms for the country. Instead, they were to engage in labour for the military. Although the labour service was not set up specifically for Jews, by December 1940 Jews serving in the military were being moved into labour units. A new decree, announced in April 1941 and implemented in August 1941, known as Order 27 300, stipulated that Jews could serve only in labour companies, and all Jewish military officers were stripped of their ranks. By definition, Jews were now regarded as unworthy of bearing arms for Hungary. The same decree also called for the wearing of yellow armbands by Jewish labourers and white armbands by Christian labourers who were considered Jews by a racial definition. The last step in the separation of the Jews from other men in the Hungarian military came with the order of March 17, 1942, calling for Jews to no longer be issued uniforms or be allowed to wear them, but to wear only civilian clothing with armbands.

By September 1942, over 70,000 men served in the labour service. In the area of military operations on the Eastern Front, there were 151 units, with about 38,000 men. Out of these units, 130 were comprised of Jews, six of Christians by religion but of Jewish origins, and fifteen of people considered politically unreliable. In addition, on the home front another 33,000 men had been drafted for labour service in another 152 units. Nearly half of these 152 units, seventy-three, were made up of minorities — Romanians, Serbs, Croatians and Ruthenians; the rest were primarily Jews. According to the first serious research on the subject by the late Elek Karsai, about 100,000 Jewish men were eventually drafted into the labour service. About 45,000 served on the Eastern Front, and of that number 80 per cent died. From Hungary, some 6,000 mostly Jewish labourers were also sent to work in the production of copper in the mines at Bor, Serbia, which is the subject of Andai's memoir.[1]

---

1   Robert Rozett, Conscripted Slaves, *Hungarian Jewish Forced Laborers on the Eastern Front during the Second World War* (Jerusalem: Yad Vashem, 2013), 44–49.

The Hungarian forced labourers were under the authority of Hungarian officers, non-commissioned officers and regular soldiers, who were responsible for the companies. Nonetheless, the forced labourers were not considered to be soldiers, even though they were subject to military authority and discipline. They were not free to leave their service and when they did so they were considered deserters.[2]

The basic task of the men of the labour service was to perform labour of all kinds. Some with skills — like electricians, carpenters, mechanics, interpreters, and sometimes physicians — used their knowledge, and generally received somewhat better treatment than other forced labourers. Most men, however, were made to perform work that required no special skill and was backbreaking. In Hungary proper the labour servicemen were made to work in agriculture, factories, construction, and road building and maintenance.[3]

On the Eastern Front, the labour service engendered great suffering and became deadly because of a constellation of factors. First and foremost were the unbridled brutality of the war and the entrenched hatred and antisemitism of many of the Hungarian staff men who commanded them. Often present in zones of battle, many men fell to the fighting, even though they were not soldiers. In a few instances Jewish labour servicemen were massacred by the SS — but there are only a handful of known incidents in the east. In not a few cases the Hungarian soldiers in charge of the men put them in patently lethal situations, like clearing minefields without proper training and equipment. Trailing not far behind these factors were the extreme weather in the occupied areas of the Soviet Union especially in winter, immeasurably inadequate housing, lack of hygiene, periods of severe hunger, rampant sickness and above all, the gruelling, backbreaking labour that sometimes also was exceedingly dangerous to perform. The punishments meted out for real or imagined infractions of the rules could also be deadly, especially when they were

---

2 Ibid., 109–113.

3 Ibid., 91–93.

implemented with maximum sadism — which was quite common. To a very large extent, survival or death depended on the treatment the men received at the hands of their officers and the soldiers who were responsible for them.[4]

Almost universally, the labour servicemen on the Eastern Front suffered from lack of food — they were malnourished to the point of starvation. Until well into 1943, the men of the labour service units suffered discrimination at the hands of the military regarding the amount and quality of their rations on an official level. After that orders were given to treat them like Hungarian soldiers, but in most cases the orders were not followed. In addition, very frequently the Hungarian soldiers attached to the labour companies stole the labourers' food. Sometimes they sold it back to them for exorbitant prices, sometimes they sold it on the black market, and sometimes they merely enjoyed it themselves.[5]

About 16,000 Jewish forced labourers on the Eastern Front surrendered to the Soviet forces and became prisoners of war. Most of these did so around the battle at Voronezh in January 1943, where the Hungarian Second Army on the Stalingrad line was pulverized. A significant number also did so in summer 1944 when the Hungarians were being pushed back into Hungary proper by the Soviet advance. Almost universally the Jewish forced labourers believed that the Soviets would treat them well, since they had been the objects of persecution. This was not what happened. Rather they were treated by the Soviets as invaders and enemy soldiers. Three quarters of the labour servicemen who became prisoners died in captivity, especially in early 1943, owing to the disastrous conditions prevailing in the prisoner of war camps. Of those who survived this ordeal, many were released only well after the end of the war — some as late as the 1950s.[6]

As Soviet forces began conquering Hungary, many thousands of

---

4   Ibid., 113–124.
5   Ibid., 93–102.
6   Ibid., 216–223.

other Jews who served in the labour service within the confines of Hungarian territory began to be sent to the Austrian border to build fortifications. The brutal conditions caused many deaths, and then in early 1945, when the Jewish labourers were moved into Austria, some were massacred, most notably at Deutsch Schützen and Rechnitz. The rest were sent to various concentration camps, especially Mauthausen, Gunskirchen, Sachsenhausen, Dachau and Dora. In these concentration camps appalling conditions and cruel treatment led to many deaths, even on the verge of liberation and in its immediate wake.[7]

The story of Jewish forced labourers working in the copper mines at Bor is a special chapter within the saga of the Hungarian forced labour service. After the tremendous victory by Soviet forces against the Germans and their allies at Stalingrad and on the Stalingrad line early in 1943, the German leadership became more concerned than ever with ensuring the supply of various raw materials that were crucial to their military effort. The Germans had acquired the Bor copper mines in spring 1941, which were taken over and run by the Siemens Construction Union and Organisation Todt, the body established in Nazi Germany to carry out large-scale construction and engineering projects. In February 1943 it was decided to increase production there. The Germans pressured the Hungarians to accede to dispatching forced labourers to Bor and the Hungarians agreed to do so in June 1943. According to the agreement, three groups of 1,000 mostly Jewish forced labourers, but also a small number of Jehovah's Witnesses and Szekler Sabbatarians, would be sent to Bor in three waves during July. Over the course of the following months and into the summer of 1944, some 3,000 more men were sent there, making it over 6,000 all told. Some of the forced labourers sent to Bor had already served on the Eastern Front.[8]

---

7 Ibid., 241–245.

8 Randolph L. Braham, *The Politics of Genocide: The Holocaust in Hungary,* vol. 1 (New York: Columbia University Press, 1981), 330–335.

Andai writes that he was drafted, at the age of nineteen, into the forced labour service on May 16, 1944, just as the first wave of transports of Hungarian Jews began to be sent to Auschwitz-Birkenau. There were several different camps for the forced labourers at Bor: Westfalen, Laznica, Rhön, Bregenz, Berlin and Heidenau, which were administered jointly by the Hungarians and Organisation Todt.[9] Andai mentions spending one night at the Berlin Lager before being sent to the Heidenau Lager, where he would remain during his incarceration.

As on the Eastern Front, the Jewish labourers in Bor worked hard and suffered greatly primarily because of the brutal antisemitic harassment of the Hungarian soldiers stationed with them. By the time Andai arrived in the camp, Lieutenant Colonel Ede Marányi had been the commander for half a year, having taken over from Lieutenant Colonel András Balogh in December 1943 and having instituted a much harsher regime. Andai writes of him: "Marányi encourages his officers and subordinates to commit atrocities…. Alleged offences are punished with beatings, trussing-up, being thrown in pits, hog-tying."

By September 1944, owing to the military situation, it was decided to evacuate Bor in two stages. Andai describes this evacuation and the uncertainty surrounding it. On September 17, the first group of some 3,200 inmates left Bor along with about 100 Hungarian guards. They were marched by way of Belgrade to Zimony, reaching Titel on October 4. At Cservenka, with the collusion of the Hungarian guards, German and Bosnian SS men killed about 680 men on the night of October 7 and 8. Later, as the remnant continued their march, the Hungarian guards shot stragglers and additional smaller massacres took place. The survivors were marched toward the Austrian border, and many ended up in the German camps Dachau, Buchenwald, Oranienburg-Sachsenhausen or Flossenbürg.

---

9 Adina Drechsler, ed., *Bor, Sipuro Shel Machane Leavodot Kfia 1943–1944, Mivchar Aduyot* (Jerusalem: Yad Vashem, 2015) [Hebrew], 22.

The remaining forced labourers from Bor left the camp on September 29. Soon afterward, near the town of Majdanpek, Communist partisans serving under Josip Broz (Tito) freed the forced labourers and killed many of their guards. Some of the liberated labourers joined the partisans as fighters, whereas others tried to reach Romania, which had left its alliance with Germany previously in August. Andai was part of this contingent and describes in detail being freed, his decision not to join the partisans, and his subsequent "wanderings."

The most famous victim from Bor is probably the poet Miklós Radnóti. Andai frequently mentions Radnóti, the poems he composed at Bor and readings of his works. In this, Andai illustrates the efforts of prisoners to retain their humanity in the face of the inhumanity of Bor.

As Andai writes, Radnóti was taken from Bor in the first group to be evacuated. Although he survived the massacre at Cservenka, Radnóti was later shot as a straggler sometime between November 6 and November 10, 1944, and buried in a mass grave in Abda, near Győr in Hungary. When his body was exhumed after the war, his last writings were found on him.[10]

Miklós Radnóti was born on May 5, 1909, in Budapest. Orphaned of his mother at birth and of his father when he was twelve, Radnóti began writing poetry while a teenager. He also kept a journal for much of his life. Before the age of twenty he was a published poet, and in 1937 he won the prestigious Baumgarten poetry award.

Radnóti had a rather ambivalent attitude toward his Jewishness. He rejected traditional Judaism, was deeply steeped in Hungarian literature and culture, and was drawn to liberal Catholic ideas and socialism. His poetry reflected the danger he felt at the growth of the far-right throughout the 1930s and early 1940s. It seems he was profoundly moved when he saw Picasso's painting *Guernica* in Paris

---

10 Braham, 337.

before the war. Nevertheless, in his poetry, he never addressed this situation from an overtly Jewish perspective. [11]

Radnóti was called up for the labour service in September 1940 and was stationed in a number of places on the Romanian border and in Romania itself. He was discharged on December 18, 1940, after having suffered both physically and mentally from his service.[12] In July 1942 he was drafted for a second time. Remaining in Hungary, he nonetheless suffered from depression during this round of his service. From his journal entry of February 15, 1943, it is clear that he had been considering conversion to Catholicism for a while. He converted on May 2, 1943, and shortly after he was discharged from the labour service. Whether he converted from conviction or to rescue himself from the labour service, or some combination thereof, remains unclear.[13] Conversion, however, did not ultimately protect him. Three days after Andai received his draft notice in May 1944, Radnóti received his third summons to report for forced labour. This time, he was sent to Bor.

In Bor, as Andai attests, Radnóti continued to compose poetry about his plight and his longings. According to his biographer Zsuzsanna Ozsváth, "The extraordinary beauty of Radnóti's lyrics reached a new plateau in his Bor poems. Composed in *extremis*, these lyrics demarcate the rise of a new genre in poetry that has been defined by subsequent generations of authors and literary critics as Holocaust literature."[14]

The Hungarian forced labour service was not established in order to murder Jews, but especially on the Eastern Front from 1942 until 1944, in Austria toward the end of the war, and at Bor, the system

---

11 Zsuzsanna Ozsváth, *In the Footsteps of Orpheus, the Life and times of Miklós Radnóti* (Bloomington: Indiana Press, 2000), 1–5, 24, 117, 123.

12 Ibid., 150–153.

13 Ibid., 170–180.

14 Ibid., 203.

became quite deadly. For the labour servicemen who managed to remain in Hungary proper until the end of the war, it was not nearly as deadly. In fact, during the first mass wave of deportation from Hungary to Auschwitz-Birkenau (May 15, 1944, to July 9, 1944) and to a lesser extent during the Arrow Cross period from October 15, 1944, until the Soviet conquest of Hungary, being in a labour unit within Hungary actually protected many men from deportations.

Nevertheless, there is no question that the story of the Hungarian Jewish forced labourers is part and parcel of the experience of Jews during the Shoah. They were thrust into the vortex of this experience because Hungary embraced racial antisemitism and persecuted its Jews according to that ideology.

The story of Bor reflects the trajectory of the forced labour service. From the beginning it was generally harsh but not necessarily deadly, tainted strongly with antisemitism and sometimes extremely cruel. As events unfolded, however, it became more and more deadly. At first, service in Bor also was very harsh and coloured by antisemitism, but it was only after Marányi took command that it became much more brutal. At Cservenka and in its aftermath it became explicitly murderous for many of the forced labourers from Bor.

Andai's memoir sheds much light on the experiences of the labour servicemen at Bor and adds to our understanding of the camp, the labour service itself and the Holocaust of Hungarian Jewry. No less important, his memoir also stands as a testament to those who did not survive the ordeal.

Robert Rozett
Senior Historian,
International Institute for Holocaust Research, Yad Vashem
2020

Editorial and Translation Note

We are proud to publish the English edition of *Mint tanu szólni: Bori történet* (To Bear Witness: A Story of Bor) under the new title *In the Hour of Fate and Danger*. The original title of the book comes from a line in the poem "Eighth Eclogue" written by the renowned Miklós Radnóti. Canadian Holocaust survivor Ferenc Andai (1925–2013; born Ferenc Goldberger) wrote his memoir in Hungarian several decades after the events it describes and had the book published in Hungary in 2003, where it won the Radnóti Miklós National Prize the following year.

The translators and editors faced an array of issues particular to Andai's text. In this translation our intention was to preserve the original literary prose style, while finding English equivalents for its many similes and other figures of speech. Although the historical present is an unusual grammatical tense for a memoir in English, we decided to stay true to the original Hungarian by using it wherever the author did. The story is written as though a nineteen-year-old Andai is relating the events as they happen, but the erudite mind of Andai the historian and teacher of decades later is evident through-out the memoir.

This is not only the detailed account of the author's experience of Nazi and antisemitic atrocities, but also a vivid depiction and power-ful celebration of Jewish life and culture in that era. Andai eloquently describes a community of Hungarian men — artists and intellectuals, with the charismatic Miklós Radnóti, the famous Hungarian poet, among them — who were deported to a forced labour camp in Serbia, where they strove to nourish their spirits and intellects despite the cruel conditions. For the excerpts of Radnóti's poetry that Andai included, we sought out the best available translations.

Following the editorial style for our series of memoirs, we have only added explanatory footnotes where they were absolutely necessary to clarify or correct a historical fact while keeping true to the original narrative; any additional footnotes provide a timeline for the Radnóti poems that Andai used in the memoir. As is standard for all of our books, a glossary of historical terms is included. We have standardized the spelling of place names in Serbia, Hungary and Romania to the contemporary form and also included brief English translations in the memoir itself, where the original memoir had used non-Hungarian terms — transcribed fragments of speech in Serbian, Russian or Yiddish using a Hungarian phonetic system. The original memoir was separated into three long sections, and we have chosen to divide it into eleven chapters, creating new chapter titles. We have added a new introduction by historian Robert Rozett, as well as a moving and illuminating epilogue written by the author's daughter, Diana Andai.

We trust that this translation finds the right balance between fidelity to the original Hungarian text and accessibility to the English reader.

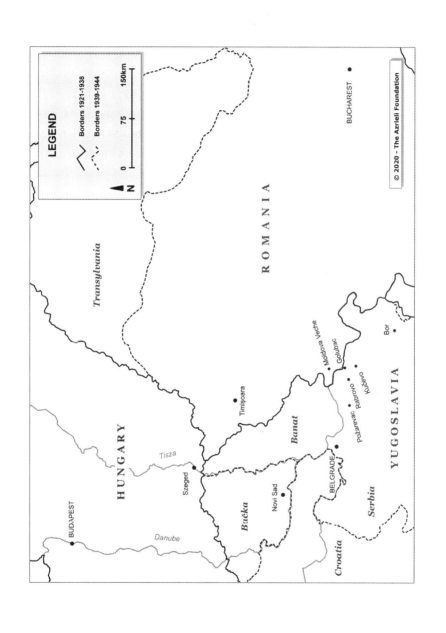

LEGEND

Borders 1921-1938
Borders 1939-1944

0   75   150km

N

HUNGARY

BUDAPEST

Danube

Tisza

Szeged

Bačka

Novi Sad

Transylvania

Timişoara

Banat

ROMANIA

BUCHAREST

Moldova Veche

Golubac

Požarevac

Rabrovo

Kučevo

Bor

BELGRADE

Croatia

Serbia

YUGOSLAVIA

And still you question why your heart
Is cramped and anxious in your breast?

　　Goethe, *Faust*

They were a hundred men at arms.
When the sun rose in the sky,
They all took a step forward.
Hours passed, without a sound:
They didn't bat an eye.
When the bells rang,
All of them took a step ahead.
So the day went, it was evening,
But when the first star blossomed in the sky,
All at once, they took a step ahead.
"Get back, get away, foul ghosts:
Back to your old night."
But no one answered; so, instead,
They took a step ahead, all in a ring.

　　Primo Levi, "Erano cento"

The Call-up Notice

On a Thursday morning at dawn, only a few sturdy German and Bulgarian soldiers wearing dusty boots are on duty at the railway station in Zaječar, Serbia. Prisoners are arriving in cattle cars on the wide-gauge tracks from Vác, Hungary. All of a sudden, the station comes alive. With the help of the German and Bulgarian uniformed men, the guards herd the stiff prisoners to the cars idling on the narrow-gauge tracks. Two pint-sized, rickety steam engines at the front and two at the rear are whistling away. The first engine is already snorting and spitting out dirty puffs of smoke; the two little engines keep hauling and pulling the coal cars deep into the mountains of the Serbian Erzgebirge, the Ore Mountains.

This time, it's not coal but people being transported by train from the station in Zaječar to the copper mine located thirty-five kilometres away. The more resourceful fellows have managed to find seats on the wooden benches. The landscape is astounding: the little "coffee grinder" — this train with its unusual cargo — winds through wild forests, rocky cliffs, valleys bursting with wildflowers. The tracks run along steep mountainsides, full of unexpected hairpin turns, with frightening slopes and inclines. The countryside is a tourist paradise.

In one of the strawberry-red coal cars — there must be about twenty of us here — a man with striking features and a friendly smile is holding forth. He is wearing knee breeches and a beige trench coat.

Every now and then, the mountain breeze ruffles his wavy brown hair. He is slim, with sparkling eyes. The ember has gone out in his English pipe. He is angular, with a somewhat prominent jaw and smiling eyes, and restless. He talks like a teacher.

We've been ascending, winding up a serpentine course for more than an hour, in a northwesterly direction. Where will this distressing odyssey end? We have already heard about the horrors of the copper mines. In the coal car the topics keep swirling around like colours in a kaleidoscope: Is there going to be a Soviet offensive? And when? Are there any Chetniks lurking in the area, or only Tito's Partisans? Does the Siemens Construction Union or Farbenindustrie (IG Farben) have a stake in this? What about the invasion? Is there going to be an invasion? And when? The pessimists and optimists are wrestling with a jumble of guesses and suppositions: What will become of us?

The young man in knee breeches seems to be an optimist. As he leans against the rotten boards at the side of the car, his eyes scan the majestic landscape that falls away into infinity. People throw questions at him in hopes of getting reassuring answers, the way a gravely ill person would badger his doctor. The man doesn't exaggerate, but he does try to allay their darkest fears. At times his eyes suddenly glaze over for a moment, but soon they become soothing again, with the slightest hint of a mischievous smile. Then it's his turn to ask questions, and he continues to offer us reassurance.

I don't ask and I don't answer. In this company, I am clueless as a calf. I am wet behind the ears, a simpleton who still hasn't realized where fate has landed him.

A tight ring forms around the man in the trench coat. I join the rest of the onlookers; I watch as he twirls his pipe and rubs it with his fingers, all the while talking without a pause. A small, pudgy man of about fifty nudges me, and I sense the respect in his tone. "That is Miklós Radnóti, Radnóti the poet."

From a distance of nearly sixty years, I still fault myself for my lack of culture. This was the first time I had heard his name, huddled together in the coal car on the way to Bor, Serbia.

My fellow labour serviceman — *muszos* man — went on to say, "He is also a teacher." Maybe he didn't know more about Radnóti either.

~

May 16, 1944. Very early on Tuesday morning, I received an SAS, which stood for Hurry, Immediately, Urgent — in other words, a *dringend*, urgent, call-up for so-called public-interest labour service. A zealous courier has brought the draft notice to my bachelor flat in an ancient apartment building in Budapest. In his hand is an indelible pencil, which he licks then shoves under my nose, so that I can sign the receipt. What else can I do? I scribble my name. The delivery man puts his lead pencil back in his bag and rushes off.

I live with my mother, just the two of us. Mum is standing beside me, still in her nightgown, pale as a ghost, and I see that she's trembling. The superintendent, Mrs. Thury, fusses over Mum, trying to calm and console her.

I'm looking at the draft notice: public-interest labour service. What sort of public interest do they want me to serve? And in whose interest is it anyway? I'm to present myself in Vác on May 18. The day after tomorrow. Good Lord, what do you need when you're called up? The neighbour, a well-meaning retired tram conductor, suggests the shop on Vilmos Császár Avenue that sells outdoor gear. I rush over to Vilmos Császár Avenue: windbreaker, mess tin, spoon, fork, knapsack, sturdy boots. There is a huge crowd in the store. Lots of noise, pushing and shoving, scrambling to get ahead, a bizarre cacophony in our ears and a jangling strain on our nerves. They've got mess tins, spoons and forks, but no sturdy boots. They ran out. Maybe next week. Oh my God, what should I do? All I have is a pair of walking shoes, with a hole in the sole that I mended from the inside with cardboard. You can't join the army in walking shoes. Yet I have no choice. I could really use a duffle coat, some kind of a warm jacket. The store has duffle coats for sale, but the hundred pengő my mother borrowed from the superintendent is all gone. Where have they disappeared to?

I have no idea. How time is flying! I only have a day and a half left —
perhaps not even that much. What if I didn't report for duty? What
if I tore up this disgusting draft notice? What would happen? Where
could I hide? Who would help me?

The railway station at Vác looks like somebody poked a beehive:
lots of commotion, running around, shouting. From there we are directed to the Curia Hotel. That's what they call this big shapeless barn
of a place — Curia Hotel. It sounds good. Full house: veterans of the
Ukraine, known to me as *ukis* men, among them István (Pista) Horn,
lanky Gyuri Gara and Pista Cserhát. These are all weather-beaten and
experienced *muszos* men, for whom Vác represents a second or third
call-up since 1941. There are a few "oldies," over the age of fifty, and
some youngsters, such as myself. The hotel at Vác is already full, so
the newcomers are sent to another small town called Sződliget.

How long are we going to stay in Vác? Where are they taking us?
The rumour mill starts turning. We are going to the copper mines
at Bor, to relieve the *muszos* men there who were called up in 1943.
"Never mind relieving them — they've all bitten the dust by now,"
says one of our well-informed mates. "We are going to replace them."
All of a sudden I feel a sharp pain with the thought that I have become a motherless child. Why? I have no idea.

From the talk around the soup cauldron, the *muszos* men find
out that back before April 1941 when the Germans invaded Yugoslavia, Germany had obtained the rights to the Bor copper mines from
the Mirabeau Bank of Paris. The mines had originally belonged to
the stockholders of the Société des Mines de Bor, administered by
the Mirabeau Bank, and it was French stockholders who enjoyed the
profits.[1] But once the Nazis got hold of the stocks, the Bor Kupferberg-

---

1   According to Randolph Braham in *The Politics of Genocide: The Holocaust in Hun-
    gary*, after the Bor mines were acquired by the Germans following April 1941, the
    mines were "taken over by the Prussian National Bank (Preussische Staatsbank)
    on the pretext that the mines were supplying war materials to Britain." (New
    York: Columbia University Press, 2016. Vol. 1, 3rd ed., 387.)

werke und Hütten AG (Bor Copper Mine and Metallurgy Company) owned the mines, and it was the responsibility of the Organisation Todt (OT) to increase productivity. The Serbians were considered unreliable, and the "danger of Partisan activity" had become constant.

The Jews of Yugoslavia had been obliterated, and so it became time to make use of the Hungarian Jewish labour force. Colonel General Ruszkiczay-Rüdiger, the deputy minister of defence, made an agreement with Organisation Todt on July 2, 1943; and that's how the name of Bor got written into the history of Hungary.

~

From the hotel I send a postcard dated May 24 to my Christian brother-in-law in Pest. Hurried lines scribbled in pencil: "as soon as you receive my card, please come here and bring me a parcel. Sturdy boots!! Winter duffle coat, foot rags…. We will be here for a few more days…. It's a matter of life and death that you come. Don't say a word to Mum."

May 27. The soccer field in Csukatelep, at the crack of dawn. The *muszos* men from Sződliget and the village of Kosd are already here. A seasoned sergeant with a handlebar moustache forms a company out of the crowd of men. The sun is beating down on us, our canteens are drained dry. Soltész, who has a heart problem, faints. The enlisted men stand on the sidelines smoking, the officers are chatting away; commands and instructions are issued non-stop. There are two thousand conscripts of various ages scattered around the field, instead of twenty-two soccer players.

They are looking for tradesmen: "Tailors, shoemakers, truck drivers, carpenters, joiners, step forward!" barks the sergeant. But out of the milling crowd, furriers, locksmiths, blacksmiths, leatherworkers and upholsterers also step forward, as well as the brazen fibbers, who all of a sudden call themselves tradesmen. No one is asking for papers. They hardly send anyone back from among the imposters.

The cathedral bell strikes noon. The selection has finished. The final companies and platoons have formed. The selected tradesmen stay behind. What would have happened if I had signed up as well?

The officers from the Jutas training camp give the command, sending the group with knapsacks to a line of cattle cars at the Vác railway station. They begin loading the cars right away. A chaotic throng on the tracks and railway beds; shouted commands and swearing. The *muszos* men are being crammed into the boxcars; the guards are yelling and shoving the timid fellows.

"Aryan" friends laden with small bundles slip through the cordon of guards; they keep rushing up and down beside the cars, panting, calling out names, showing photographs: Does anyone know him? Does anyone know where he is?

There are forty of us in one cattle car. I'm squatting on manure-covered straw in front of the open iron door. I spot the figure of my brother-in-law, wandering around in the chaos outside, ashen-faced. He is being shoved from left and right, and keeps turning his head in all directions. I shout at him as loudly as I can, "Döske, Döske, I'm over here! I'm over here, Döske!" He notices me and runs toward the car. The train has begun to move.

The wheels of the train screech. A soldier takes the bundle from my brother-in-law and throws it into the car. The doors slam shut, the locks click in place, the prisoners' cage is closing.

There is a pair of boots in the bundle.

Five days in the cattle car. At night the *muszos* men can only fall asleep in a huddle. Sweat, foul odours, asthmatic rasping, epileptic fits, pervasive stench. The younger men are crying; they devour their supplies of canned food.

The train keeps stopping along the way: Eszék (Osijek), Ruma, Karlóca (Sremski Karlovci), Zimony (Zemun). Air raid, bombs hit the ground and explode, anti-aircraft guns rattle away. The prisoners huddle more tightly together in the closed cars. We reach Belgrade. The locomotive puffs on down the Balkan Peninsula; past Niš, the iron doors open in Zaječar. We are near the Bulgarian border.

There are only a few German uniformed soldiers and one or two railway men hanging around the Zaječar station. They herd the newly arrived *muszos* men toward the coal cars. "Schnell, schnell!" (Fast, fast!) they scream, more at the Hungarian guards than at the *muszos* men.

There are about fifteen hundred of us. The tradesmen, almost five hundred in number, stayed behind at the Csukatelep sports field. I'm still beating myself up for not having tried to pass as a tradesman. My God, where have I arrived in just a few days? Such a diabolical place.

The first of June: brilliant sunshine. In the open coal car, the clear mountain air refreshes our lungs. The locomotive winds through the Serbian Erzgebirge for another half hour. Suddenly, dark rain clouds swirl above us; by the time we arrive at Bor, a stormy wind is howling. Night is falling.

A new set of guards receives us at the Bor station. They direct us to the Dresden Lager, a forced labour subcamp of Bor near the Eastern Orthodox cemetery. Angry, impatient outbursts; guards use their rifle butts to move the men along and utter commands intended to scare us. Then a roll call and they issue orders. We set our knapsacks and blankets down in the corral behind the barracks before lining up for our first dinner in Bor. Italian prisoners, former soldiers of General Badoglio, are the cooks; they slop a bulgur gruel, called *burizs,* which smells like pig swill, from the cauldron into the mess tins of the men standing in line. The hungry *muszos* men, especially the young ones, are overcome by disgust and nausea. I am seized by impotent anger. I try to calm myself, my stomach in knots. Only the seasoned veterans of the Ukraine guzzle down the greyish liquid; in vain they warn the young men that they must eat.

Next morning at dawn, the new arrivals are herded to the neighbouring Berlin Lager. Surrounded by barbed wire, the Berlin Lager is the antechamber of hell. Tattered inmates with lead-grey, blood-caked faces and festering wounds on their feet and arms shuffle past poles for trussing-up. Clad in rags, they drag their scabrous bodies along like the prisoners of war who were slaves in the mining camps in ancient Rome, or like the Native Americans in the Spanish colonies who were whipped until they bled. All of a sudden I feel as forsaken as the convicts in the Middle Ages who wasted away in castle dungeons. I quote Dante's lines from memory: "So bitter is it, death is little more." Bald, human-sized wrecks stare blankly ahead, their harrowed bodies scarcely obey them anymore. We are strictly forbidden from talking to them, as they know. They are also Hungarian labour servicemen. Hungarian? I no longer believe that we're Hungarian. The sadistic Hungarian guards heap vile curses on the tattered crew. Just to amuse themselves, just as a routine. These ragged men arrived in July 1943 to mine copper ore in the mountains.

Just as addicts need more and more morphine, the Germans need more and more copper for the continuation of this bloody war. In 1943, the Germans were still hopeful of winning the war, of wiping Jews from the face of the earth and of becoming the acknowledged masters of the world, superior gods ordained by nature. You need copper for cannon balls, cartridges, machine guns, tanks, Mauser rifles, Stuka dive bombers and for God knows what else.

The Yugoslavs have already been subjugated, but their people are untrustworthy and mostly hostile toward the Nazis, who are well aware of this. Yugoslav people of all ages have taken up the fight against their occupiers. Tito's Partisans continue to attack the German troops; they blow up the tracks under the German military transports. Where else would the Reich turn for a labour force if not to neighbouring, collaborationist Hungary? Who is the labour force for slave labour? Jews, naturally. After all, Jews are not even considered Hungarian anymore. What Jew would even dare to claim to be Hungarian? They are Jews. And what does the "New Order" desire? The "extermination" of the Jews. The extermination of Jews throughout the whole world. And the extermination of the Blacks, the extermination of the Gypsies (Roma), the extermination of the Jehovah's Witnesses — extermination, extermination, extermination.

Gerhard Fränk, the vice-president of the Organisation Todt, demanded thirteen thousand labourers from the Hungarian government in February 1943, to replace the dangerous Yugoslav prisoners of war, who were engaging in more and more acts of sabotage in the mines and in the surrounding area.

Negotiations took place between the German and Hungarian governments. The requested thirteen thousand shrank to three thousand for the time being. This was approved by Hungarian Colonel General and Chief of General Staff Ferenc Szombathelyi without the knowledge of Vilmos Nagy de Nagybaczon, the Hungarian minister of defence. The minister of defence was not a semitophile, but a soldier who saw things clearly: the Hungarian government fully in the grip of the Germans. He knew the Nazis were going to lose the war, that it would be a matter of a year or two, no doubt about it. Vilmos Nagy de Nagybaczon resigned. The new minister of defence, Lajos Csatay, is a total bootlicker.

The Germans struck a splendid bargain. They receive a labour force for the mines, they sell copper to the Hungarians, who will process it, and the Germans only have to pay on delivery. Such is the Hungarian fate. But the Hungarian friends of the Nazis would not see themselves as absolute losers: they managed to get rid of three thousand more Jews.

Numerous pits have been excavated in ledges behind the Berlin Lager. Open-pit mining is evident on the yellowish-reddish-brown mountainside, which has stepped terraces carved into it up to a height of twenty metres. Mine cars roll along the tracks laid over these terraces; red tongues of flame from glowing foundries light up the dusk. The banging of pickaxes, the clattering of excavators and the chugging of small train engines day and night can all be heard from far away.

~

Before dinner, the newly arrived men meet Lieutenant Colonel Ede Marányi, the commander of the Bor forced labour camps. Immaculate uniform, riding crop beating against riding boots polished to a high shine, haughty gaze, Marányi stands surrounded by his officers, barely thirty metres away from the lined-up *muszos* men. The Hungarian guards keep shouting; Marányi and company are chatting, sneering and offering each other cigarettes from their cases.

Unable to sleep, we spend the night tossing and turning in the filthy corral. The mine operates day and night in two shifts. "By dawn we'll be in the mine shafts, too," wails a puny *muszos* man. It's terrible to think that in a few weeks, or perhaps in a month or two, we will be as pitiful and heart-rending wrecks as the conscripts of 1943.

At dawn on Saturday, June 3, all-terrain trucks arrive. Everything always happens at dawn. Before — indeed not that long ago — what a beautiful, lovely and idyllic mood dawn used to inspire in me. Now dawn brings only fear and dread to us prisoners.

Commands fly, and the chosen company is formed into columns, which then clamber onto the open trucks. Where are they taking us?

We have absolutely no idea. It's not possible to ask anyone, and it's not advisable either. So we are not going to load *csille*, mine cars, in the copper mines of Bor? "I would rather drink bor [wine] in Chile," remarks Pista Cserhát on the truck. Stupid, morbid joke. But it gets a lot of smiles.

We spend only one night in the Berlin Lager. We don't know where they're taking us, but we breathe a sigh of relief at leaving the dreadful camp behind. The convoy of trucks with their German drivers and cargo of *muszos* men winds its way toward the northwest on the steeply inclined road into the interior of the Homolje mountain range. The road is fissured and full of rocky debris. It's really hard on the engines. Our truck is open, so we have a view of the landscape; there is hardly any traffic. Nature, in all the fresh green shades of spring, is enchanting and wonderful. As we make our way upward, flocks of sheep appear along the road, locals in their peasant footwear, on small, one-horse carts. Apart from this, the only thing that disturbs the silence is the sound of our vehicles thudding into the potholes and over the stones, and the whirr of the wheezing engines.

A scant ten to fifteen minutes after setting out, on the left side of the winding road, a prison camp comes into view, painted a sombre green: "OT Innsbruck"; the convoy moves on past it. What a sacrilege to name a slave settlement after the breathtakingly beautiful Tyrolean university town. And after this comes a series of other camps: the Vorarlberg, München, Graz and Bregenz Lagers. Then, on Kupinova Glava Mountain, a thousand metres above sea level, our future quarters, OT-Lager Heidenau, suddenly pop up on the left, in a clearing.

They stop the engines. The *muszos* men jump off the trucks, carrying their full gear on their shoulders. A few of them can only climb down with great difficulty.

There could be about four hundred of us. In front of the Lager there is a huge clearing. We take in the crisp mountain air and luxuriant shrubbery around a grassy area. The trucks' engines start whirring again; the dusty vehicles turn laboriously back toward Bor. Suddenly the scene grows still, but only for a few moments. Then rough commands chase the *muszos* men into the green field.

Reserve officer Second Lieutenant Antal Száll is the omnipotent commander of the Heidenau prisoners. He is a blond pretty-boy of about thirty or thirty-five. He looks like the bon vivant in an operetta, à la László Szilassy. He is a stern, indifferent civilian parading in a uniform. With his azure blue eyes and feigned dignity, he looks straight through the slaves of various ages under his command.

We form up on the field. The guards snap out their commands. They make straight, horizontal lines out of the *muszos* prisoners. The shrill command to stand at attention resounds on the square, a command echoed ominously by the mountains. Without mincing words, Száll informs the company that we are in a war zone, there are Partisans lurking about, escape is punished by execution and "minor" offences — that's how he says it, minor offences — by trussing-up, which means being strung up to a pole and suspended from it with one's hands tied behind one's back. I wonder what a minor offence could be. Who makes these laws? Will they post the list of minor offences or will they pass sentence as they see fit?

The Second Lieutenant's deputy is Ensign György Turner; he is a short, skinny little man, under five foot seven. He is probably the same age as Száll. Turner orders, "Spread out the blankets." The *muszos* men undo the blankets attached to their knapsacks with nimble fingers. Turner's voice barks again, "Empty knapsacks, coat, jacket and pants pockets! Everything, understood? Put all valuables on the blankets — jewellery, pengő, dinars, flashlights, cameras, books! You may keep your wristwatch, wedding ring, prayer book. Understood? I warn you: there is going to be a body search, and anyone found with forbidden items on his person will be punished by trussing-up. Is that clear?"

When we were still in the cattle cars, commercial transports that had been converted into moving prisons, in Eszék the Hungarian guards ordered us to hand over any money we had in excess of forty pengő. They threatened anyone who failed to obey with severe punishment. "We will send the money back to your relatives," they said. They walked through the stationary cars with paper and pencil in hand, jotting down home addresses with great seriousness and collecting the banknotes hidden in our pockets and jackets. Quickly, carefully, almost politely, they gathered up the bills of smaller and larger denominations. How childish and gullible men can become when they're in trouble.

After the underhanded looting had finished and the wagons were sealed again, we suffered on in the cramped car; the stench was all-pervasive. The *ukis* men were doubtful that the money would ever be sent to their relatives. The optimists were hopeful; they wanted to believe that the money would reach their wives, their parents.

That devious collection of money was a cordial prelude to the circus now taking place on the clearing in front of the Heidenau Lager. As soon as Ensign Turner's "Is that clear?" is heard, a commotion starts in the rows. Guards holding on to the leashes of furious German shepherds scrutinize the items tossed on the blankets. More odds and ends land on the blankets. At a leisurely pace, the fellows recruited from among the sappers of Szeged paw curiously through the hodgepodge; one of them fingers a thin little gold chain and another keeps counting dinars while licking his thumb. It is evident that they are satisfied with the booty. They prepare a list of the surrendered items. Here again the paper and pencil come out, to lend an official appearance to the "fun." The body search never happens.

But it's too late for regrets. I don't have any money, neither dinars nor pengő. I don't have a watch or a gold chain that I could have tried to keep. Only a prayer book. I sense what a nonentity I have become amid the collective insanity. For a long time, in his ranting speeches, Hitler has been saying that the Jews are the parasites of humanity that need to be "exterminated" like noxious vermin. By now I know I am a noxious pest; my mother committed a crime by giving birth to me, so I ended up on the list of those to be exterminated.

Corporal Sisák, a sly individual with hair black as ebony, is circulating a sheet stating: "Escapes or attempted escapes are punishable by death." To make the threat complete, they have each *muszos* man sign his name. The pencil is passed from hand to hand. Our boots are confiscated, which also reduces the temptation to escape. We have to write our name on the outer edge of our new footwear, clumsy wooden clogs.

The command is given: March into the Heidenau Lager. We keep stumbling awkwardly in our wooden shoes on the gravel road toward the Lager situated on the other side of the clearing. Rows of green-painted barracks are enclosed by an oak fence topped by barbed wire. It's a horrible, frightening prison. Inside the gate, on the right, the *muszos* men line up and we are then distributed among six barracks. Corporal Horváth does the sorting. The men with yellow armbands, which signify that they are Jewish, and the Szekler Sabbatarians and the Jehovah's Witnesses are directed to the first, second and third barracks of the first row, and the fourth and fifth barracks of the second row. Christians who had converted from Judaism, who were nevertheless considered Jewish according to the anti-Jewish laws, wear white armbands; they are placed in the sixth barracks, near the building with the showers.

The medical office, kitchen, food storage and military staff barracks are on the left side of the arched gateway; the quarters for the camp commander and the officers are more spacious. The supervisors from the Organisation Todt are assigned a separate living area in the staff quarters. Across from the prisoners' barracks, at a distance of thirty metres, is the rectangular shaped, unpainted latrine. The padlocked building that contains the generator is beside the showers, and the tool shed is to the left of the barracks.

From among the *muszos* men Second Lieutenant Száll selects several overseers. He seems to favour the ex-reserve officers. Dr. József (Jóska) Junger, who is an ex-ensign and a former lawyer and vice-president of a Hungarian Zionist organization, becomes the chief overseer. He is a dapper and energetic young man, no older than Second Lieutenant Száll, and he has served in the Ukraine. Junger is the intermediary between the prisoners and their keepers. Former lieutenant Zoltán Kovács and former ensign György (Gyuri) Gara are his assistants, having lost their titles when all Jews were stripped of their military ranks by decree of the Hungarian Ministry of Defence in 1941.

I end up in Jóska Junger's barracks, which has rough triple-decker bunks. He is in a middle bunk in front of the door; I am on his left, in the bottom bunk. I already made the acquaintance of Gyuri Gara, Pista Horn, Pista Cserhát and several other men in Vác. I'm still very shy, just like most of the other young labourers here. The *ukis* men are all over thirty, but I'm not even in my twenties yet. I study their words, their gestures; I separate out those with friendly faces, those who give well-meaning advice. We arrange our belongings, spread out our blankets, place our knapsacks and duffle coats under our heads, at least those who had managed to get such a coat. I don't have a duffle coat, since the money we borrowed from Mrs. Thury was only enough to buy a trench coat of a cheaper quality.

The experienced *ukis* men hammer L-shaped nails into the beams beside their bunks, for hanging their bundles. I find that most of the *ukis* men are well equipped. They have a lot of little items that can come in handy in our prison: needle, thread, pliers, pieces of string, gauze and even L-nails emerge from their satchels. They hang up their bundles in case of rat infestation. Ákos Grósz from Jászberény is brushing his teeth; Péter (Peti) Szüsz is wailing; the veterans are telling young Szüsz off. My immediate bunk neighbour, Károly Háy, meticulously lays down his blanket on the rough board and puts on a spinach-green jogging suit; he is getting ready for bed. I make a dash for the latrine before lights out. After that it's forbidden to go outside.

The night descends on the camp. We want to surrender our tired bodies to sleep on the rough planks. "I lie aplank, an animal captive amidst vermin, the fleas / renew their assault, while the host of flies retreats."[2] Sleep eludes us. Bloodthirsty bedbug brigades emerge from the cracks of the bunks, the rotten cavities of the beams and the fissured ceiling, and attack — like wild beasts — our noses, mouths, ears, navels, thighs; they bite our groins until we bleed. The previous occupants of the Heidenau Lager — the ones Radnóti referred to as loud Italians and heretic Serbs — and more recently Greek prisoners of war, left behind a disgusting mess and an indescribable stench. The whole Lager is infested with filth and vermin, and the bloodsuckers are getting fat on our feet and arms.

---

2 Miklós Radnóti, "Seventh Eclogue." Heidenau Lager: in the mountains above Žagubica, July 1944.

In These Mountains

We hear the five in the morning reveille, the signal to get up. We line up with our mess tins. In the kitchen, József Kardos, the cook, is serving a black liquid. Two *shamashim*, assistants, hand out rectangular half-kilo loaves of bread, the portion for two days. It's mouldy. We clean up our area in the barracks, rush to the huge, communal latrine. Shoving and urging each other to hurry up, a depressing lack of privacy. From *Homo sapiens* we turn into animals in no time flat.

The army of slaves sets off to labour. On the side of the road to Homolje, on a cloddy field strewn with broken rocks, the company marches along in clunky wooden shoes that are secured to our feet with string. The mountain air is almost freezing in the early morning; the valley, the area where we work, is covered with an icy mist.

The first work day. The wind swirls and howls. Schleghorn, a thick-set, bowlegged man of about fifty, the local head of Organisation Todt, negotiates with our barracks leader, Junger, who is interpreting Schleghorn's orders. We have to form teams of four: for mine car, pickaxe or wheelbarrow work. The hardest work is digging and excavating to build the railway. One of the Todt men, a guy from Burgenland, the easternmost state of Austria near the Hungarian border, can also speak Hungarian, slowly drawling out his sentences. With his big, callused, spade-like hands, he demonstrates to the greenhorns, us new labourers, how to grip the pickaxe and takes special care to ensure that the wheelbarrows are loaded to the hilt.

The Kupinova Glava Mountain is set in a bleak landscape criss-crossed by mountain ranges, forests, gorges and deep valleys. The majestic mountain peaks seem to be floating in a veil of clouds.

At noon the field kitchen rolls into the valley. Although the dawn was freezing, by noon the sun is burning fiercely. Bulgur gruel is distributed. Only one ladleful is slopped into our mess tins. The one-hour lunch break even affords us time for a short rest and for picking wild strawberries.

In the afternoon all hell breaks loose. Backbauer from the Organisation Todt, a rude and irritable guy, is waving his rifle butt around like a foaming madman, screaming angrily, "Schnell!" (Fast!) and "Schweinerei!" (Filthy mess!) Rage colours his warty, swollen face scarlet red: "These miserable wretches haven't a clue about railway building or even about digging." What did this fat work fanatic expect? Maybe he was hoping that top-notch tradesmen would arrive here, experts in excavation, in blasting rocks and rock walls, in removing the roots of huge trees, in laying down rails for mine cars, and they'd work at a killer pace in wooden shoes and their own clothes just to meet the quota.

We find out from the slow-speaking, patient man from Burgenland that the prisoners will first have to tamp down the earth for the tracks that will later be laid on top. The planned mountain railway will speed up the transport of copper from Bor to the Danube River. But every now and then the Burgenlander loses his temper: "Gotta pay attention, understand? No hurry-scurry…. What a bunch of bozos!"

Every day thereafter, the monotonous navvy work — shovelling, loading wheelbarrows and mine cars — is a repeat of the first day. The Nazis' deranged plan seems improbable in this steep, craggy mountain region. Besides, we couldn't care less about the railway. The *muszos* men heave their pickaxes and empty their wheelbarrows all day long, apathetically and at a snail's pace. However, the pace quickens as soon as Schleghorn or Backbauer approaches.

The food is inadequate for hard physical labour. We no longer devour our bread right away, instead we let it get soggy in our mouths; our tongues play with the crumbs just to prolong the taste. Cooked food is even scarcer. We fantasize about food more and more often.

The monotony is broken by Liberator bomber planes. A squadron of these bombers flies majestically overhead in the direction of the oilfields in Ploieşti, Romania, and as they return toward their airbase, we can hear their engines in the sky again. Some of the engines are giving off smoke or whining. We keep counting the airplanes, anxiously rooting for their success, and when they return intact we heave a sigh of relief. In the midst of slave labour, this is our little secret; it feeds our hopes.

At 6:00 p.m., Schleghorn gives the signal to knock off work. Wakeup call was at 5:30 a.m., and we left for our workplace at 6:30. We've had enough. We line up the pickaxes in the shape of a pyramid and push the mine cars into the shed. We stumble back into our corral like so many draft oxen.

We receive low-calorie food: in the morning, a murky black liquid and German army bread, the taste and texture of sawdust, decorated with greenish-grey mould, a quarter of a kilo for the whole day. At noon and in the evening, a thin soup with cabbage, every now and then enriched by tiny bits of potato. Dangerously little for physical labour in the mountain air. Every ten days, they hand out twenty Morava cigarettes and twenty sour candies.

The slaves of nicotine exchange candy for cigarettes. We carry water in tin buckets and perform a quick collective ablution; anxiously, we exchange what we refer to as "cauldron news," sharing what we know in whispers as we clean ourselves; at nine o'clock, it's lights out. We lay down our weary heads. "In these mountains, amidst rumors and vermin…. The camp's asleep."[1]

---

1   Radnóti, "Seventh Eclogue."

The prisoners are not allowed to have newspapers or to listen to the radio. It's forbidden to ask questions, and it's also dangerous. The guards don't engage in conversation with the prisoners — they only give orders. Occasionally we hear news that gets our hopes up: On June 6 the Allies landed in Europe; Tito's Partisans are scouting nearby. Or a different type of news: The Jew-gobbling Marányi, proud recipient of the National Defence Cross, makes his guards sell cigarette paper, and he embezzles a large part of the parcels of cigarettes, canned goods, marmalade and margarine provided by the Wehrmacht; the Bor black market is full of Marányi's wares. Rumours circulate about Marányi: he is torturing prisoners in a potato pit, we hear.

Albin Csillag, the forced labourer artist of Bor, drew cartoons of the drunken Lieutenant Colonel surrounded by women in lewd positions. He was hoping to get the drawings to Hungary through a clandestine channel, but someone snitched on him and the drawings ended up in Marányi's hands. From that time on, Csillag has been trussed up twice a day and beaten half to death. When trussed up, his feet are not allowed to touch the ground; the henchmen keep laughing at his misery. At the end, Csillag is thrown into the potato pit to join the twenty-two other prisoners who have been languishing there for weeks. Marányi is a sadistic and fanatical antisemite who incites his officers and guards to commit atrocities.

Accompanied by armed guards, some of the prisoners go to Bor, but mostly to Zaječar, to purchase food. Ensign Turner selects these buyers from the older *muszos* men, on heaven knows what basis. Béla Wellesz, a former druggist from Vilmos Császár Avenue, is one of them. It's from him that we learn the Chetniks led by Draža Mihailović are lurking around the Heidenau Lager; a bomb has exploded at Hitler's headquarters; the Germans are facing resistance in the Balkans.

We shiver as we hear all this news: we don't know whether these events mean our lives are going to be saved or shortened. Grey-haired

Uncle Ede, a militant socialist, spreads the news about the approach of the Soviets. Dr. József Bárdos, a physician with a reddish moustache, the son of Artúr Bárdos, the theatre director, bemoans the scarcity of medications. He is trying to use Demalgon and Karil, generic drugs, to cure headaches and hemorrhoids. The other two physicians of the Heidenau Lager, Zoltán Vécsei and László Spitzer, also complain about the lack of medications. There are a lot of injuries and hardly any bandages. Dr. Bárdos likes to talk politics: he considers Hitler a military genius and staunchly believes in the success of the German wonder weapons, especially the V-2 rocket. He is convinced that there is absolutely no doubt about the final victory of the Germans. Bárdos smiles as he talks about this; he is almost always smiling. He is beside himself with joy, and we are starting to avoid him.

~

In the first days, life in the Lager thoroughly disoriented us: our heads were spinning from the cacophony of commands and orders. The surprising and barely comprehensible events kept multiplying; here nothing corresponded to any known norms. The Lager has become the throbbing of a thousand excited and tangled nerves. Although we've all been sharing the same desperate situation, some dissension has already begun: the young and the old don't get along well. We are suffering from the captivity and from the knowledge that our slave-keepers, the representatives of the "pure and superior race," can commit excesses at will. We have no way of defending ourselves against the spate of unexpected, disastrous blows.

Day after monotonous day passes: the days are exhausting, and at night we wage war against the bugs. Even Goethe mentions his disgust with them in one of his *Venetian Epigrams,* listing bedbugs among the things he finds more repugnant than even snakes and poison.

On the advice of our veteran confreres, the youngest peer group, the nineteen- and twenty-year-olds, walk around with a neutral gaze, lest the guards find fault with us. We fear Corporal Sisák and, most of all, Corporal Horváth, Marányi's informer. Those two have a penchant for picking on the lanky prisoners and the knock-kneed ones with their duck-like gait. Their repertoire consists of kicks in the ass, jabs with rifle butts, trussing-up and hog-tying. Yet no matter how bad things are, they can always get worse. In life everything is relative: our situation, for example, is pretty good compared to that of the prisoners in the Berlin Lager.

On a Sunday morning, Lieutenant Száll gives us permission to exterminate bedbugs. The disassembled bunks are singed with candle flames outdoors, which is how the *muszos* men destroy the eggs and burn the armies of bloodsuckers running around in a frenzy. They drip hot wax into the cracks of the boards and try to fill the openings with the weeds that flourish in the fens.

Reassembling the bunks in the barracks proves more complicated than taking them apart. The campaign against vermin turned out to be a failure. The next night, millions of bugs that managed to escape mount a revenge-thirsty attack with their merciless jaws. The parasitic beasts suck our blood with ferocious rage.

As the days go by, starvation becomes ever more unbearable. The system starts to digest its reserves. The young ones — mere babes in the woods, most of them penniless greenhorns — fight among themselves ever more frequently. A few of them haven't even turned twenty yet, the ones born in 1924. As it turns out, I am one of the youngest in the Heidenau Lager, or even in all the Bor Lagers, since I was born in 1925. I had my nineteenth birthday in April. What a tragicomical claim to fame this is! Have I landed here by mistake? But each one of us arrived at this antechamber of hell by mistake.

The malnourishment, the defencelessness, the corporal misery, have steadily taken their toll. Tormenting starvation drove one of the fellows to steal bread. Let him remain forever nameless; let me add that it was my piece of bread he snatched in an unguarded moment: he was upset about it, claiming that he couldn't restrain himself, and he begged for forgiveness. Junger and company quickly restored order in the barracks, lest the guards find out about the theft, which would have been a good reason for trussing-up.

Corporal Sisák is a big joker. He and two of his buddies toss mouldy slices of bread in the sand the way you would throw slop for pigs in a trough. What makes the fun even more interesting is that the bread tossing takes place right next to the stinking latrines. The prisoners can only pick up the bread using their mouths; it is forbidden to touch it with their hands. The young men rush over in a pack for the measly slices of bread. There are only a few filthy pieces of bread left in the hands of Sisák and his gang; they tear them up into even smaller pieces to prolong the circus, almost killing themselves laughing at the degrading sight. The winners' mouths and noses are filled with sand and dirty bread crusts. How low we've sunk in the last two months. How deep into this hell we've been shoved by our keepers. It has been said that camels that have been driven to exhaustion last longer if they are sung to. Will we last longer if they are cruel to us?

By now we are bald, because the provisional Lager barbers shaved our heads to the number zero setting. Lajos, a quiet guy with a limp, directs the amateur Figaros; he used to be a hairdresser in Femina, a downtown salon, the darling Lajoska of the beautiful ladies. Now that our noggins are bare, both escaping the Lager and getting lice are more difficult.

The *ukis* men relate how the barracks were set on fire in Berdychiv, in the Ukraine, while *muszos* men suffering from typhus were still inside them. They also tell us about bloodbaths in Zhytomyr and Fastiv and the massacre in Voronezh, and that the journalist György Bálint died as a forced labourer in the Ukraine.

Not a day goes by without *ukis* men recounting some horrendous story from the Ukraine days. For the prisoners, it's not the eleven-hour work days of digging, the thirst or the increasing starvation that represents the greatest torment; it is the threat of death that draws ever nearer. If we fall asleep, the sound of the death rattle wakes us, and we cannot get the thought of our impending death out of our heads.

On our outerwear, our trench coats, on both the front and the back, there is a garish twenty-centimetre yellow star. They cut out a pattern from cardboard and painted it with oil paint, and in an instant two equilateral triangles, one pointing up and one pointing down, were transferred to our coats. The Star of David had been used for many things before: the first sighting was on the gravestone of a man from Sidon, two thousand seven hundred years ago. During the wedding of King Matthias in 1476, the Jews of Buda saluted the glorious ruler with a flag emblazoned with the Star of David. Now the sad prisoners are emblazoned with the Star of David.

ᵒ∽

We are getting to know each other. The prison camp, like many ad hoc communities, is a cross-section of society. Here you can find a butcher from Zombor (Sombor), an Orthodox rabbi, a few physicians, teachers and lawyers. Some are from Pest, others from the countryside: a sewing machine mechanic, duvet maker, theatre prop man, stamp merchant from Váci Street, general storekeeper from Upper Hungary. There are poor men and others who are well-to-do, servants and masters; young men dreaming about being admitted to university; theologians, mathematicians, painters, musicians, men of letters, PhDs and the uneducated.

As the fellow prisoners warm up to each other, mocking nicknames are spawned: we call Walter Hirschberger "Baron Munchausen" for telling tall tales; Pista Breuer, who is forever sniffing around for food, becomes "Pinocchio," the king of second helpings; Zoli Heller is "Shaggy-sloth"; the sous-chef Szabados is "Gravedigger"; white-blond-haired Gertler is "Albino"; and so on.

Miklós Radnóti and the *ukis* man Emil Sági are pushing wheelbarrows in tandem. Two other men from their barracks do the shovelling for them. Radnóti is in the whites' barracks, the one for

Christian converts, in the same room as Sági. (I heard from Sági decades later in 1984: Miklós had the bunk in the middle near the window, to the right of Sági's bunk.) A huge yellow star blooms on Radnóti's trench coat as well; the dividing line between "Whites" and "Yellows" has disappeared, as we are all marked with the star.

I wield the shovel along with Emil Rubinyi, the son of Mózes Rubinyi, the famous linguist and ex-president of the Hungarian Pen Club; Péter Szüsz and Feri Duschinszky push the wheelbarrows with us. All four of us live in barracks five. Emil is the oldest in our team at twenty-five; Duschinszky and Szüsz are both twenty.

When the clanking of the mine cars and the banging of the pick-axes quiets down at lunchtime, we seek refuge from the blazing sun in the shade of tall oaks and beeches, near the babbling brook, Lipa. Here we rest, half-naked, enjoying the cool and daydreaming. Our keepers are also dozing nearby; they sometimes seem to be more tolerant at lunchtime than normally.

We keep really quiet; we only have a few minutes left. Around us are the "proud ferns, cool in the heat," described by Radnóti. There is no talk of literature now. We dream about cottage cheese with sour cream and icing sugar on top. We fantasize about sitting in Buchwald chairs by the bandstand in Elisabeth Square, with our knees pulled up to our chins while the drum major raises his baton on high and the military band plays Strauss waltzes. Or, like Radnóti, we daydream of the plum jam cooling on the verandah. Past concerts in Károlyi Garden come to mind; and conversations about French and American movies, Jean Gabin, Danielle Darrieux, Judy Garland and *The Wizard of Oz*. Or we are children again, playing "Guess That Celebrity," and joking around with the little rabbi, rattling off the tongue twister about the priest from Ibafa.

Samuel Pepys noted in his diary on January 4, 1659, "Strange the difference of men's talk!" In the prison camp, shared interests draw people together in smaller and larger groups; more intimate friendships form as well. The prisoners search out those with whom they speak a common language, with whom they can discuss their impressions, to whom they can pour out their hearts, whom they can confide in and ask for advice. The young men, Péter Szüsz, Pista Löwy, Feri Duschinszky, the blond Mayer, Bandi Reiner, Emil Rubinyi, all surround Radnóti, just like the students who surround Plato in *The School of Athens*.

We did not receive work clothes from the Organisation Todt, so we use our own, the ones we were wearing when we arrived at the Lager. Radnóti wears the same brown knee breeches that he had on in the coal car, on the way from Zaječar to Bor. When we gather around Miklós during the rest period, he no longer has his wavy blondish-brown hair, his head shaved to the skin like the rest of us. Through greenish-brown eyes, he gazes at us young fellows with an enigmatic fondness. His high, clear forehead, radiating intelligence, is crossed by a frown every now and then. Sometimes sorrow flashes in his eyes, then all of a sudden, a lightning smile. The face of a daydreamer and an intellectual, kind, genial and considerate — we are getting to know each other.

Older men also join our "round table"; they are Radnóti's age, around thirty-five to forty: the violinist Miklós Lorsi, the jurist Olivér Hollós, the art teacher Károly László Háy, the polymath József Junger, the amateur theatre critic and Lager physician József Bárdos, along with György Turán, Károly Gárdos, Andor Vajda and a few others in their fifties.

My bunk neighbour Kari Háy is twirling a charcoal pencil in his hand as he lies on his stomach on the rough planks, drawing. He makes sketches of medieval castles, cliff-top fortresses, knights in armour riding battle horses, stalwart warriors and bewigged ladies dressed in evening gowns. I watch his nimble fingers as he uses his pencil to conjure fluffy clouds, babbling brooks and stately bastions into his sketchbook with wizardly skill. But most of all he draws roosters, proud ones, with stiff spurs, combs and open beaks.

Kari brings his sketchbook with the roosters, castles and knights preparing for tournaments to our Sunday afternoon get-togethers behind the showers that rarely work. We stretch out around Jóska Junger and Radnóti in a semicircle on the grassy mound beside a trickle of water from the Mlava River, at the far end of the camp. A few of the fellows find no room in the semicircle and are cooling off in the shade of the old cherry tree nearby.

Junger tells biblical stories about the enslavement of the Jews in Egypt and their miraculous liberation. Jewish slave labourers worked on building the cities of Pithom and Ramses; their exploitation and torment ended in a miracle. Next Miklós Lorsi plays the violin. His instrument was not confiscated by the guards, who regarded it as a worthless trinket. At first Lorsi makes funny squeaking sounds, then he turns to Kari Háy and launches into the song, "The rooster is crowing, the dawn is breaking..." Kari's roosters seem to come to life.

The young men are fond of La Fontaine's fables. When Lorsi finishes, Miklós takes up the rooster theme, telling how the rooster played a trick on the fox. He doesn't reveal the punch line of the tale, as the young guys are supposed to guess it. Then another story: how did the cowardly rabbit escape the king's wrath? Emil Rubinyi's high-pitched voice takes the cake.

Miklós and others recite from memory poems by Endre Ady, János Arany and Attila József. When someone gets stuck, Radnóti helps him out. Gyuri Kádár recites verses from the collection *The Complaints of a Poor Little Child* by the Symbolist Dezső Kosztolányi. When we falter — and we falter often — we struggle together to come up with the missing words and rhymes.

Radnóti lights a cigarette and blows smoke rings. As is his custom, he gazes off toward the old cherry tree with his head tilted to one side.

One Sunday afternoon, Radnóti's circle plays Kornél Esti's favourite game, Twenty Questions, referencing Kosztolányi's novel *Kornél Esti*. Radnóti teaches the game to the lads with the enthusiasm of a professor. Some of the older fellows know it and join in. Junger recites a poem by József Kiss, "Against the Tide":

> If you defend — then you offend;
> If you are silent — cowardice!
> If you cry out — you're sensitive;
> Even a sigh draws prejudice!

Olivér Hollós refers to works by Frigyes Karinthy and Ernö Szép. At times the focus shifts to dramas: *Phèdre* by the Jansenist Jean Racine, the depiction of love in the tragedies of Corneille and Racine. We discuss *The Thibaults* by Martin du Gard, asking which of the Thibault sons is more heroic, Jacques or Antoine? An older partner in misfortune analyzes the giants of the Trecento, Dante, Petrarch and Boccaccio. He emphasizes the haughtiness and pride of the first one, the intellect of the second and the wit and humour of the third. We recite Kazinczy and Berzsenyi; Miklós often recites Apollinaire.

On Sunday afternoons, the young inmates, fresh out of high school, are getting acquainted with names and literary trends they had never heard of before: Gyula Illyés, Cocteau, Aragon and Jules Romains, who only writes about positive protagonists; the jester Max Jacob and García Lorca; Dadaism, Surrealism and the Expressionists: Lőrinc Szabó and Lajos Kassák. At school we studied Petőfi, Arany, Kisfaludy and Goethe, Schiller, Eötvös and Ede Szigligeti. Our German teacher told us that after Goethe's audience with Napoleon, the Corsican conqueror followed the retreating figure with his eyes and let out an ecstatic cry, "Voilá un homme!"

Back home a few of us had secretly read Marx's *Das Kapital*, hiding under the bed; in the 1940s we adored Faludy's translations of Villon, as well as the recitations of Oszkár Ascher and Tamás Major; we carried dog-eared copies of *You and Me*, Paul Géraldy's volume of poetry, in our jacket pockets. We knew little about the "isms" and nothing about the new trends. Our teachers were kind and elderly;

perhaps they didn't know about the world of modern literature either. Peti Szüsz sweet-talks Lorsi into letting him use his violin, he plays a Mozart sonata that shines like a pearl and is as fine as Brussels lace. Wild mountains, dark grey cliffs tower above us in Serbia's mysterious bosom.

It will soon be evening. Time to line up by the cauldrons. How quickly the magic of the afternoon has vanished: our harsh reality includes trussing-up, vermin invasion, dreaded lice infestation. The burning down of barracks in the Ukraine hangs like a sword of Damocles over our heads.

The weakened company now suffers from chronic inflammation of the bladder, and diarrhea. We live like animals — from daybreak until late into the night, the large part of our existence is filled with starvation, exhaustion and fear. We've become irritable, frequently squabbling over trivialities. There is neither time nor occasion to think, to ponder, to show signs of affection. Is it possible that our moral standards are changing too?

Jóska Deutsch from the Kőbánya district of Budapest, who is struggling with infections and varicose veins, falls into the latrine. Bashful Mayer cannot control his bladder; at dawn he sneaks to the latrine, intending to pour out the urine he's been saving in a can through the night. Poor clumsy Mayer is caught by the guard on duty, who makes him drink every last drop of the pee from his infected kidneys.

The next morning, twenty-year-old Mayer stands in the lineup with a face as pale as death. He doesn't say a word, he doesn't cry, his face is expressionless. He hands over the morning black liquid to his pal and gives his bread portion to the guy behind him. He can't manage to swallow either the bread or the filthy black swill. On the third day, Dr. Spitzer lays him down on the bunk in the medical room. Before the twenty-minute trussing-up of Zoli Budai is over that evening, Mayer dies quietly. The number of forced labourers in the Heidenau Lager has dropped to 401. Our rabbi sneaks into the medical room and recites Kaddish without a *minyan*. I recall Radnóti's phrase, "On the peaks of Serbia full of woe." *Alav ha-shalom*! "Rest in peace," says the rabbi softly.

At the end of the work day and on Sunday mornings, Serbian women and men clad in felted wool vests, from the Žagubica area of eastern Serbia, loiter along the fence. They offer us a sheep cheese called *bryndza*, corn bread, frozen lard, bread, bacon and Drina cigarettes. Very few prisoners still have any hidden money that they managed to keep from the guards, so instead they try bartering. In exchange for better quality underwear, they'll give you a small piece of corn cake or a round loaf that was worth about four hundred dinars in the middle of June 1944. As the days pass, the exchange rate keeps increasing. A perfect shirt is worth a lot: one kilo of lard, one kilo of bacon, with a thick slice of goat cheese thrown in.

"Zdravo, druže." (Hello, comrade.) We greet the Serbian mountain dwellers from inside the fence, and when they appear on the other side of the barbed wire, we ask them, "Did you bring salo" (lard) and "do you have hleb" (bread)?

"Daću ti hleb za sat" (I'll give you bread for a watch), says one of the beanpole Serbs. The vendors like to exchange things for watches best of all: as our starvation deepens, the temptation among watch owners increases. The ration we receive from the camp guards is inadequate even for the least needy prisoner: our reserves have been almost completely depleted. We've been attacked by an insidious enemy, dangerous, sly, deadly — hunger.

Turning a blind eye, the guards avoid the area where the rag fair is taking place. The bourgeois prisoners of Heidenau devour the white frozen lard with a tin spoon.

The Jews from Subcarpathia are skilled at trading. Miklós is no good at it; the young guys even less so. Radnóti exchanged his shirt for *bryndza*, bread and *Avala*s, a type of small cross-ruled school notebook; I bought corn cake from a girl with curly blond hair in exchange for my worn-out angora scarf.

By August we calculate the value of our stuff strictly in lard, bread, bacon and *kukuruz*, corn. We evaluate each other's worn-out clothing the same way: "Laci Kende is wearing two kilos of bread, one kilo of goat cheese and twenty Drina cigarettes," and so on. It's a demeaning association. Secretly we are ashamed of ourselves, but we do these sorts of calculations almost inadvertently.

~

József Junger is a popular man in the Lager: he speaks several languages and is a theologian and a jurist. He administers justice among quarrelling parties with the wisdom of a Talmudic scholar. Junger addresses trivial complaints, soothes ruffled feathers. He walks around among the prisoners in his duffle coat complete with yellow star, using a crooked cane he carved himself; he encourages the despondent and helps the downtrodden.

From the very first day of our life in Heidenau, a strong friendship was formed between Radnóti and Junger, which has grown into an even closer bond. After the distribution of dinner and before lights out, Miklós can often be found in our barracks; he climbs up to Junger's bunk and lets his legs dangle over the side. Then out comes an *Avala*, and in the stifling summer twilight he reads to us from what he has written in it:

Can you see, it's getting dark: and the wild fence of oak, edged
with barbed-wire, and the barracks, hovering, evening absorbs.
The listless gaze, the frame of our captivity lets go,
the mind alone, the mind alone knows the wire's tension.
Do you see, dear, how only now imagination's loosed so,
and dream, the deliverer, sets free our broken bodies
and all at once the prison camp sets off toward home.

We of barracks five are the first audience of the "Seventh Eclogue," one of Radnóti's Bor poems. Miklós reads his poem in a warm tone, quietly and with feeling. He has several *Avalas*; he makes corrections to his poems and copies them to a new notebook. Kari Háy draws illustrations to complement the poems. We are already familiar with these lines and Kari's drawings when they are presented to the group on Sunday afternoons.

As the number of bombers increases in the fleecy clouds of the Serbian sky, our hope for change grows too. Starting even as early as the middle of August 1944, we think we can hear dull cannon blasts from the direction of Bulgaria. The Serbian vendors keep hinting that the Germans are ready to pack it in.

The prisoners are overcome by ominous premonitions. Does fate hold a better or a worse future for us? Our thoughts seem to be paralyzed: the present grips us with wolf fangs, and we cannot tear ourselves away; we wonder what our keepers have in mind.

Miklós sits right beside me on Kari Háy's bunk, on the checkered blanket. Junger crouches alongside us. Miklós reads loudly from the *Avala*, gesturing occasionally:

Power flashes in the root
that drinks the rain, lives by earth,
dreams the snow-white dream

And then:

Flower once, root now below,
dark earth presses down hard
on me, and so it is written:
the fatal saw wails above me.[2]

2 "Root." August 8, 1944.

Marching Orders

The rumour mill goes into overdrive. The men from Todt and the guards are growing visibly anxious. The sentries place machine gun stands around the bunkers. Corporal Sisák is shouting non-stop. Corporal Horváth is cursing a blue streak. Guards with savage German shepherds march us to our place of work. We putter around the mine cars like sleepwalkers, dragging our afflicted bones around in a daze. With blood-blistered hands we keep lifting our axes. Backbauer, that deranged Todt man, swings his truncheon at us. "You insolent, sabotaging riffraff," he growls, his eyes flashing with rage. "You will all end up in hell! Schnell, schnell!" Backbauer runs up and down, mercilessly hitting anyone he can reach.

We listen to these rude tirades, half asleep, exhausted. We are lethargic. We are starving and we daydream that we are eating. It's a cruel dream; we suffer the torments of Tantalus. From time to time our jaws begin a monotonous motion; we picture the food in front of us, we smell its exquisite aroma, then we abruptly wake up to a furious voice. We each feel a spasm rush through our bodies, but we keep on toiling.

"Meshuggener mamzer…mich shrekt men nit" (You crazy bastard, you don't scare me), whispers the little rabbi through his teeth, in Backbauer's direction.

Our keepers fear attacks by Tito's Partisans. The prisoners dread the Chetniks led by Draža Mihailović.

~

On Sunday, August 20, St. Stephen's Day, the occupants of the Lager get their boots back. Rumours are rampant. The Lager is buzzing like a beehive. Junger and Sergeant Tóth try to reassure the agitated men. Even Sisák's rage has subsided.

In the afternoon, Miklós reads his poem "À la recherche" in our barracks. He wrote it in the days before we got our boots back. The next day, Monday, we don't do any mine car work or navvying; instead, we are sent out for tree cutting. The Partisan threat continues to grow. The guards fear a surprise attack, expecting the Partisans to appear out of the forest. It's been months since we've had shoes on our feet, so we keep sliding and stumbling on the uneven surface full of clumps of earth and rocky debris. We lug the giant stumps in groups of eight, straining ourselves to the breaking point, because they are driving us hard; our arms and legs are covered in scrapes, our clothing is in tatters. Bandi Reiner, Sági, Radnóti and I chop down the dense forest on the same team, hoping that the Partisans will find us. For a fleeting moment, we hope for the miracle of liberation.

On August 22, Lieutenant Száll receives a command: "Get ready to march." At night we hear sporadic shooting from the direction of Žagubica. Sergeant Kovács points his binoculars at the mountains and spots Titoists on the horizon. We hear loud cannon blasts from Bulgaria and the rattle of machine guns from far away.

Lieutenant Száll receives a new command: "Cancel the marching orders." Radnóti's words ring in my head, on the peaks of Serbia full of woe. The highway leading to Požarevac comes to life. The cracked, neglected road to Bor swarms with men, animals, carts, the captured Italian soldiers of General Badoglio and truck convoys packed with Wehrmacht soldiers.

Haggard prisoners from the Westfalen, Laznica and Rhön Lagers beyond Heidenau come into view, drenched in sweat and stumbling on the bumpy road. Only the elderly and those unable to walk were sent on their way in the company of armed guards from the Lagers beyond Heidenau; the remaining prisoners still have to work. The Todt foreman prescribed a very strict production quota. In the Rhön Lager, they are not trussing-up as frequently, a clear sign that something is up.

More cauldron news: Romania has withdrawn from the war; Antonescu was arrested in a coup. Hungary is ready to act. The Red Army is approaching, making flanking movements through the Balkans. Many men from the Laznica Lager have escaped to join Tito's forces.

We also feel the urge to escape, but we are fearful: we've been told many times that if someone flees their nearest barracks mate will be executed right away. We know that if we don't end up with Tito's Partisans, our fate will be sealed. It is said that the Chetniks will kill us without hesitation, before we can utter a word; Milan Nedić's Serbian State Guard will hand us over to the Nazis. The majority of the prisoners don't speak Serbian, though some of us could say a few halting words.

$\sim$

The men in Heidenau wrote a card home when we could. None of us ever received a reply. What has become of our homes? Are our families still alive? In "À la recherche," Radnóti asks, "But where are the suppers / made wise with wine?"[1] The Todt man from Burgenland occasionally "loses" his *Donau-Zeitung* around our work site. At lunchtime, we'd read in these accidentally abandoned German newspapers about the extremely rapid advance of the Soviet army.

---

1 "À la recherche." August 17, 1944.

It's raining; it has been pouring relentlessly since dawn. We are drenched like orphan sparrows on telephone wires. We line up in the morning for the usual black liquid and soggy, mouldy *Zwieback*, a kind of twice-baked bread. A tiny wooden tag bearing an identification number hangs on the right side of each of our hats. We are still alive, but we haven't had a name for a long time — we are only numbers. "Here!" we shout when we hear our four-digit number. This morning, for the first time, there are small pieces of pasta in the black swill. Is this to give us strength for the days to come? I fish out the thin noodles with my tin fork; my spoon was lost a long time ago, or was it stolen, who knows? Here in the camp everything is a cherished treasure, even extremely dirty worn-out clothes stained with mud, blood and lard. We don't have lice yet, but at dawn when we get up we are teeming with bedbugs. We continuously scratch ourselves without even being aware of it.

Terrible things happened last night. The Lager was awakened by the sound of gunfire. Pitch dark, icy fear: the guards' dogs are barking eerily. Is it Chetniks? Tito's Partisans? SS death squads? After an exchange of fire that lasts an hour the guns suddenly go silent. Radnóti's "shattered heart and lung"[2] can hardly bear the excitement. No one says a word. No one knows what happened, who fought whom during the night.

Each day since Lieutenant Száll cancelled the marching orders, it has been rumoured that we'll start marching the following day. Starvation is worsening, if that's even possible; the food depot's reserves have been completely exhausted. The "supply run" has become dangerous; the buyers can no longer travel to either Bor or Zaječar. Kari Háy and Gyuri Gara trade their Morava cigarettes with the smokers, who give them scraps of bacon in exchange, according to the going rate on the clandestine stock market.

---

2   From "He Could No Longer Bear." February 29, 1944.

We cherish the memories of our former lives — dear faces, child-hood friends, young loves secretly guarded in our hearts, now appear to us through a haze. For brief moments my grandmother's garden in Szatmár full of apple trees, by the gently sloping hillside, flashes across my mind's eye, as do summer vacations, hiking in the Buda hills, grape harvest festivities in Gyál, wine treading, the stomping of the grapes, at the tiny vineyard of my friend Tibi's parents. Bicycling with Vera in Buda: speeding down the steep slope of Hegyalja Road without brakes to the cog-wheel railway terminal. My mother's face appears to me every day, always in the evening, a few minutes before lights out. She looks at me with her serious, sad blue eyes, just looking at me.

The guards' hate-filled shouts; we are so worn down that we can't even feel fear anymore. But now we draw strength from the sound of the cannons, the commotion, the bombing — as if we were hearing the rumbling of the approaching end.

Toward evening, Miklós is in our barracks again; his pale, stubbled face wears a teacher's smile. He has just finished an eclogue. He needs a bit of cajoling to recite his poem. Those who are interested gather around Junger's bunk. Miklós opens up his cross-ruled notebook, and the poem, in his small, neat handwriting, comes into view:

POET

Hail to thee, fine old fellow, easily making your way down
this wild mountain road: be you hounded here or flown?
you're ire-driven, wing-lifted, lightning flashes from your eyes,
hail to thee, agéd one, I can already see that you belong
to that ancient race of great-raged prophets. Say which one?[3]

---

3   "Eighth Eclogue." Heidenau Lager: in the mountains above Žagubica, August 23, 1944.

The precious minutes fly by. We hear the command for lights out. Miklós cannot finish his reading, as he must return to barracks six immediately. Junger borrows the *Avala* from him. The next day at dusk, Junger reads the "Eighth Eclogue." He recites it more beautifully and with better diction than Radnóti:

PROPHET

Which one am I? Nahum I am, of the city Elkosh born,
against that vile city, Assyrian Nineveh, I sang the word,
I, become a sack full of wrath, sang the holy word.

Junger recites poetry standing up. This wise Torah scholar, who is the same age as Radnóti, holds the *Avala* in his left hand, while leaning on his knobbly cane with his right. I wonder about who Radnóti used as a model for Nahum, the prophet of Elkosh.

Kari Háy is sketching with incredible ease; along with the usual roosters, I can already see the castles of Drégely and Eger in his sketchbook. Now he is drawing the prophet Nahum surrounded by glowing embers and angels.

On August 28, a lot of wrung-out *Häftlinge,* prisoners, are hanging around the barbed-wire fence. Serbian black-market hawkers arrive bearing packs of food. A wristwatch has already changed hands. A pair of brown walking shoes surfaces from who knows where. The law of supply and demand is in force. The prices have gone sky high. *Kol'ko dinara?* How much? the eager prisoners ask the vendors. One of the kerchief-wearing women has *kozji sir*, goat cheese, for bartering; in the blink of an eye, a deal is struck. *Kol'ko dinara?* The prisoners pelt the sellers with questions. They then quickly calculate the amount in terms of shirts and underwear.

I watch the turbulent spectacle with rapt attention. I've got nothing to barter, but I still linger among the traders. The experienced Ukraine veterans started out on this trip better prepared than us young fellows. They brought along a lot of stuff that could be used for trading here in the mountains of Bor.

The blond girl who sold me a corn cake the other day in exchange for my worn-out scarf notices me standing there longingly and motions me over. I say and gesture that I have nothing left. She smiles and presses a sizeable loaf of corn bread into my hand, then signals for me to wait. She runs off and returns a few minutes later with a small bundle. It is cheese and goat cheese curds wrapped in a napkin. She hands this over as an extra, and blushes.

Kako se zoveš? I ask her name. "Radmila. Radmila Mudrić," she replies, and blushes even more.

A new command zings by. The guards flick their hands to shoo the vendors away; they do the same to the prisoners beside the barbed-wire fence. Radmila stands straight and tall beyond the fence, along the Na Crnom Vrhu road, among the Serbian women wearing polka-dot kerchiefs, and she waves: *Vidimo se opet prijatelju* (See you again, my friend). I can still hear her voice as she recedes, see her waving. She is teary-eyed and keeps waving until the prisoners disappear from sight.

The following day, Tuesday morning, the company is ready to leave — this time for real. At dawn, new uniformed men arrive from Bor to ensure a smooth departure. The Lager is filled with feverish preparations, people scurrying around like disturbed ants. The *ukis* men wrap boot rags around their feet and advise the young men to do the same: "With socks in your boots you'd end up with bloody blisters," Miki Kun instructs them. The young guard we call "Parsley" gives us permission to fetch wheelbarrows from the depot for the ailing older men. Two or three of them may put their belongings in the wheelbarrows. The physicians don't have any medicine left. Radnóti is suffering from a toothache. In the first week of August, one of his teeth got so inflamed that they transported him to the Rhön Lager to see the physicians there to deal with his high fever. Dr. Müller — we later learned his name was actually Dr. Béla Mária — acting as a dentist for the occasion, extracted Miklós's bad tooth. But Miklós is tormented repeatedly by his teeth and has frequent stomach cramps. Pista Hajdú passes bloody urine. Zoltán Zilahi, the former punctilious bookkeeper, moans and groans. Junger, wearing baggy cotton pants, carries a small knapsack; he has a satchel slung over his shoulder and the indispensable knobbly cane in his hand.

Lieutenant Száll gives the command to line up. We start marching toward Bor. The tattered death brigade of Heidenau Lager stumbles as they march on the cracked road. The wheelbarrows wobble along. Our soles are developing blisters, our shoulders are growing numb under the weight of knapsacks, blankets and duffle coats. Three months of toil have carved deep furrows in the brows of the marching men; months of loading mine cars, cutting trees, building railways and navvying; months filled with starvation, constant night battles with bedbugs and fleas, feuding, suspicions and accusations.

The exhausted prisoners stomp along in a forced march with their bundles and blankets on their backs, the Star of David blooming on their trench coats. István Gáti, who suffers from goitres, collapses on the ground; two men reach under his arms, they put his knapsack in a tip-cart; István "rises and walks again / Ankles and knees moving… as if wings uplifted him, sets out on his way."[4]

Before we started off on the forced march, Ensign György Turner, Lieutenant Száll's adjutant, read us the riot act: "It is forbidden to step out of formation; it is forbidden to fraternize with the local population. It is forbidden to salute the German soldiers; it is forbidden to ask questions. Understood? There will be no more beatings or truss-ups. Anyone who tries to escape will be shot in the head on the spot. Understood?"

Forbidden, forbidden, forbidden. In spite of it all, the mood of the company is not mournful. It is cautiously optimistic, since we've

---

4 From Radnóti's "Forced March." Bor, September 15, 1944.

heard the cauldron news: we are going home. This abominable war will soon end, the warring parties will make a peace agreement, the losers will be punished, the liberators will be celebrated. The victims will be commemorated then forgotten; the atrocities will fade away.

We keep tripping over the razor-sharp mountain stones. We've been marching for a long time. The guards in the front dictate a fast pace. Muscular Emil Sági supports Radnóti. Miklós lugs a bundle for Soltész, who has a weak heart. The pace is better suited to a forced march for young recruits. Among us are many older men, in their forties and fifties, who were suffering from asthma, heart valve disease, high blood pressure and God knows what other conditions at the time they were called up. We weren't even given medical exams; everyone was thrown into the same sack, like laundry you pay for by the pound.

The weary men from Heidenau get shoved to the edge of the ditch by Wehrmacht convoys and peasant carts from Zaječar making their way up the hill, packed to the hilt with plundered goods. Weakened and limping, old men try to keep in step with the others; if they stagger, a rifle butt lands on them swift as lightning. Only a few stale drops of water slosh around in our canteens.

Shepherds in traditional footwear stare mutely at the pitiful company. The guards scan the winding roads surrounded by cliffs with their binoculars: they still fear Partisan attacks. Word has spread that Tito's Partisans know about us, and we are filled with hope that they'll liberate us. What would we actually prefer right now? Certain liberation or the return home that the rumours promise?

Lieutenant Száll orders a short rest in the vacated Vorarlberg Lager; the *ukis* men warn the guys who are young, or just clueless, not to remove their boots, because they wouldn't be able to put them back on their swollen feet. For those who lack discipline, the voice of experience falls on deaf ears. The minutes of rest seem like mere moments. Dragging ourselves to our feet is more difficult than marching.

The company sets off again. We trudge along, the rocky debris crunching under our feet. First the Innsbruck Lager appears on the right, then the deserted München Lager. The scenery is slowly changing, the savage wind dies down, the mountains become tamer by the time we arrive at the uncannily quiet Dresden Lager. Its occupants have already left for Bor. The empty barracks make a hollow sound. The vermin-infested bunks beckon our stiff bodies. Lieutenant Száll gives us permission to sleep outdoors, if we want. The majority of the Ukrainian veterans, the young men, Kardos the cook, Junger, Pista Rajna, Radnóti and I spread out our blankets on the Lager's bumpy meadow. The boots have blistered our feet, our foot rags have disintegrated into threads, our feet are throbbing with blood blisters.

The scenery here is beautiful: lush vegetation, bright red wild strawberries growing along the broken-down fence; intoxicating, moist mountain air all around us. The prisoners are so exhausted that sleep, sweet therapeutic sleep, eludes them.

We had been marching since dawn without eating or drinking. We are worn out, lethargic. We are the living dead, reposing in the world of shadows. Homer once wrote that for men the most grievous of all deaths is to die of hunger.

The scrawny little rabbi is davening, praying quietly; Junger leafs through his Bible. Miklós's long, slim face is hollowed, his eyes are sorrowful; the pale poet is scribbling in his *Avala*:

From Bulgaria, wild and swollen, the noise of cannon rolls;
It booms against the ridge, then hesitates, and falls.
Men, animals, carts, thoughts pile up as they fly;
The road rears back and whinnies, maned is the racing sky.[5]

When I finally manage to fall asleep, I dream that I'm munching on white berries that taste of honey, picked from the dusty fruit trees along the road from Gyál to Péteri.

---

5 "Postcard 1." August 30, 1944.

On Wednesday, August 30, in the early hours of the morning, the miserable band of the downtrodden continues on its agonizing way toward Bor. For the first time we see SS soldiers on motorcycles with sidecars whizzing by on the road; we also encounter poor locals driving one-horse peasant carts. The daily quota for the forced march is thirty kilometres. If a person slows down to do his business, he is lucky to get away without a beating. Walter H. faints. Two or three men lift his heavy body into a wheelbarrow as they proceed. Dr. Bárdos tries to revive him, Walter comes to.

It is early afternoon by the time we are herded through the gate of the Brünn Lager in Bor. Brünn is a thousand times worse than Heidenau was. There are prisoners dangling with taut arms from trussing-up poles; their toes barely touch the blood-soaked ground. The penetrating stench around the latrines mixes with the smell of cyanide. We lay our threadbare blankets on the designated bunks in the gigantic barracks. The guards bark commands in the huge hall, demanding that everyone who passes by them stand at attention. Out of the chaotic babel, new faces, old acquaintances and old friends surface. All were brought from the neighbouring Lagers and forced to squeeze into this hellish place called Brünn.

Swarms of flies buzz around the filthy cauldron; we receive a ladleful of thin soup in our tins; we slug down the tepid liquid eagerly. After leading the life of a beast for months, days filled with fear and exhaustion from dawn till dusk, exposed to the vagaries of the weather, we have no energy left for thinking, pride or love. We are living among strange smells, pressed up against strange bodies, and even our dreams have become very strange.

Lights out. When I was a child I was told that if you sleep in a new room, before falling asleep look at the four corners of the room, and what you dream about will come true. Dead tired, I am searching for the four corners of this humongous barracks, but I'm afraid, I'm very much afraid of the dream, I'm afraid it will come true.

Clouds of bloodthirsty insects, "parachuting bedbugs," hail down on our shoulders, mouths and eyes; they know we still have blood in our veins. There is no mercy. Then at dawn all hell breaks loose. The guards, perhaps sensing the proximity of Lieutenant Colonel Marányi, inflict extreme brutality — they administer swift kicks to groins and genitals.

We are building bulwarks along the barbed wire. The work is directed by the men from Todt, and at times Wehrmacht soldiers also show up on the site. Marányi, the megalomaniac, is seen frequently around the Brünn Lager. He issues orders to his officers, but the labour force men are beneath his notice. Marányi's whole attitude makes it clear that he has totally bought into the superior man mythos; he derives an almost sensual pleasure from playing the role of the demigod atop the hill of the wretched. His disciples, the excited guards, jump like trained seals at a wave of the master's hand. There is no trace of rationality anymore; after all, we are the scum of the earth, the tumour that needs to be excised.

Marányi encourages his officers and subordinates to commit atrocities. With an arrogant, haughty face and a dashing pose, he makes his cronies laugh at his jokes. From where, I wonder, has this perverse murderer been unleashed on the world. Alleged offences are punished with beatings, trussing-up, being thrown in pits, hog-tying. Torture has its own techniques. Marányi and his henchmen have raised this ancient rite of the human-beast to an art form. Slave drivers are beating the men who are working on the bulwarks; it's the same way the slaves who built the ancient pyramids were treated. Starvation — I have talked about it so much already, and somehow I cannot stop talking about it — is getting more and more horrible. The kitchen staff throws rotten cabbage in the bottom of our mess tins; a horrendous stench permeates the air around the barracks.

By the beginning of September, three thousand prisoners have been crowded into the Brünn Lager. Fellow sufferers from Vác and Sződliget; *muszos* men conscripted in the previous year, 1943, from

Szeged, Tasnád, Székesfehérvár, Jászberény, Zombor; Jehovah's Witnesses, Szekler Sabbatarians, friends from home, classmates, relatives,
all find each other. Emil Rubinyi embraces his brother. Radnóti meets
up with his sociologist philosopher friend Sándor (Sanyi) Szalai and
the social-democratic writer Pali Justus. We count among us the writer Gyuri G. Kardos, the neurologist Béla Mária, the poet László (Laci)
Tabi, the theatre critic László Balásti and the cellist Gyuri Horváth,
and many others from the scientific and artistic communities, the
opera house, from the universities, colleges and high schools. Péter
Szüsz, Gyuri Horváth and I represent the community of the József
Eötvös High School of Budapest in the Brünn Lager.

In the evenings, once again, we squeeze around the bunk of Jóska Junger. The old friends, writers, artists, arts aficionados and we
younger guys constitute Radnóti's circle of friends, the name we gave
ourselves in Heidenau. Out of respect, we voted for Junger to have
the upper bunk, which is close to the small cobweb-covered window.
Kari Háy is complaining; he has no paper left and his pencils have all
worn out as well. But he is also scared to make drawings ever since he
found out that the sadist Marányi is torturing Csillag for his cartoons;
Csillag is buried half dead. Miklós, like a fanatic, keeps writing quietly; he is copying his latest poem into *Avala* 5:

> Oh if only I could believe that everything of worth
> Were not just in my heart — that I still had a home on earth;[6]

Pali Justus, a translator of Shakespeare's sonnets and a wise and
always pleasant sociologist, reads the first "Razglednica," postcard,
aloud. Szalai and I recite the "Eighth Eclogue" from Radnóti's *Avala*.
Sanyi is the poet and I am the prophet. We both have trouble correctly pronouncing the Rs. We totally ruin the effect.

---

6   From "Forced March." September 15, 1944.

Portents of Death

Destitute days in September. We've been suffering in the Brünn Lager for two weeks now. The agitated Todt and Wehrmacht men are swarming around the bulwark construction sites. They are fuming with rage; with guns drawn, they drag the weakened prisoners from one worksite to the next. Twelve-hour shifts of furious, rushed work with a thirty-minute break at noon; there are no Sunday siestas like we had in Heidenau. From far and wide we hear about the atrocities committed by Marányi. We hear rumours that in the second half of July he sentenced two young prisoners to death in the Berlin Lager. The boys had tried to escape. To set an example, Marányi ordered several thousand slaves to witness the execution.

Miklós Lorsi has not played any music for a long time; he hides his violin locked in its case as if it were a precious Easter egg. It would be so nice to listen to its velvety sound; it might calm us down. Cervantes once wrote: "Where there's music there can be no evil." But here in the savage Lager you can only hear the strident sounds of the murderers.

Radnóti's eyes don't smile anymore; his face is ashen, like those of the conscripts of 1943. Miklós seeks out the company of the Zionist Junger and a few of the younger men. Emil Rubinyi recalls old stories about his father, Mózes Rubinyi, the outstanding linguist. I talk about my teacher at the Eötvös High School, Manó Kertész, the Hungarian,

Finnish and Estonian language scholar, and about the afternoon sessions of the József Kiss literary circle for youth. Miklós listens attentively; we can see that for a few moments he forgets about the bleak present, just as we young fellows do.

Anti-aircraft guns are mounted at the Bor crossroads; tanks with caterpillar tracks rumble on the road, along with armoured vehicles carrying steel-helmeted Wehrmacht men who are armed to the teeth. Trucks laden with stolen goods speed toward the north, madly fleeing the sinking ship.

Portents of death are trembling in the air. The Germans and their henchmen dislike waking from their long dream of being rulers; they can't conceive of being losers. Their flight and their new circumstances only increase — if such a thing is possible — their immeasurable hatred and hostile behaviour toward us. It suddenly occurs to our jailers that we are not stupid. They see the joy of upcoming retribution on our faces, and in their nervous state they imagine that our eyes reflect malicious mockery. It has dawned on them that we all belong to the other side, to the side of those who scour the blue skies with Liberator bombers day after day to rain bombs on their enemy, our enemy: them.

Waffen-SS formations appear in the vicinity of the Lager. We hear that Lieutenant Colonel Marányi, who gets a sick thrill out of torture, had the prisoners in the potato pit, the artist Csillag and twenty-two others, executed.

The spectre of mass slaughter looms. After all, we know about the bloodbath in the Ukraine, the burning of prisoners in sealed barracks. Why should they treat us more mercifully?

We have the feeling that no one can escape anymore. Yet, I still dream that I have escaped: I am at home again in the ground-floor apartment with my loved ones, and I talk to them about the horrors. They listen incredulously; perhaps they don't believe any of it and act as if they aren't even interested in hearing about it.

An unexpected lice and scabies inspection. In our section, this is carried out by the three physicians from Heidenau. We hear rumours now that the several thousand prisoners of war are going to be taken home. Heartening words. But how? Could this be a phantasm?

~

The Partisans blast the railway tracks; the Germans have let their Serbian helpers go, suspecting them of being Titoist infiltrators. The local population takes part in the sabotage; we can feel passive resistance in the air. The Bor prisoners' early morning drill gets steadily more cruel. The local SS formation, like a big-bellied giant spider, is expanding the reach of its pincers. At times, the silence of the undernourished switches to senseless chatter. Bread distribution slows down. The *Häftling* army is living on maggoty bread; we are on the brink of collapse.

In the Brünn Lager, there are no hawkers along the wire fence, like there were in the "good old days" at Heidenau. Truth be told, there is hardly anything left to barter.

From the kitchen comes the lunch call; we start salivating just like Pavlov's dogs. To a hungry stomach there is no such thing as inedible food. My tin spoon vanished back in Heidenau, and now, like an eager Puli dog, I lap up the stinking cabbage broth from my grimy mess tin.

On September 15, a Friday morning, Marányi's bloodhound, Sergeant Major Császár, who is famed for his cruelty in the service of the tyrants, barks out the order to fall in to the companies from Heidenau and Rhön. Császár, with his crooked moustache, has been sent by his boss from the neighbouring Berlin Lager to Brünn. Sergeant Major Császár's reputation as a dreaded murderer has preceded him; we learned his name a while back from our buyers in the mountains.

Sergeant Major Császár commands the inmates from Heidenau and Brünn to go to the Berlin Lager. I wonder why we were selected out of the crowd. The Berlin Lager is reputed to be the most horrible Lager of all.

We've been standing around idly for about an hour in the courtyard, mulling over our worst fears. From the headquarters building, Lieutenant Colonel Marányi is heading our way. Military medals gleam on Marányi's uniform; he is a professional soldier, with a stocky build and a pug nose; he keeps sniffling frequently, as if he were taking snuff. He inspects the horde with an air of indifference.

We stand shivering in the drizzling rain. In the square, Marányi issues these commands: "You will leave for home soon. You will proceed to Požarevac on foot; from there you will continue your journey to Hungary by train."

This time, Marányi — we can't believe our ears — addresses us as politely as if he were having a conversation in the officers' mess with his chief of staff: "It takes five days to reach Požarevac, one hundred and fifty kilometres. It will be a forced march. The Berlin Lager will start first, Brünn will follow later. The sick will stay behind. Those who feel they cannot walk must not start off. There is to be no falling behind. We are on a battlefield; the enemy is lurking all around us. Those who cannot endure a march of thirty kilometres a day should stay here in Bor and await further instructions. Those who fall behind will be shot."

Marányi, in his immaculate uniform, has finished his sermon on the mount.

Moved by his words, the ragged band cheers the mass murderer. "Did you hear it?" The prisoners start hugging each other. "He said we are going home! Home…"

Like thunderbolts from a clear blue sky, fresh rumours start flying around. These rumours keep changing, like confetti in a kaleidoscope. There appears to be an excess of personnel. For strategic reasons, it is not possible to dispatch all of the prisoners from Bor at once. The officers try to smooth the men's ruffled feathers: "In a few days, the men left behind will also set out for Požarevac escorted by guards. Part of the trip will be done by truck, so they will need to walk less."

We don't believe these enticing words. We want to get home as soon as possible. "The Heidenau Lager stays behind; they will be sent out on the second transport," sounds the devastating command.

We don't believe for a minute that the second transport, or, as it's called in military jargon, the second contingent, will be sent home. We don't take their promises seriously. The Organisation Todt is already clearing out its offices; they load *Vulkanfiber*, laminated plastic, suitcases full of papers, files, ledgers and typewriters onto the waiting trucks. They pack feverishly, non-stop. Trucks roar around the Todt barracks, their brakes screeching; there is a lot of shouting and swearing. The Germans are running around like headless chickens; and that's how it should be, because to our way of thinking, they are the living dead already. But first it's our turn to die: they make the "V" sign while laughing maliciously, and they call us *Stinkjude,* stinking Jews, with a sneer.

Then the Einsatzkommando, the firing squad, arrives in the area.

The Germans don't make us work anymore; they have stopped punishing the slaves. A strange, indescribable, depressing mood takes hold of us, the like of which we have not experienced before. Perhaps it's how condemned men feel before their execution.

The fellows from Heidenau exhort the non-commissioned officers, Company Sergeant Major Lajos Szép and Sergeant Kovács, and, with Junger's help, the more humane Lieutenant Száll, to talk Marányi into squeezing the Heidenau group in with the first contingent. The wealthiest prisoners promise to amply reward the non-commissioned officers if they can arrange to have them included in the first group to leave. They know that the first transport means life, and the second, annihilation. Ervin K., a fifty-year-old grocer from Tátra Street, offers the sergeants the gold crowns he removed from his teeth.

For two days the weather has been windy, with drizzling rain. The men with rheumatism or gout especially suffer from the dampness that penetrates their bones. We are waiting around idly in the middle of the sea of mud, in the spongy muck by the wire fence, when we are told to fall in to receive a new command: Heidenau has been joined to the first contingent. It seems that the manoeuvrings of Lieutenant Száll and the sergeants have yielded results. Hooray! We are leaving for home too! Including those from Heidenau, 3,600 prisoners will set off shortly, the remaining 2,400 some time later.

The faces of the dispirited men from Heidenau flush with joy when they hear the news. "We are going home after all!" is their jubilant cry. *Kam derlebt*, says our little rabbi in Yiddish — "That was close!" Walter Hirschberger, our Baron Munchausen, pictures himself promenading in Paris with the seamstress he hasn't seen for a long time, and our crafty Pinocchio heads off in the direction of the food depot, bent on thievery; he sneaks around without being noticed, like a black panther in the dark forest.

Although he is even paler than usual, Miklós Radnóti is nonetheless animated, as if his mood has brightened. All of a sudden, we start making plans; life returns to us as to wilting flowers after the rain. Miklós, perhaps for the first time, talks about his wife, Fifi, and about his old friends. As for me, I am hopeful that I will be admitted to university and will be able to continue my studies. We are going home! Yes, we are going home.

While we were toiling away in the mountains, and later as we suffered through the building of the bulwarks, we hardly had time to think; the images of our families, our loved ones and our old homes faded from our memories. Our souls are alive again, we are spilling over with words, with old memories. Nostalgia is kindled in us, and we are shocked to realize that we haven't forgotten a thing from our past; we think yearningly about our everyday lives in former times.

Lieutenant Colonel Ede Marányi issues a new command: The headcount for the first contingent is too high, so the old, the sick, the wounded, and whoever else is designated, cannot leave. The list of those staying behind will be prepared by the non-commissioned officers.

The elderly, who are generally debilitated, strike comical poses to show off their muscles to the inspectors; the sick regain their strength; the wounded hide the pus-filled sores that cover their bodies. The wealthier men once again offer promissory notes that can be cashed in at home, mentioning fabulous sums. In desperation, the intellectuals try to appeal to the emotions: to get on the list of the first contingent means life, to fail means death. The spectre of the SS death squad hangs over us. Exhausted human wrecks who subsisted on a daily diet of eight hundred calories are now pleading, begging the henchmen of the tyranny.

The selection process drags on; Laci Boros gives himself a lightning-quick shave so he'll appear fresher; the well-to-do continue to murmur the magic words of bribery in the guards' ears; Junger goes back and forth between the *muszos* men and the non-commissioned officers tasked with selecting. No one can escape the selection. A desperate struggle to stay alive is going on. Our stomachs are in knots from anxiety, as we wait to see who will and who won't.

By Saturday, September 16, the list of those in the first group is ready at last: the first ones to leave for home are those who were taken away in 1943. The majority of them are from the Berlin Lager. They want to send off half of the forced labourers from Bor in the first contingent, around three thousand people. To the conscripts of 1943 they add not only the prisoners from the Innsbruck and Heidenau Lagers, but also the Jehovah's Witnesses and the Szekler Sabbatarians.

On hearing the news, the men from Heidenau suddenly see the future through rose-coloured glasses. The *Häftlinge* are caught up in feverish preparations. We hang around on the grounds of the Lager. We bump into acquaintances, friends: lisping Laci Somos from grade school, Uncle Abonyi, the father of Edit, the girl with the turned-up nose from Irányi Street. What a strange place fate found for our encounter!

On Saturday afternoon, unexpectedly, we are ordered to fall in and given a new command. Devastating news: the headcount has increased, and so we must reduce the numbers. This also includes the Heidenau Lager.

Deathly silence. You could hear a pin drop. The minions of the Third Reich shout out names. This time we are no longer numbers but "names" again.

Kádár…Olivér Hollós…Károly Háy…and the list goes on: Wellesz, the buyer, Pinocchio, the king of second helpings, myself, and another fifteen to twenty people from the Heidenau Lager end up in the second contingent. The bearers of the called-out names are rooted to the ground, just like Lot's wife when she looked back at Sodom. Before we recover from our fright, the non-commissioned officers and the guards chase away the scabies infested band with vile curses.

The departure of the first contingent is imminent. We learn from Miklós, as he talks to some of the younger guys, that originally he'd been assigned to the group that would stay behind, but Junger arranged for him to leave with the first contingent. "Those who have a wife and family waiting for them should have priority," Junger reasoned convincingly with the non-commissioned officers.

The men of the first contingent, including those from Heidenau, are preparing feverishly. Radnóti is happy, but he's got a bad conscience about having been included in the first group by using pull. Time is short; Miklós copies his poems from Bor into a cross-ruled notebook. Aware that Sanyi Szalai got grouped in with the ones staying behind, Miklós asks him to safeguard his poems. Junger also copies lines from the *Avala* into his own notebook.

A wall has descended between those who are about to leave and those who must stay behind. The Heidenau men of the first contingent would like to set off; they find it painful to bear the sad looks of those left behind.

We are saying our goodbyes. The men of the first contingent can scarcely conceal their joy. They vow to notify our families at home right away that we are okay, that we are alive and will soon be leaving as well.

Nevertheless, Miklós's mood is sombre, as many of his friends are staying behind: Kari Háy, Sándor Szalai from the Rhön Lager, the majority of the single men, myself among them.

I think about the many hours I spent with Miklós on Sunday afternoons, on the banks of the Mlava River in the Serbian Erzgebirge. He read his poems, and I told him enthusiastically that I also wrote and was going to be a teacher. He smiled, slowly exhaling smoke, and kept nodding.

We are now standing in the relentlessly drizzling autumn rain, in the mire, trying to say goodbye. Szalai walks glumly over to us. Miklós embraces both of us. "There is still half a loaf of bread under my pallet," says Miklós, "divide it between the two of you. They will hand out more to me when I leave."

We can only stammer at this display of generosity; we are not able to properly thank him. Miklós sees that I'm shaking. Because of the steady rainfall all day, it feels like every inch of my body is shivering. Radnóti comforts me, as a father-confessor would comfort a condemned man about to be executed.

"I am not afraid," I croak. I'm trying to play the hero in front of Radnóti.

The central square of the Lager is a hive of activity; it's where everyone is gathering and jostling each other. It makes me think of the caravans in fairy tales.

Junger approaches me and sees Miklós consoling me. And then, quietly but with determination, he says, "I'm handing my place over to you. You go with the first contingent."

I look at Junger, flabbergasted, and my first thought is that I haven't heard right, that I'm hallucinating, that mischievous elves are playing tricks on me. Junger looks at me calmly and benevolently. "Go with the first contingent, I will arrange for the switch."

I am freezing in the howling wind; my teeth are chattering; I feel sick to my stomach. "I'm not afraid," I repeat to Junger. Of course, I am just saying that. Because I really am afraid. I am struggling with an oppressive, primal anxiety. I would happily give my right arm to be able to leave with the first contingent. But I cannot agree to take his spot, to force Junger to stay behind.

They are ready to march early the next morning, on September 17, a Sunday, the three thousand prisoners of the first contingent, among them Jóska Junger and the poet Miklós Radnóti from the Heidenau group. Surrounded by a hundred armed guards, they start off on a forced march with wheelbarrows and tip-carts along the bumpy road in the direction of the Erzgebirge, toward Požarevac station.

The first contingent is led by Lieutenant Pataki and his deputy, Lieutenant Juhász. The belongings of the officers and their deputies are pulled on peasant carts stolen from the Serbs, by young, broad-shouldered *muszos* men. They are marching in rows of five. They are getting further and further away.

That was the last time I saw Miklós.

Jews with the Star of David and converts to Christianity who follow the gospel of Jesus, Baptists, Jehovah's Witnesses, Szekler Sabbatarians, believers and atheists: all march along together.

The death brigade of Bor.

Tonight is the eve of Rosh Hashanah. Tomorrow is the first day of the Jewish new year.

The fate of every creature is decided during these days.

A Fragile Liberation

It has been a week since the first contingent set off. Those of us who have stayed behind keep working, engaged in totally purposeless make-work activities: we are building a shed and we carry the tools from the copper mine to this structure. The next day we dismantle a depot, then we lug the iron chains of excavators and cutting machines to the southern perimeter of the vacated mine. The copper mine, which only two weeks ago was in full production day and night, now has the look of an exploited, barren mountainside, like a yellowed moon crater.

Now we are carrying bricks beyond the Lager gate, near the Eastern Orthodox cemetery, escorted by guards. The buildings beside the Berlin Lager are clearly visible from here: they are the Hungarian military headquarters, the infernal domain of Lieutenant Colonel Marányi. The adjacent building houses the command centre of the Organisation Todt for Bor; to the right of it, we can see our old "inn," the Brünn Lager.

One day we dig ditches for the defence of the town; the next day we stretch barbed wire around the Lagers. The trees of the small town are losing their leaves, and we toil, chilled and soaked, in the cold, monotonously drizzling rain. The Germans are scrambling, the Wehrmacht men are speeding around in trucks, the SS henchmen are cleaning their boots and weapons, totally oblivious to us. Luckily.

We pile bricks along the sides of the cemetery, about five hundred metres away from the Berlin Lager. The guards are chit-chatting, paying no attention to us. From the other side of the narrow road, a short, muscular-looking man in a grey raincoat approaches. The look he gives us galley slaves is sympathetic. The man looks about thirty to thirty-five years old, with dark brown hair. He sneaks a look at our keepers, but the guards are deeply immersed in their conversation, so they don't even glance toward the stranger.

We know it is forbidden to salute anyone in a German or Hungarian uniform, or to talk to them, and it is strictly forbidden to talk to a civilian. Nevertheless, this time we chance it. We pretend that we're working while we exchange a few words with the man. His name is Miloš and he's an engineer; before the German occupation, he worked at the mining company. Out of curiosity, we ask him where he works now. With a kind, sorrowful smile — as if he hadn't heard our question — he changes the subject. "At lunchtime, go to the cemetery… see how beautiful the graves are and bring back some souvenirs from there."

We are perplexed by his remark; we think he's speaking nonsense.

Miloš speaks "little Hungarian." His brother-in-law is Hungarian and lives in Petrovgrad (Zrenjanin), Serbia. Miloš mixes Serbian with his "little Hungarian," and we somehow manage. The guards glance over at us, but they don't say a word.

Miloš gives us details about what's going on in Romania. We had already heard from the buyers in Heidenau that the Romanians withdrew from the war on August 23; in our closed world, this was just a stray bit of news, nothing more.

The Serbian engineer informs us that King Michael of Romania arrested Antonescu, Romania's commander-in-chief and prime minister; General Sănătescu formed a new government. The coup succeeded, and Romania turned its back on the Germans.

We were amazed that the fascists had given up on them so readily. Our new acquaintance seemed to read the doubt in our faces.

"The Germans launched a fierce attack against Bucharest and surroundings right away," Miloš continues, "but the disciplined and well-equipped Romanian army drove off the German troops. Moscow radio announced the German fiasco in Romania on August 27."

Miloš would like to give us more good news — he is an educated man who speaks quickly — but the guards interrupt the brief idyll: "Get on with it, get on with it, you lazy bunch, goddammit!"

We haul the red bricks to the front of the Todt building. On each trip we have to carry eight bricks. Are they even planning to build something? This is completely senseless — just like everything else.

"Boring work in Bor," mutters one of the *muszos* men under his breath. He totes his load, puffing, sweat streaming down his forehead. We're happy to see that Miloš is still hanging around us; it's a miracle the guards haven't chased him away.

"The position of the Nazis in the Balkans is shaky," whispers Miloš. "The way for the liberation of Yugoslavia, Bulgaria, Hungary and southern Poland has opened up. Big event, boys…there was a decisive victory." Then quietly he adds, with a wink, "The Nazis will soon be kaput."

Our engineer's appearance near the cemetery was sudden, and he leaves just as abruptly; his figure, like a modern-day Scarlet Pimpernel, disappears into the misty, grey distance in the direction of the mine.

At lunchtime, we are ordered back to the Lager; the Italians, we call them *badoglios*, in reference to the general, distribute the cabbage broth. The Italian boys are only "semi-" prisoners of war. They were allowed to keep their hair, and they spread margarine on it to make it shine.

The Italian prisoners of war are our cooks; they are the ones who slop the early morning black swill and the late afternoon meal into our mess tins. Our cook from Heidenau, Kardos, and the rest of the kitchen staff left with the first contingent. I wonder where they are now. There is no news of them.

The autumn rain falls relentlessly. At night, in the howling wind, it keeps beating down on the roof of our barracks.

Early the next morning, we continue to carry bricks. This time we have to lug the bricks from alongside the Todt building back to the fence around the entrance to the cemetery. The guards come up with these crazy ideas for work all by themselves; organized central orders for work stopped coming long ago. We carry the blocks back and forth. We're covered in brick dust, famished, ragged and reeling from exhaustion. We are tough, having managed to endure the tribulations so far, and we won't give up now. I wonder when they are going to send us home.

I suspect we are nearing the last act now.

Near the cemetery gate, we catch sight of Miloš in his grey raincoat.

Our guards are more brutal than yesterday. They confront Miloš with their rabid German shepherds. "Get out of here!" they bellow at the Serbian engineer.

Our messenger looks right through the soldiers, unfazed, as if they were puppets. He turns to us in a friendly fashion and asks, "Did you see the graves in the cemetery?" Like someone who feels right at home, our engineer moves past the guards with confident steps. Dumbfounded, they stare as the stranger departs.

At night I have confusing dreams. The Roman poet Cato advised: "Pay no attention to your dreams."

The foul-smelling Berlin Lager makes me think I've entered the realm of Hades. Within the confines of the Lager, the guards feel safe; they can inflict cruelty to their hearts' content.

Ten days after the departure of the first transport from Bor, the Subcarpathians and the other religious forced labourers wanted to commemorate the Day of Atonement. Yom Kippur is the most sacred holiday of the Jews. According to the Jewish calendar, the Day of Atonement is on the tenth day of the seventh month, and in 1944 it started on the evening of September 26 and lasted until sunset on September 27.

The Berlin Lager prisoners who were observing the holiday asked Jenö Duschinszki, the rabbi from Rákospalota, to conduct the service.

Moses spent forty days on Mount Sinai and returned to his people on Yom Kippur.

Yom Kippur is the day of love and forgiveness.

Rabbi Duschinszki, with the prior permission of the guards, calls the faithful to prayer in the barracks used for meal distribution.

Every man's, every creature's fate is sealed on Yom Kippur.

The legion of rags and tatters listens to the rabbi in awe:

Baruch atah adonai…. (Blessed are You, Lord our God….)

In an unexpected clash, a pack of enraged guards push through the door and window; they kick us in the groins and kidneys; they hit us on the head with cudgels and rifle butts; they heave Duschinszki through the window into the sea of mud.

"Here's the Yom Kippur you asked for! You scum…. You're all going to die like dogs!"

We are aghast. Bandi Reiner, Zoli Zilahi and a few others are standing around near the barracks when the rabbi is thrown out. Poor Duschinszki thuds down unconscious in between the piles of cast iron rails and crossties.

We had hauled the tarred beams and rails to the Lager from the mine so they could be used to build barricades against Partisan attacks. The guards consider themselves demi-gods; they ape their officers. They are the intrepid emperors of the fleeting moment, holding life and death in their hands.

We carry the bricks by the Eastern Orthodox cemetery again. A lanky, freckle-faced lance sergeant is the senior guard; we haven't seen him before. He speaks to us using the polite form of address, and that surprises us. "Carry six bricks at a time, not eight!" orders the lance sergeant. The other guards give him a strange look, but they don't say a word.

At noon, the Italian "cauldroners" roll the field kitchen to the cemetery entrance. It doesn't take them long to portion out the cabbage broth and then head back to the Lager. We carry our mess tins, these prized treasures, with us at all times, just as we carry the yellowed photos of our loved ones. In the Lager, neither we nor our valuables are safe.

During our half-hour lunch break, we finally have a chance to sneak into the cemetery. The lance sergeant vigilantly watches our steps, as if he wants to say something, but then he remains silent and waves it off; it's evident he's turning a blind eye. On the graves there are decorated metal baskets of various sizes: they contain corn cake wrapped in colourful kerchiefs, *bryndza*, round loaves, bacon and white bread, along with other tasty treats. The temptation is incredible. We don't know the rituals of the local religion: maybe they pay their respects to the dead by offering food.

Suddenly Miloš the engineer's advice springs to mind: "Go to the cemetery and take home some souvenirs." Yes, these tasty, feast-worthy morsels were prepared for us by the locals. It's possible that it is a ritual to put food on their loved ones' graves, but Miloš's message leaves no doubt in our minds that they are for us.

We snatch the food with savage hunger. Feeling pangs of conscience, we divide the spoils and devour the corn cake, the cottage cheese, the lard. We're insatiable, just like the peasants in Zsigmond Móricz's novels who have been starving their whole lives. Our bellies are bloated, we even feel dizzy. It's strange, but we don't feel satiated. Rather, we are worried that tomorrow we'll be starving again.

During the afternoon shift, Miloš shows up again; he walks by us slowly and repeats several times as he passes: "See you again, my friends…see you again."

~

Frantic scurrying in the Berlin Lager. Peasant carts lining up at the entrance. The officers' assistants carry bundles, bags, suitcases, radio equipment, uniforms and boxes of files to load on the carts.

We have already built the bulwarks; the Berlin and Brünn Lagers are surrounded by barbed wire, and the SS have installed machine gun stations around the Berlin Lager. We sense that the end is approaching.

The officers and staff are getting ready to flee the sinking ship and leave us to the mercies of the SS men.

It's too late to attempt to escape. There is neither time nor opportunity.

To our surprise, on September 28, in the early morning, we see Wehrmacht soldiers in the Lager: they distribute cans of peas, one-kilo loaves of bread, *mahorka*, a kind of cheap tobacco, and cigarette paper to the poor starved creatures who are lined up. The SS men standing nearby watch this all unfold with total indifference.

We think to ourselves: this is our "last breakfast," like the condemned prisoner's last meal before his execution. The fatalists are lamenting that we cannot change our destinies. The optimists are hoping for a miracle.

After the unusual distribution of canned goods, one of the Hungarian officers issues commands to the Bor prisoners. The Wehrmacht and the SS men have disappeared from the camp unobserved. The dashing officer relays the information in a strong baritone voice: "We will evacuate the camp tomorrow at dawn. Only the healthy men will march out with us; it will be a forced march, no stopping. The sick and those who can't withstand such a hard march will be taken over to the Brünn Lager to await further instruction. The second contingent will be ready to take off tomorrow at dawn. The Wehrmacht ration is for two days, make it last. That's all."

The officer turns sharply and leaves the tattered band in haste.

The Lager has already started falling apart. There is hardly any water coming from the faucets. Stormy winds have torn the doors off their hinges; the draft keeps making the windows bang. The latrines are filled to overflowing, and the *Häftlinge* keep doing their business anywhere at all, like ill-trained dogs.

"Where are we really going?" The doubting Thomases are trying to pick holes in everything.

"The officer didn't say that we were going home," objects one of the unfortunate wretches.

"Rest assured that we are going to Hungary," answers the well-informed Gyuri Kádár.

"Who told you they were taking us home?" The others argue with Kádár.

"We were told that we'd be going with the second contingent… don't you remember? Marányi said so." Gyuri Kádár is trying to convince himself and the others.

Several men are considering signing up to stay behind. The *ukis* men, who have been through the Soviet forced labour camps, again bring up the bloodbaths at Zhytomyr and Fastiv, the massacre in Voronezh, and the burning down of the barracks in Berdychiv, where the weakened inmates were slaughtered en masse.

"I'm not staying here," announces one of the "old" guys with a bent back. "If I am going to die, why should it be here in this hellish copper mine?" Despite this, perhaps a hundred or a hundred and fifty of these bone-weary, wretched men, hardly able to shuffle along on their aching feet and unable to work, decide to stay. They surrendered, they gave up the fight, they couldn't take the misery anymore. They are staying put. It's a numbing feeling to be helpless, subject to the whims of fate.

György Fehér, the physician, remains with the infirm.

~

It's our last evening in the Berlin Lager. Tomorrow at dawn, the men who are staying behind will be taken over to the Brünn Lager, and we will set off. We, the ones who are leaving, are preparing feverishly. The Lager is like a riled-up anthill. The guards scarcely pay any attention to us, since they too are busy packing.

At dusk, along the wire fence surrounding the Lager, the Einsatz-kommando, the SS killing squad, reappears. On the last night in Bor, exhausted, we lie down to sleep on the disgusting, bedbug-infested bunks. I fall into a heavy sleep; muddled nightmares spin around in my head. In my dream, Radnóti is filling his pipe, Junger is sipping draft beer, Peti Szüsz is slurping coffee with whipped cream at the Požarevac railway station. I also dream that they are upbraiding me: "Why didn't you come with us? You imbecile." I'm waving my arms in desperation — look, I'm here! But my friends keep on scolding me needlessly.

Szüsz gazes at me sorrowfully: "Tell me, why didn't you come? Jóska Junger offered to stay behind in your place."

"I'm standing right here, can't you see?!" I'm shouting at the top of my lungs. "I'm begging you, look at me…can't you see that I'm here?"

A pale, blond SS soldier keeps shoving me over to the ditch near the railway embankment. He is hounding me impatiently, "Schnell, schnell!" If I don't stop fooling around he'll shoot me.

Warum? "Why?" I ask imploringly.

Darum. "Just because. Because I hate you!" He shrieks at me like a jackal, and his gun goes off.

⁓

The second contingent is sent on its way on Friday, September 29, at dawn. Second Lieutenant Rozsnyai, Ensign Torma, the commander of the Rhön Lager, officers and non-commissioned officers head up the raggedy caravan of more than two thousand men.[1]

It's a shameful, pitiful army. Some of the men could pass for scarecrows.

----

1 According to the United States Holocaust Memorial Museum's *Encyclopedia of Camps and Ghettos 1933–1945*, vol. III, this convoy was led under the command of Lieutenant László Schäffer and included more than 2,600 men. See "Bor" on page 320.

The prisoners are tramping on the steep slopes of the Erzgebirge. We are getting close, for the second time now, to our old camp, Heidenau. To the left and right, Schnitzer and another two dozen guards keep watch over the "public-interest" labourers dragging dolefully along.

After a few hours of marching, the column that started off as a unit has spread out to cover a kilometre and a half. The eyes of the bulldog-faced Company Sergeant Major, Császár, blaze with hatred; he is a cruel, foul-mouthed peasant, a favourite butler of Lieutenant Colonel Marányi. We first heard of him in Heidenau, and we got to know him in person in the Berlin and Brünn Lagers. His vocabulary of obscenities is inexhaustible. He pops up either at the front of the line or behind the last stragglers, howling like a mad dog and issuing crazy, sadistic *ukases*, his grand decrees that attempt to incite hatred toward us in his soldiers.

The guards listen to Császár's hysterical outbursts with indifference. They scan the winding road and the dense forest on both sides; they eye the rustling foliage of the centuries old oaks; each time a twig cracks, they grip their guns tighter.

Just before we reach a bend in the road that appears suddenly, four of our fellow captives rush into the woods on the right. One of the soldiers notices the escapees; in the blink of an eye, he removes his gun from his shoulder and gets ready to fire. His mate Corporal Kocsis, a square-built giant of a man, grabs the soldier's shooting arm and makes a gesture that seems to say, "Let them go, it's not worth the effort."

We never see the officers, because they are at the front of the column, but we watch the nervous guards surreptitiously. They act as though they are afraid of the deep dark forest; they talk in low voices, have given up on their slave-driving and their cursing has subsided.

Our empty stomachs enervate us; thirst drives us mad. Our mess tins are empty. We have devoured all of the salty canned food; what remains of our bread is stowed in our satchels. The rain is falling incessantly, and we slip and slide on the bumpy, winding road. Our boots are wet, as rainwater has seeped through the flimsy soles. They are so entirely soaked through that we can wring the water out of our foot rags.

The thousands of marching prisoners reach the Heidenau Lager. In the late afternoon light, we view the site of our summer suffering for the second time. But all we can see are the scattered shards of the burnt-down dark-green gate and the wrecks of the blown-up barracks. The shower room is still standing, abandoned, with doors agape; the generator has been removed, so there is no water and no lights.

The officers order us to camp out overnight on the bare clearing in front of the former Lager, the same clearing where, when I was a greenhorn, Lieutenant Száll and Ensign Turner gave their sermon, and where the guards greedily stole our small treasures from our coat pockets and knapsacks.

Out on the road, German trucks loaded to the gunnels rumble in the direction of Bor, or at times toward the mountains. There are also horrifying SS units patrolling the road.

More than two thousand tattered men, aged beyond their years, try to settle down to sleep; we endeavour to catch a few hours' sleep on the wet grass, amid knobby stumps.

A putrid, pungent vapour rises in the air.

Worn-out human bodies and souls.

We never see our officers and only rarely, the enlisted men.

SS men with machine guns keep a stealthy watch on us from nearby.

When we turned in, the late September rain let up, fortunately; by dawn the sky was clear. Our ominous premonitions have faded — we survived the night. The SS units lurking in the vicinity have vanished without a trace. Once more we start hoping that we too will be taken home. We will reach the Požarevac railway station in two or three days.

Yesterday, at our departure, we even saw Marányi in the Berlin Lager. He was gazing haughtily at the scabies-infested, persecuted people; his eyes radiated an ancient, Scythian disdain.

The fascist lieutenant colonel issues swift orders to his officers, who are ready to set out. Before our dawn departure, Ensign Torma declares with laconic brevity: "To stay behind or to step out of the column is forbidden. Partisans are lurking in the area. Anyone attempting to escape will be shot in the head."

Whispers are circulating: at night, under the shroud of darkness, about twenty guys flew the coop; they fled into the dense forest. Not a soul is looking for them.

This was the opportunity I had been waiting for. "You idiot," I scold myself, "why didn't you take off too?" My mood is dark. I feel that we are in terrible danger, that we have reached a dead end. My heart races, and my stomach is killing me. The constant spectre of execution has taken an extreme toll on the forced labourers, who have been reduced to human wrecks.

Shortly after seven o'clock, the tattered army of the second contingent is marching toward Požarevac. We have left behind the charred remains of the blown-up Heidenau Lager. We are stumbling, shuffling our feet on the twisty mountain road full of sharp bends, declines and inclines. It's a miserable slog. The tight formation we began in at dawn now stretches out again to more than one kilometre, and the quick pace on the serpentine route makes even the well-fed guards sweat.

After yesterday's bleak weather, the sunshine's caress feels nice. Not even two hours after our departure, we slow down visibly, like tired wanderers before the gate of the old city. We don't know why the pace has slackened and are not even interested. We march on in resignation, but in our peculiar life, it's a small joy that for the past little while we've been almost marching in place.

Just as we have completely caught up with the head of the column, we spot, on the left side of the bend, a strong, slim young man looking down on us from the top of a hill covered with rocks and brush. His gaze is confident; he has a quick-firing gun in his hand and is wearing a black felt cap with a red star on the front. He stands all alone on the peak. A few times, he motions toward the bottom of the hill with a wide sweep of his arm, as if he were signalling our arrival to his army.

The man is a Tito Partisan. He aims his weapon at the deathly pale guards. "Put your rifles, handguns, magazines and bayonets in the middle of the road!" he shouts with blood-curdling determination, and we hear him cock his gun. No sooner has the Partisan finished giving his orders than the soldiers guarding us throw down their weapons helter-skelter. They stand around the discarded weapons looking lost: without their guns, they are naked. They are whining and there is fear in their eyes; they are afraid of retribution.

The second Partisan, who has just appeared on the top of the hill, gives instructions to us in Hungarian, "Collect the guns and stack them in a pyramid shape. Use separate piles for handguns, hand grenades and magazines. Don't lay a finger on the guards."

The despondent prisoners are about to be seized by the urge to start lynching.

The Adam's apple of one of the sergeants is bobbing in his throat; his handlebar moustache is trembling. The foul-mouthed corporal who wanted to leave us rotting in a dirty rathole now begs us for civilian clothes. He has already cast off his uniform, along with his soldier's honour; he starts blubbering, imploring his former prisoners to hide him and give him some clothes.

As if the Holy Ghost had entered some of the older men, the limping pharmacist pulls out a T-shirt that mice have gnawed holes in to give to the corporal. He is about to hand over the raggedy garment, but the others attack him, angrily berating him and calling him a filthy traitor.

If someone were to make a movie now, he would observe what a poor, pitiable, ghostlike bunch of people we are; we simply cannot process what has happened to us. The orderly rows have broken up, but it hasn't dawned on us yet that we are liberated from bondage, from the murderers and their henchmen, from those who filled us with anguish, from the thieves who sold the bulk of our provisions on the black market.

The two Partisans on the hilltop direct the rescued men impatiently from the road to the mountain path covered in shrubs and wildflowers. We retrieve the weapons and ammunition from their stacks and distribute them among ourselves. The guards now march in the middle like a flock of sheep. Deathly pale, they walk as slowly as altar boys before Mass.

We are in the Erzgebirge, in the woods of the Homolje mountains, somewhere near Žagubica; the other village, Laznica, cannot be too far off.

~

One year before I was called up, in the spring of 1943, I was cramming for my matriculation in Algebra, Ars poetica, Cicero and János Arany's poem *Toldi,* at a school desk in my downtown high school. A large sign advertising *His Master's Voice* was flashing through the window of the institute. I gazed with envy at the people leisurely walking by.

In those days I knew precious little about Tito or Partisans. I had my noggin buried in the sand like a long-necked ostrich. I was only interested in books, sports and girls. Our teachers steered clear of sensitive topics; they rarely spoke about the course of the war or world politics. By that time it was dangerous to discuss political theories or give opinions.

Our Serb-speaking fellow inmates from the Délvidék, or southern land, a part of the country annexed by Hungary, first informed us about the Chetniks: we needed to be wary of them, since one of their groups consisted of fighters who were German sympathizers. Were we to end up in their hands, they would murder us right away or hand us over to the SS.

Of course there were two more groups among the Chetniks: one supported the collaborator Milan Nedić's government; the group backing Draža Mihailović, on the other hand, wanted to restore the monarchy. Among the three Chetnik factions, dissension and chaos reigned.

The Partisans — so the southern *muszos* men told us back when we were navvying and loading mine cars or during our precious minutes of lunchtime — were organized by Josip Broz, also known as Tito. He was the first to start fighting in Yugoslavia against Hitler's invaders. The fiftyish, Communist-leaning Tito was already a legendary hero in his country when we arrived at Bor.

The Germans and their Hungarian military henchmen stationed in Yugoslavia shivered at the sound of the word *Partisan*; we, on the other hand, were waiting for them like the biblical Jews for the Messiah.

We have been marching for more than an hour on a path lined by a dense thicket, slipping and sliding on slopes strewn with rocky debris. We are panting as we struggle up the steep inclines, and thorns and dead twigs scratch us as we go.

The guards, who only recently became prisoners, have transformed into a band of people who look scared, furtive and exhausted. They walk along submissively, feeling that they have turned into a mob of outcasts.

A few of the *muszos* men start kicking the blond corporal, and they beat the detestable lance corporal from the Innsbruck Lager with a cudgel. The guards don't defend themselves; they know that any move on their part would only inflame the mood of the revenge seekers. The more level-headed men impede further beatings; they appeal to common sense and advocate seeking retribution by lawful means.

When the armed Partisan made his sudden appearance at the bend and signalled by moving his arm in a wide circle, we suspected that there was a sizeable Partisan unit behind him, ready to fight. The guards threw away their weapons without hesitation, like the cowards they were. Resistance, lining up in formation, seeking entrenchments, charging the Partisans or even just fleeing into the dense forest never occurred to them; they were paralyzed, practically hypnotized.

Still marching through the forest, we don't see Partisans anywhere. Our Partisans had also disappeared; it's possible that they went to the front of the line to guide us over the extremely difficult terrain.

Where are we, to which mountain village is our path leading us? We keep guessing whether we have left Vlaole and the other nearby village, Tanda, behind. Are we far from the Timok River? Where are the Partisans taking us?

Just as suddenly as the armed Partisan sprang up beside the road, we come upon an enormous clearing in a valley surrounded by dark grey cliffs. Huts made out of hastily thrown together branches are scattered about the grassy plain, like so many giant caterpillars.

Young Partisans are busying themselves around us. All two thousand of us refugees are now sitting in the meadow. We scour our knapsacks for a bite of bread; our parched lips yearn for a gulp of water.

Partisan women also show up in the valley, young creatures wearing duffle coats, seasoned in combat. It's our first time seeing a female fighter with a weapon on her shoulder. Over their thick brown hair, the girls wear Titovkas, the khaki-coloured cap with a five-pointed star on the front.

The majority of the Partisans are clad in felt trousers and a duffle coat, just like civilians, and only their hats and weapons indicate that they are resolute fighters who attack the fascist invaders fearlessly and obstruct their operations wherever they can.

Two uniformed Partisan officers step out of one of the camouflaged huts. They can hardly be more than thirty years old. A golden badge of rank blooms on each of their greyish-green jackets. We begin guessing at their ranks; the men with military experience think one of them is a second lieutenant and the other a major.

The officers, with the help of the Hungarian-speaking Partisans, make the two thousand liberated prisoners sit in a semicircle and then wait until everyone is settled. It is no easy task. Everyone wants to draw near to the officers, as if this way the information they are about to impart would be of greater value. It takes a few minutes for the racket to quiet down. The crowd looks at the officers expectantly.

The morning wind sweeps along the sun-bathed valley, blowing the yellowish-brown leaves of the trees over to where we are sitting.

The senior officer gives a speech to the assembly. In his introduction, he states that he knows "little Hungarian." In that instant our jaws drop as it hits us that we are seeing Miloš again — Miloš who, during our wretched captivity, encouraged us to visit the Eastern Orthodox cemetery.

Only a few of us recognize Miloš, the mining engineer, namely those of us who once toiled at lugging bricks and are now here as members of the second contingent. The Partisan commander doesn't recognize me or Kari Háy; in the officers' eyes we are merely a colony of ants, a scratching, thirsty, hungry crowd in dirty clothes and with unshaved faces.

"The Partisan headquarters found out that you'd been sent on your way," starts Major Miloš, assisted by a translator. "Not just us but the whole population of Bor followed your cruel fate most attentively. We decided that if we found out the SS was starting some atrocities at night, we would interfere, and since this did not materialize, we decided that we would liberate you today, here in the mountains."

"Vivat! Vivat!" Ecstatic, the tattered army claps and cheers. It's a long while before Miloš is able to continue his speech.

"Unfortunately, this area is very poor, as are the people in the nearby villages. They have very little food, and they use it sparingly, so that they can help the Partisans fighting around here. According to Red Army reports, the Soviet forces will reach this area within days, and then we hope the difficulties regarding food will diminish. I would like to let you know," continues the major, "by our estimate, we will chase the Nazis and their henchmen from this country in a matter of weeks. We will fight until final victory. We have an un-limited need for anyone who is sympathetic to our cause and willing to help. Those who feel they want to fight with us, we will welcome with open arms."

All of a sudden, our dear major switches to elevated language. "Our commitment is unshakeable; we are one with the people who are united in their fight against the enemy!"

Miloš then hands it over to the Partisan doing the translation. "My friends," begins the Titovka-wearing Partisan in a baritone voice — you can hear a soft southern accent in his speech — "three of us escaped from the Berlin Lager. After some adventurous wandering, with the help of the locals we reached the camp of the Titoists, where we were taken in. We became free men again. We now fight together with them, and we feel that our life has a purpose once more."

He raises his voice as much as he can. "My friends, my former fellow inmates! I am conveying our commander's message: Those who want to join the Partisans, those who wish to fight with us, we will receive as our brothers in arms. The final fight still awaits us. The enemy is still ravaging; it is possible that we will fall in battle."

Our young interpreter is warming up. "Peace does not happen on its own. You have to fight for peace. I don't like hateful words, yet I have to tell you: I cannot imagine more vile brigands than the Nazis and their henchmen. I would like to keep on living, just like all of you. But I'd rather choose an honest death than cruel and debasing slavery."

Now almost shouting, the Partisan addresses the inmates from Bor sitting in a semicircle. "Those who want to join the Partisans raise your hands!"

The crowd of people starts fidgeting. Should we take up the fight against the fascists with our weakened bodies and filthy necks, in these lice-infested rags? The Germans turned us into the walking dead, so we no longer even consider ourselves human.

"Those who want to join our ranks raise your hands!" The young armed man repeats the call.

The throng of two thousand is shrouded in deep silence. We look around, casting a furtive glance to the left and right to see whose hands are raised. For seconds, everything is as silent as a crypt. Around us the mountains slumber in deceptive peacefulness. Suddenly we realize how easy bravery is for a brave man and what a pitiful group we are.

When not even a blade of grass moves, the men who are fixed to the ground, paralyzed, begin to stir. The first hand shoots up in the air, and then, as if that were a signal, one after the other more hands are raised. A few men hesitate, considering what to do. Everyone would like to follow his own secret recipe for staying alive. Although it's shameful to admit it, many of us recall that it's impossible to stay alive without some moral compromise. Virgil taught us: "Abide, endure, and keep yourselves for coming days of joy."

Fates Decided

Out of a head count of two thousand, about three hundred join the Partisan camp. The recruits form quite a mixed company: there are the battle-tested, the young adventure seekers, men fuelled by revenge, fascist-hating fanatics and those who are always ready to sacrifice their life on the sacred altar of justice and honour.

The crowd lets out a timid sound. "We want to go home," I can hear them imploring, "We would like to go home."

Major Miloš takes over from the young Partisan. "We will hand over the weapons, hand grenades and ammunition of the Hungarian soldiers to those joining our ranks."

The commander adjusts the handgun holster attached to his belt, then explains in a flavourful mix of Serbian and Hungarian sentences, "You are all free; our patrol from the 23rd Division liberated your column from captivity. We have already separated out your slave drivers, the guards and officers, who will be prisoners until further notice."

As if the major has sensed what the crowd would like to get further guidance on, he continues his speech: "There is still some hard fighting ahead; the desperate enemy won't accept defeat easily and they will persevere to the end. You are all under our protection, and we will do everything in our power to enable you to get home."

The ragged, hungry multitude shouts hurray and cheers his speech.

The major and his adjutant leave. The young Hungarian-speaking Partisan, Sándor Háber, and a few of his companions stay with us.

The tension seems to abate. The weather-beaten, suntanned young man is pelted with a thousand questions:

"When will we get some food? We are hungry. Where are we going? Where are we? Are there Germans nearby? When are we going home?"

Then come the personal questions: "When did you escape and from which Lager?"

Sándor Háber tries to answer the spate of questions patiently, with a smile. Soon the two armed Tito Partisans standing beside Háber, Gyuri Sági and János Nyerges, join the conversation. Sági and Nyerges escaped from the Laznica Lager. They'd been plotting their escape for a long time, when on a pitch-dark August night about twenty of them carried out the plan. They cut the wire fence with pincers stolen from the tool depot and hid in the forest before dawn.

The questions fly thick and fast. The men would gladly listen to the Partisans' stories, but from the commander's hut the command to leave arrives. We get ready to move again, trying to guess when our misery will end. The eternal optimists keep repeating, "Soon peace will prevail in the world and we can return to our everyday lives."

The sick and mortally exhausted company is now proceeding in a disorganized fashion, walking again along the serpentine forest track. It seems that we are moving toward Laznica, and according to some we must be close to Jasikovo, a little village sheltered in the mountains.

We have left the valley behind; once again we are plodding in the heart of the Erzgebirge. Here and there we see huts made out of twigs and brushwood, and then some huts made of wind-blown foliage; we see old people in lambskin hats and peasant footwear.

The guards march at the front of the column, under Partisan escort. A few people keep wondering what fate has in store for them. The majority, though, don't care. We are still stunned that in a fraction of a second we were saved from the hell of deportation and that we are no longer the most unfortunate people in the world.

Tiny mountain settlements pop up with astonishing suddenness on the winding road; this terrain is incomprehensible to the foreign invaders, but it provides safety to the Partisans defending their country. We have been marching for long hours; our journey is infinite; we no longer have hope that it will ever end. Just when our faith is at a low ebb, Mother Earth smiles at her wise son, as the saying goes. A few hundred metres ahead, there's a clearing in the forest, from where the little town of Majdanpek is visible.

Looking back from the glade, I can see sombre mountains reaching to the sky. The wind is blowing, but just enough to somewhat revive the worn-out men. The Partisans give the command to take a rest in the clearing. The utterly exhausted refugees mill about excitedly, looking for friends and acquaintances; those who are sick search for physicians; rumours are swapped. Like ascetics mortifying their flesh, we've been dragging ourselves without food or drink for two days now, gnawing on twigs and wetting our lips with drops of dew in the morning.

The clopping of hooves can be heard; the hoof-beats draw nearer. Major Miloš sits erect on his grey horse. This time he is surrounded by two Partisan officers, a few Partisans in civilian clothes and a few armed men who got hold of the guards' rifles. They are conferring.

The officers instruct those forced labourers with weapons to prepare a list of the most brutal guards. Instantly, the armed men spread out in the crowd; they make inquiries, gathering information from the prisoners of the different Lagers to find out who suffered grievous ill treatment, who had undergone torture inflicted by sadistic guards. The names of the most infamous brutes are known by many; the second contingent consists of prisoners from fifteen different Lagers in Bor and the vicinity. The tortured prisoners recall their tortures, truss-ups and other horrendous atrocities. They remember being thrown into the potato pit or the latrines, being cudgelled, the thefts, the murders. The more reasonable men try to calm the hotheads; they mention the names of guards who behaved humanely under the circumstances and did not participate in the lawless brutalities. The majority stand up for the decent Hungarian soldiers. But when it comes to the guilty ones, animosity flares up; only yesterday these murderers were the absolute rulers over our fate.

A bestial corporal ended up being listed among the bloodthirsty. As a young conscript, he participated in a series of murders in Novi Sad and surroundings in the winter of 1942. He took pleasure in killing Serbians and southern Jews with his rifle. He was the imaginary emperor of Novi Sad, and he and his accomplices slaughtered more than three thousand men[1] on "orders from above," in cold blood and as a matter of routine.

How do such worn-out, tattered people know all these facts, here on the vast clearing in the shadow of giant cliffs near Majdanpek? At lunchtime, the corporal used to beat the forced labourers with the butt of his rifle, while bragging about his previous acts of heroism, then jokingly, because he was a funny guy, he kept on repeating, "I haven't finished the job yet…. Now it's your turn, you piece of filth!" And then he would unleash a string of savage obscenities.

In the Lagers, when we were slaving away at the monotonous navvy work, we were whipped by slave drivers, like racehorses by their jockeys. After heavy labour, the selected *schlemazels*, the unlucky, would be hanging unconscious on the trussing-up poles, for the entertainment of the out-and-out scoundrels. Slaps on the face, fist blows, curses, screwing with us — these things had become so routine that nothing was considered strange or terrible, except for hunger, thirst, having our feet covered in festering sores or other

---

1   Although over three thousand people were murdered in massacres in this region in January 1942, according to Randolph Braham in *The Politics of Genocide*, closer to nine hundred were murdered in Novi Sad itself.

illnesses. In the Lager, our senses had dulled; we ignored the penetrating stench of our dirty bodies, as in our dreams we were clad in
snow-white linen and strolling peacefully on a velvety lawn in a rose
garden.

How fast everything happened! It took only a fatally short time
for us to resign ourselves to that captivity, like trained dancing bears;
we were jumping around for our trainers like chimpanzees on a tight-
rope, even though we knew that we had ended up in the grip of evil-
doers who would never set us free.

Why did we put up with it? Why didn't we rebel? After all, there
were four hundred of us in the Heidenau Lager and only fifteen or
twenty guards. Among the inmates of the Lager there were some
tough, battle-seasoned men: Lieutenant Zoli Kovács, the ensigns
Gyuri Gara and József Junger, Ákos Grósz, István Horn and quite a
few others who were strong, muscular young men at the time we were
called up to Vác; experienced men who had been in the Ukraine, former soldiers and officer candidates. And there were the rest of us:
inexperienced but muscular young men, ready to act. We held the
former soldiers, the Ukraine veterans, in high esteem, and had they
rebelled, we would have eagerly followed them with fire in our hearts.

Ten to twenty guards with rifles. Four hundred of us with spades
and pickaxes.

Livy of Padua, writing two thousand years ago, teaches us that this
is the nature of the multitude: it either humbly serves or arrogantly
dominates. We were exploited prisoners, branded with the Star of
David, living on swill soup. Like cowed animals, we yielded submissively to being trained by the guards.

The list of the murderers is being prepared. We no longer wear
blinkers, we are no longer beasts of burden driven to exhaustion. The
complaints keep gushing out. We enumerate the terrible crimes of
our captors.

"Torma…Ensign Torma!" the former inmates of Rhön noisily insist. The Rhön Lager, five or six kilometres higher in the mountains,

was the neighbour of Heidenau. This is where the author, journalist and well-known humourist László Tabi and Sándor Szalai were prisoners among many hundreds of forced labourers.

Ensign Torma, a ruddy-faced reserve officer and long-time Marányi disciple, is known far and wide as a leading expert on torture. He made his henchmen truss up victims in such a way that their feet couldn't touch the ground. When one's toes are swinging in the air, the pain increases exponentially.

Ensign Torma's disciplinary exercises, his fiendishly clever techniques of torture, served as a textbook example for the sadists of the Bor Lager system. The commander would put two or three poor wretches in the pillory every day, based on drummed-up, trivial infractions. He had them hung up high on the poles in front of the kitchen, using thick ropes.

Sitting in a straw rope armchair and attended by Cadet Szaulich, who reeked of alcohol, the clown pretending to be Nero took pleasure in watching the jerking dance of the men hanging from the ropes. The two would laugh maliciously, and as if they were at the races, make bets on which of the unfortunates would pass out first. Every now and then, the unwashed stench of the trussed-up men would make Ensign Torma and his stooges grimace. They would hose down the torture victims to bring them around, and the sickening spectacle would continue. Ensign Torma would sit there in his armchair, chewing on a greasy pork chop and hiccupping from laughter; the whole time he'd be cursing and berating the sunken-eyed victims swinging there, with their loose rags and emaciated limbs. Sly and heavy-set Schnitzer filled the role of the technician.

Who knows how and why this sentence comes to mind: "Everybody can take pain except the one who's feeling it."

The complaints, the myriad grievances keep pouring out of the inmates of the Rhön Lager. The bestial commander deprived the prisoners of their Sunday rest: Marányi, the chief executioner, had his sights set on commendation. Cutting down forests, building bulwarks, cleaning latrines and stretching wires were all part of the holiday agenda.

On one occasion the engineer from the Organisation Todt rushed out of his room, foaming at the mouth; he was totally shocked at the sight of his workers being tormented on the trussing-up poles. "I won't tolerate this!" he shouted, extremely upset. Then he grabbed his service pistol and pointed it at Ensign Torma's head.

A thousand horror stories come to light on the outskirts of Majdanpek. In the next few hours, here in the Erzgebirge, we seek redress for the atrocities that were committed. Our blood is racing, just like that of soldiers on the front line before being sent into action.

Our hearts are beating wildly because we have never exposed murderers before. We must administer justice, and that's not easy. Because he who passes sentence has to have two attributes: first, he needs to possess a certain equanimity, and second, he needs to have an imperturbable belief that he has made the right judgement once he has brought down his decision.

The time for payback is approaching.

In front of the tent that serves as the Partisan headquarters, a long table has been hastily knocked together, and some benches put around it. They already have the names of the criminals in their hands: Ensign Torma, Lance Sergeant Kecskés, Second Lieutenant Rozsnyai, Lieutenant Juhász, as well as the corporal who committed the mass murder in Novi Sad.

Disguised in civilian clothes, Ede Marányi's favourite jailer, Company Sergeant Major Császár, the Dracula of Jutas, is brought forward. The Partisans had long been familiar with Császár's atrocities. As soon as we got to the clearing, they started looking for him. Where had Császár disappeared to in the throng? Everybody had seen the screaming sergeant major among the guards when we set off, but when the armed Partisan appeared at the bend, in our joy, in our surprise, in our extreme excitement, we didn't notice that the infamous Császár had disappeared.

From God knows where, Sergeant Major Császár had gotten hold of a worn-out jacket with the Star of David on it and a pair of tattered felt pants that covered his boots. Who had assisted this barbarian cannibal in disguising himself? Who sympathized with him? It's worrisome and disheartening to even think that someone among the *muszos* men was capable of doing that.

The Partisans do not question the provenance of either the jacket or the felt pants.

⌒

Some of us idly wander about the barren clearing, driven by unknown impulses. We are just walking aimlessly, hungry, fantasizing about food, almost tasting it on our tongues; our dulled instincts are playing with us the way the wind plays with fallen leaves.

The young men are pestering the Partisans for food. The Serbian men are embarrassed; they keep saying that they themselves are hardly getting any food at this point. "Patience, patience," they say kindly, trying to calm us down, "people from Majdanpek will bring you something to eat soon."

The officers summon those who volunteered to join the Partisans that morning to the commander's tent. The recruits gather by the long table in front of the tent. Some, after the first rush of enthusiasm, have changed their mind. Many others only now decide that they want to fight — what an exquisite feeling it is that we can act of our own free will again.

Major Miloš announces that he would be glad to accept the support of tradesmen and craftsmen and doctors. "We can use every helping hand." The major continues, "Here in this clearing, I promise you again that we will drive out the heinous fascist occupiers. God willing, the war will end soon, and you can return to your family and to your children."

His words strike a chord with us. Do we still have a country? What has happened to our families? Are our children still alive?

Bakers, tailors, shoemakers and mechanics sign up at the long table. Béla P., the epileptic watchmaker who ended up an invalid after a beating by the fascist brutes, lines up too. A good number of people respond to the invitation to join; people ashamed that up to now they'd been walking like sheep to the slaughter are coming back to life from their paralysis, bent on revenge. Physicians also volunteer: the surgeon Pál Rubányi, Béla Müller-Mária and a dozen other excellent doctors. The Partisan officers are touched and somewhat surprised to see how many men are joining them.

Major Miloš has a good understanding of human nature. He senses that some of the men only joined the ranks out of a sudden burst of enthusiasm; physically, they are incapable of climbing the crags of savage mountains, of scrambling down slopes, of keeping pace with the Partisan troops on their varicose legs.

The commander announces tactfully: those who cannot handle the hardships of Partisan life may be discharged at any time. We, the remainder of the Heidenau group, Gyuri Kádár, Bandi Reiner, Kari Háy and the others, are conferring; we want to join the Partisan fighters. Szalai wants to get to Romanian territory as soon as possible, to fight the fascists with words. Kari Háy is unusually pale and sick; he doesn't take on the struggle. The young men accept Gyuri Kádár, the experienced fighter trained in the Ukraine, as their adviser.

It's very difficult to see clearly in the chaos of the moment. We don't know yet whether the coming days will bring us peace or misery. Right now, we are under the protection of Tito Partisans, but all around us there are Wehrmacht soldiers fighting with determination, as well as SS murderers. In a matter of seconds the tide could turn. The Nazis can attack and shoot the whole lot of us.

"Let's wait for tomorrow morning," suggests Kádár. "We'll see what plans the Partisans have for us."

The young men listen to the older Kádár. Ancient wisdom teaches us: "Youth, don't listen to the old people; the only thing they can teach you is what they have been doing badly up until now."

Unexpectedly, rifle shots are heard, a commotion starts. There is only a short pause between shots. Suddenly the crowd goes silent; they look in the direction of the shots with frightened eyes, paralyzed. Many grab their worn-out belongings, ready to flee; the fear that has only recently left their faces returns. The series of shots ends. Deathly silence. The Partisan tribunal has carried out their sentence. The murderers have received their punishment.[2]

We have travelled a long way from Bor. We put most of the Homolje Mountains behind us, left the road full of razor-sharp rocks called Na Crnom Vrhu, which wound between Bor and Žagubica. The blown-up Lagers have disappeared from view; we are now in the vicinity of Neresnica, on the outskirts of Majdanpek, in the vast mysterious forest of eastern Serbia.

A cool autumn wind blows through the clearing where we have stopped, causing eddies of dry maple leaves to swirl up into the air. The sharp air rushes through our threadbare clothing. On the undulating mountain road horse-drawn carts appear, coming from the direction of the little town. They are quite close to us now, loaded with bundles. A whole caravan. We keep counting: four, five, six carts.

They are getting closer and closer, and we can now hear the squeaking of the wheels, the thump of the hooves. The volunteer drivers stop one behind the other in front of the officers' tent. Elderly farmers sit in the drivers' seats; beside them are women in kerchiefs, with deeply lined faces.

We're pretty sure that they have brought us food to keep us from starving to death. Our first reaction is to rush over to them, but one of the Hungarian speaking Partisans sharply shouts "Stop!" at the hungry pack about to storm the carts. His command brooks no

---

2   According to the United States Holocaust Memorial Museum's *Encyclopedia of Camps and Ghettos*, which cites a memoir by survivor Yehuda Deutsch, Császár was executed after a Yugoslavian trial after the war, and not, as Andai implies here, by Partisans in the woods.

contradiction; it rivets them to the spot, halting the surge of people ready to attack.

"There is food enough for everyone," announces the Partisan in a calm and encouraging voice. "Two people will be distributing food at each cart. Line up with your mess tins and canteens; you will also get plenty of bread."

The starving, including those who were stopped in their tracks and those who were simply trying to muster the strength to get up off the ground, gather around the carts unsteadily. The Partisans diligently direct the crowd, showing them which cart to wait beside until it's their turn. The women are handing out a little bit of bread, some dried wheat, *bryndza*, eggs, corn cake, polenta; they also add chunks of cheese and some cake. They ladle hearty pasta soup into our mess tins from large tin canisters. The farmers dole out the water and the women are in charge of apportioning the food.

This region has a long tradition of people helping each other out in times of trouble. From the beginning of the war, they have provided food for the Partisans in their area and are now sharing their reserves with us.

"There is no better or nobler people in the world than the Serbs," effuses Laci G. Many nod in agreement.

The men who have been served already are squatting in the clearing; they bite into the food with an almost religious reverence, savouring it with their eyes closed. After a few tasty mouthfuls, they take a deliberate swallow from their canteen, going about it carefully to make the water last longer. Our bellies are getting full, but, strangely, the feeling of hunger stays with us.

Only now do we notice that additional men and women have joined us in the clearing. Shortly after sundown, many of the inhabitants of the small town came up here to offer us corn cake, goat cheese and savoury pastries wrapped in linen kerchiefs. A few of our group are from the southern land and speak Serbian well; they engage in cordial conversations with the locals. Even I can stammer "a little Serb," and so I manage to make some acquaintances too.

After emptying their goods, the food carts leave the clearing and slowly head back toward the little town. To the northeast, behind the pale grey peaks of the Erzgebirge, an improbably brilliant moon has risen. Far from the commander's tent, the moonlight, like a stage spotlight, illuminates the agonies of a trussed-up man. Two Hungarian Partisans stand on guard beside him.

I am talking to an old man named Marko Popovićty. Actually, he is doing the talking, and I am trying to understand him. He joined the Partisans in 1941 and fought with them around Gorski Kotar and Zlatibor. He also laid landmines under convoys of trucks transporting Wehrmacht provisions on the road between Niš and Leskovac. He suffered serious injuries, and it took him half a year of treatment before he could walk again. After that he returned to his old trade; he has a blacksmith shop in the eastern part of Majdanpek. Insiders are aware that he is engaged in producing arms and bullets for the Partisans in his workshop.

Although old Marko is thirty-six years old, he looks more than fifty. His forehead has a thousand wrinkles, his work-worn hands are dotted with crusted scars; his sweet smile reveals missing teeth. While we talk, the moon moves past the midpoint of its path across the sky, its light shining all the way to the edge of the town. Marko invites us to spend the night at his place; we can sleep on the straw in his barn. Kari Háy, Kádár, Bandi Reiner and I take up the offer.

Gradually the crowd in the clearing disperses. The men who signed up to be Partisans gather around the commander's tent; they are chatting, smoking and getting acquainted. They form clusters of various sizes, old friends and new Lager pals are making plans for the future.

The luckier, more resourceful people have already set off with their host toward the town. The more ineffectual fellows are out of luck, like girls with two left feet at a dance. Some of them shrug their shoulders and start off toward the settlement without an invitation, hoping that something will turn up. Many are already slumbering on their raggedy blankets, their bellies full.

Marko is walking ahead of us on the sloping road; we near the little town with anticipation. On arrival, we see a lot of men in tattered clothing with yellow stars on the main street; they have bundles in their hands and are engaged in conversations around the neatly painted small houses.

The main street of Majdanpek, at the foot of the mountain, is kind of like a village street. There are poles made of pine along the road, children's crying can be heard from the courtyards of the houses. A knock-kneed mule stands morosely in the middle of the road. Compassionate people — girls, grandmas, young wives — are attending to the new arrivals.

It seems like all the yapping dogs were just waiting for our arrival. Now we've come to Marko's house; his workshop is at the far end of the courtyard, with the barn right beside it. Our host can tell that we are utterly exhausted. He opens wide the barn door, quietly bids us goodnight and leaves us on our own.

We are mute. Fatigue and the events of the day have put us in such a daze that we can't even say a word to each other. We lay our heads on the straw and fall into a deep sleep right away.

By the time the first flickering light of day appears, we are all awake. From the window of the barn we gaze into the pale dawn, into the budding morning opening up before our eyes. At six o'clock the sun is already well above the horizon, and its sparkling golden rays have crept into the barn. Our kindly host, Marko, soon puts an end to our silent reverie: "I bet that was the best sleep you've had for a long time. You can wash yourselves at the well and use the outhouse at the end of the courtyard. Afterwards, come into the house and we'll have a bite to eat."

From under eyebrows that meet in an obtuse angle he observes us with velvety eyes; his interested gaze moves from one of us to the other. It seems as if he's trying to read our wishes from our sleep-swollen faces, so that he can accommodate us fully.

In the spacious room of the house, two friends of Marko's, farmers in peasant footwear, and the *popa*, the Eastern Orthodox priest of the region, sit around a bare table. As soon as we enter the men make room for us in a friendly fashion, and the conversation starts immediately.

The women, Marko's wife and a young girl, bring corn cake and polenta and coffee in a Turkish-style pot without delay, while our host passes around water, dried fruit and tobacco. The narrow-necked jug of *rakija*, a Serbian fruit brandy, is plunked down in the middle of the table. It is soon evident that the priest is adept at directing the conversation. As we eat, we describe what happened in the labour camp. We interrupt each other as the grievances keep pouring out. Our host and his friends listen attentively to our jeremiad.

Suddenly I'm hit by a wave of guilt. Why are we complaining to our Serbian acquaintances? After all, they are quite familiar with atrocities. I've heard that since 1941, the Nazi occupiers have slaughtered more than one hundred thousand Serbian men and adolescents. They carried out bloodbaths in Prokuplje, near Niš, and in Leskovac; they killed patriots by the thousands around Smederevo and Požarevac. Drunken SS soldiers hurled babies against the wall like discus throwers. They raped the Serbian women, and if Partisans fell into their hands, they burned them at the stake.

During our lavish breakfast, our hosts tell horrible tales of carnage wreaked by the Germans and the Ustaše, Croatian fascists. In April 1941, Hitler divided Yugoslavia among Germany's allies: Italy, Bulgaria and Hungary obtained valuable spoils; the Croatians achieved nominal independence, while Nazi Germany ruled directly over Serbia and its capital, Belgrade.

The Eastern Orthodox priest describes how he fled from Croatian territory. His stories are hair-raising: the Croatians, with the consent of their German patrons, decided to "cleanse" their country of foreign elements, namely Serbs, Jews, Roma and Sinti, the Eastern Orthodox clergy and all those who sympathized with these supposed corruptors of the nation.

"The Croatians devised a diabolical plan," the *popa* relates. "They decided that they would execute all of the Jews and Gypsies and one third of the Serbs. Another third would be put into concentration camps, and the rest would be made to convert to the Roman Catholic faith one way or another."

On one occasion, the Croatian fascists drove truckloads of women, young girls, and small children from Mostar and the Čapljina area to the top of a mountain, from where they hurled the screaming victims into the gorge.

The priest was not the only one telling these stories, a flood of grievances poured out of Marko's friends as well. We heard about the burning of churches, how the faithful were shoved into the building by force and how it was set afire so that they would perish inside. According to Marko and his friends, since 1941, about half a million Serbs had been murdered by the Croatians, Germans and their boot-licking henchmen.

The priest remarked quietly, "I think it is even more than that."

Our Serbian hosts informed us that in the summer of 1944, the Hungarian Jews from the countryside were deported to an unknown destination. They mentioned the heinous crimes committed in 1942 by Hungarian soldiers in the southern lands, in Zsablya (Žabalj), Csurog (Čurug), Óbecse (Bečej), Mozsor (Mošorin) and Újvidék (Novi Sad).

The latest news, they say, is that Bulgaria, following Romania's example, has turned against the Germans; they united with the Soviet troops and are now fighting in the northeastern part of Yugoslavia, nearing Belgrade.

Marko and his friend describe the incredible amount of murderous weapons and other military equipment the Nazis have used in their fight against the Yugoslavs. The Krupp enterprise in Essen, the death manufacturing centre, has been turning out cannons, howitzers, machine guns and hand grenades every day and in vast quantities. We learn that Majdanpek and the surrounding area are still dangerous. Chetniks and boot-licking quislings continue to back the

German units fighting in the vicinity. It is feared that they will break through the Partisan lines, sweep through the city again, and then their infamously bloodthirsty fighters will carry out brutal killings.

The bearded priest is a strong man, and only now do we notice that he has a crutch beside him. He recommends that we head for Kučevo. On September 21, a Partisan brigade had liberated Kučevo and vicinity. If we reach it, we'll be safe.

Weighing our options, discussing our future fate, we pay careful attention to the locals' advice. In the meantime, the jug of *rakija* is passed around, and according to Serbian custom, we each take a swig from the colourless brandy until the jug is emptied. To refuse to sample the *rakija* would be sacrilegious and a grave insult.

At this early hour, the occupants of the house are bustling around us. Marko's wife, a small, fine-boned woman, pours hot café au lait in our mugs and puts goat cheese, polenta, hard-boiled eggs and two bottles of *rakija* in front of us. We attack the food quickly. We are ashamed of our hunger and thirst, but we cannot resist the food. We don't stop until we've demolished everything on the table. The jug of *rakija* is passed from hand to hand. At a slow pace, each one of us sips from the mild brandy. When it's our third or fourth turn to take a swig, we start getting a bit dizzy, and the world starts whirling around us.

We've become free men again: look, we can chat, they listen to us, and they furnish us with important advice about the local conditions. It seems as if our weakness and despair has evaporated. How quickly we forget. It wasn't so long ago that we felt that the trap had closed on us, that we were the prey of the SS soldiers, that the machine guns would start their rattle until all was quiet, kaput.

We are ashamed of our ravenous appetites, greedily wolfing down the food at Marko's table. Of course, we tell ourselves that it would be impolite to refuse such kind hospitality. With solicitous care, Marko's wife makes sure that no one stays hungry. I don't remember if I've ever experienced such goodness from strangers. The generous hospitality embarrasses us. A peacetime feeling of lightheartedness passes through the tobacco-smoke-filled room. Poor mountain peasants have taken care of us with genuine sympathy. Thoughts of leaving now preoccupy us. Soon we will be stumbling over tracks, across farmlands and through dense forests. We will avoid the main roads and will become wanderers.

Twilight Hopes

We gather our things and say goodbye to our hosts. Marko and his friends embrace us in a comradely fashion; the obliging *popa* gets up, leaning on his crutch, and blesses us for the journey. Our host and the priest discuss which route we should take to Kučevo. The priest draws a map, explaining the signs and warning us which sections are dangerous. We will have to steer well clear of the Chetniks who patrol the regions and are collaborating with the occupiers.

Our host's wife and an old woman with a thousand wrinkles and in grubby garments hand out provisions for the road and offer us more advice. We know that these good-hearted people were glad to give us food and shelter, but we are sorry to have depleted the larder of Marko's family. In the mountains, there is always a scarcity of food.

In the cool morning, refugees in groups of various sizes can be seen on the Majdanpek road. They are gathering in the church square. They loaf around aimlessly and sit on the benches by the road, chatting and wondering in which direction to proceed.

In front of the *kafana*, or café, we run into Sanyi Szalai and a bunch of other fellows from the Rhön Lager. They are heading to Donji Milanovac, because the man who hosted Szalai and his group advised them to go in that direction.

"We mustn't be too far from the Danube," says Szalai. "If we manage to somehow paddle our way to the other shore, we will be in liberated Romania." Sanyi is trying to talk us into going along with them.

For the first time, we remember the men who left with the first contingent.

"They must have reached Hungarian soil a long time ago," comments Deutsch, a dental technician from Upper Hungary. "Perhaps they have arrived home already — all of them."

"Radnóti and company were supposed to be put into boxcars in Požarevac," notes Szalai, always well informed. Of course, this is just speculation. Was it possible to procure cars for more than three thousand people, we wonder. We don't have a scrap of news about our friends from Heidenau and the others who were taken on a forced march to Požarevac with the first contingent.

"First contingent" — the pretentious military slang sounds ridiculous to me now.

"One thing is for sure, it must have been a really hard slog," adds Olivér Hollós bitterly. "We don't know what tomorrow will bring," he grumbles. "Heaven only knows when we'll get home…if we ever get home."

It's a cool, windy, sunny autumn Sunday. The date is October 1. We're still hesitating to leave, wondering in which direction we should set out. The little town is quiet and the mood feels leisurely, as is usual for this day of the week.

Moshe, the bony rabbi from Beregszász, mentions with a sigh, "This evening the eight-day holiday of Sukkot begins, commemorating the forty years of wandering." Then Rabbi Moshe says more to himself than to us, "Our ancestors were rambling in the desert, and here we are doing the same thing in the mountains."

The Orthodox men, who observe the religious rites, are not able to forget about the holidays even in the midst of their misery.

The Ukraine veteran Gyuri Kádár heard from the locals that there is still active fighting in Donji Milanovac, the place Sanyi Szalai is planning to head for. The Chetniks have a strong military base there, and Wehrmacht units are making incursions in the section of the Danube River below Orşova, Romania.

"You see, if we go toward Kučevo, we'll reach it in two days. There everything will change. Most likely they'll be able to give us shelter for a longer period until we get news that we can return home. And there is no doubt in my mind that we will be able to return home," Kádár says, in an upbeat mood and in a confident tone.

Gyuri has a unique way of keeping our spirits and our remaining strength from flagging. We regard him as the caretaker of our psychological well-being. Kádár is a resourceful man — he'd thrown away his leaky mess tin a long time ago, but in Majdanpek he managed to get hold of a gourd bottle and offers us some *rakija* from it.

If we join Szalai, we will reach the Danube in two days; on the other side, on Romanian territory, peace and freedom await us. It's possible, indeed highly probable, that Sanyi is right. We are struggling with the decision whether we should go with Szalai toward Donji Milanovac or with Kádár toward Kučevo. Kádár refers to the advice given by Marko and the Eastern Orthodox priest: they recommended that we head toward Kučevo, and each of them knows the region like the back of his hand.

After a long discussion, the decision is made: we'll head for Kučevo, northwest of Majdanpek. We are facing a hike of at least forty kilometres, on unknown forest tracks, far from the trodden path. Like devout pilgrims wrapped in rags, we will soon be trudging into the unknown.

Uncle Ede, a seasoned union official, also joins us. Kari Háy, who drew roosters with combs to illustrate Miklós's poems, is checking his pulse; he feels that his fever is going down, his cough has subsided too. Good-humoured Bandi Reiner washed himself from head to toe at Marko's well in the morning; in the absence of soap, he scrubbed his body with sand, and dried himself with his grimy blanket. Bandi has made up his mind: he will also join us.

We accept Gyuri Kádár, with his freckled face and his wiry

moustache, as our leader. He is an intelligent, circumspect man, who thoroughly weighs the pros and cons of every future step and discusses it with us as well.

The clusters of refugees are gathering their belongings. The main street and the church square of Majdanpek are getting less crowded, seats and benches have been vacated, and only the locals are now going about their business on the streets of the small town.

We placed our bet on Kučevo. We're taking risks like gamblers at Monte Carlo. It's a life or death adventure. *Rouge ou noir.* Are we going to fall into the Chetniks' trap or are we going to escape? Red or black. The roulette wheel is spinning — we make our wager.

We say goodbye to the homeless throng of the second contingent and separate out from the multitude; some go this way, some go that. The church bell hasn't yet struck noon when we start off.

As soon as we leave the main street of Majdanpek and reach the dense forest of pines beyond the mountain path, Kádár halts our group and starts to do exercises with us. He instructs us in how to drop to the ground, and how to get up. He shows us how to run in zigzags if we need to flee. Gyuri is confident that we will master these military exercises in no time. Uncle Ede is diligently doing calisthenics on his old legs; his snow-white moustache trembles from the effort, his thick prescription glasses fog up.

Kádár torments the group for over half an hour, repeating with fervent zeal the drills he acquired long ago. He does his best to train us. "You'll see, this training might come in handy," he says, panting, "although I hope we'll never need it."

I can say without bragging that the little bit of exercise does not faze me at all. I was a good gymnast. I can climb up a rope in a flash using only my arms and can run like a hare. I'm full of the vim and vigour of a nineteen-year-old.

Bandi Reiner and I take turns carrying Kari Háy's knapsack on the steep uphill path. Our group is often obliged to take five-to-ten-minute rests on the track where thorny shrubs invade from both sides.

During the long trek, we often reach a fork in the road that halts us, and we confer about which direction to take. The sketchy map drawn by the kindly Eastern Orthodox priest with Marko's help only gives us the outlines, and the details are missing. Should we head to the right or to the left? The wrong decision could be fatal.

We have been trudging through the dense forest for many long hours, startling at each rustle. As we go, we concoct stories in case we suddenly come across Chetniks: that we are Hungarian workers on our way home or that the Germans have commissioned us to search for mineral-bearing rocks.

"It won't be easy to make them believe us," says Uncle Ede. "We'd better come up with a more credible story." Beads of sweat gather on his forehead. He is not even fifty years old, yet he gives the impression of an old man.

We've been trying to scrape the yellow stars off our jackets for days. The star no longer protects us. Instead, it's a sign that betrays us, that gives away our true identity.

Dry twigs crack under our feet, and we scan the mysterious forest with every nerve on high alert. The trip is extremely tiring, but we stay focused on our ultimate goal: come hell or high water, we want to get home. If we've managed to stay alive this far, we mustn't fail now. The Frenchman Pascal observed: "Nothing is so important to man as his own state." It wasn't yet noon when we set out, and since then we've been marching steadily, except for the brief breaks. We don't know for sure, but we can only hope that we are moving in the right direction, toward Kučevo.

Our faces are sombre. We are utterly exhausted, but we don't complain. A man shows his true colours when put to the test. We guess that we must have covered fifteen or twenty kilometres by now. Detours, stops and quick rests slowed our progress, but we were pushing on toward our goal with determination. We reek of sour sweat; our paws are grubby, our legs swollen.

The dark shroud of the starless sky now envelops us. Evening has fallen. We lie exhausted on the gently sloping ground of a little clearing. I am half asleep when I notice that someone is staring at me. Without moving a muscle, I study the mysterious stranger. I don't see any weapon on him, or any other men with him. The man is shivering in a worn-out uniform, looking startled; his clothes are in tatters, and he has the typical dishevelled hair and stubbled face of a refugee.

Kádár scrutinizes the man from under half-closed eyelids, then all of a sudden he jumps to his feet and plants himself in front of him. The uniformed man is about thirty years old, his sunken features bearing a wild and fearful look.

We learn that he had been fighting on the side of Mussolini's opponent, the Italian General Badoglio, when the Germans captured him. In 1943, he was transported to Bor, where he worked loading mine cars in the copper mine, just like us. In the middle of September, he escaped from Bor with four of his mates. He lost sight of his comrades during a fight between the Chetniks and the Partisans; they ran off in different directions, and since then he's been hiding in the woods.

Kádár opens his knapsack without a word, and he hands corn and bread to the Italian fellow, Italo, who gives us a look of gratitude. We are shocked to see the barbarian greed with which the Italian tears into the food. Suddenly we realize that in other people's eyes we are not any better, as we have been behaving in the same way.

At dawn, when we get up, there is no sign of Italo. Before I fell asleep, I saw the Italian man lay his head on the trunk of a fallen tree. He fled — even from us. Maybe he is hiding somewhere nearby like a startled wild animal, perhaps he is afraid of us too.

Now we are gathering our things, changing our foot rags, lacing up our boots. Our little group is ready to leave. At dawn the sky was clear but by the time we set out, dark clouds are towering overhead, and soon it starts to rain. We put the contents of our knapsacks in our pockets and place the knapsacks on our heads and our blankets over top. Our "waterproof" trench coats get soaked; we are drenched through in seconds.

Luckily, we only need to do a further twenty to twenty-five kilo-metres; it's also lucky that there isn't a howling wind. There are no Chetniks in sight. Like always, we are hungry as wolves, yet somehow it seems easier to put up with trudging along the forest tracks dotted with poisonous mushrooms.

"Just imagine," begins Kari Háy, "I dreamt that I was vacationing in Italy with Radnóti, and from Capri we could see Naples. Miklós had a brush and palette in his hands. He was painting the beautiful azure blue sky, and I was tactlessly criticizing him."

Bandi Reiner is lagging behind, and he clumsily makes his way forward to catch up. He tells us he dreamt about Junger: "Jóska was wearing a lieutenant's uniform, and his jacket was covered with med-als. He was handing out delicious smelling loaves of rye bread from a wicker basket."

We take short breaks, during which we chew on our rapidly di-minishing food supply. We wring the water out of our rags. We are no longer stingy with our thoughts, and words pour out of us in a steady flow. We relate our confused dreams, wishing that the biblical Joseph could interpret our dreams, for they are often quite strange.

The rain is letting up, it has slowed to a drizzle. Our mood im-proves, and we show each other damp, faded family photos as we slog along. At noon, Gyuri Kádár suggests that we take a half-hour rest. "We can't be too far now. Under ordinary circumstances, if all goes well, we'll be in Kučevo by early afternoon, but definitely before dark," he speculates.

Uncle Ede is having a snooze. His nose is tilted upward to get more air; he's even snoring. Olivér Hollós is wheezing and scraping the bottom of his mess tin.

The rain finally stops, but no sooner does the sun make its appear-ance than it hides behind a veil of fog. Our clothes are being dried by our body heat. My boots, like the others', have become shapeless, clumsy items with damp soles. It'll be a miracle if they last until we reach the settlement.

We've been marching for three hours after our long rest when we notice that the forest is thinning out, and the landscape is becoming gentler. We can almost make out billowing chimney smoke in the distance — we are nearing our destination. This re-energizes us, and we pick up the pace, at least as much as our lungs allow. Kádár was right: we'll be in the town before dusk.

~

The small town of Kučevo is poor and uninteresting; it lies north of Neresnica and south of Rabrovo, on the banks of the small Pek River. Dusty lanes, empty shop windows, vacant squares. The torn shingles, broken windows and cracked walls riddled with bullet holes of the tiny, damaged houses seem like a stage setting; they serve as telling traces of the bloody fighting in the recent past.

The settlement seems desolate, but as we get further along, it springs to life all of a sudden, as if they'd been expecting us. It's evident that they must have seen the approach of our raggedy band from their windows.

A sturdy, forty-year-old man wearing a Partisan hat with a red star comes up to us, smiling broadly. He opens his arms as if he knew we were coming.

"Zdravo, druže!" (Hello, comrade!)

Our brand-new acquaintance leads our group into the town with waddling steps. As we walk, we pass a completely empty general store, lousy little shops, a tavern, an inn, a barbershop and a one-storey school. We stop at a well-maintained building of several storeys. Above the main entrance, a makeshift sign announces in Cyrillic letters: PROVISIONAL MILITARY COUNCIL.

In the office, they don't ask us very much. They know we are refugees from Bor who have just arrived from Majdanpek. They can see the rest: we are dirty, hungry and utterly exhausted.

One of the men wearing a Partisan hat speaks broken Hungarian; the other tall blond boy knows German, although as he mentions, he hates the Nazis and doesn't like to speak their language. "We are going to provide you with shelter," the Hungarian-speaking Partisan informs us.

He doesn't say anything else, and we set off right away. We end up in pairs in simple houses: Kádár with Olivér Hollós, Bandi Reiner with Uncle Ede, while Kari Háy, my bunkmate from Heidenau, and I share a closet-sized room that a wizened old couple, our unknown hosts, give us. The tiny room is spartan; there's no bed, instead on the floor there's a board strewn with straw, with a coarse blanket to cover us. Two low stools and a crookedy bench. After Heidenau, the pallet in Kučevo is like heaven to Kari and me. In no time we drift into a deep sleep.

Early the next morning we wake up refreshed. From our tiny window we can see trees that still bear leaves, but they are tinged with hoarfrost. We have no idea what time it is. I don't have a watch, and never had one. Back in the Lager, Kari traded his with the vendors from the mountains for *bryndza*, lard and bread.

Our soaked clothes have long since dried on our bodies, our knapsacks and worn-out blankets are still damp and stinky like a skunk.

When our new hosts become aware that we are up, they invite us to the kitchen to have some cornmeal porridge. The heat coming from the stove feels good. On neat shelves decorated with lacy paper, colourful plates and pots are lined up with military precision. The little old woman puts a jug of milk and a bowl of plum butter in front of us on the table, which is covered with a checkered oilcloth.

We have difficulty making conversation. Our Serbian sentences are jumbled, and we can't tell whether they understand what we're saying. The old man keeps nodding; he seems to be chewing tobacco. If we ask him something, he just keeps nodding. Using hand gestures, the old woman is trying to make us understand that they will gladly let us stay longer.

By the wall clock in the kitchen it's nine o'clock. We thank the couple for their hospitality and the ample breakfast, then we go to look for our buddies.

As soon as we leave the house, the ever-calm and gentlemanly Kari Háy bursts out unexpectedly, "This goddamn place! It's a cesspool, I'm telling you. For almost a week we've been wandering over hill and vale, in mud and dirt, through the dense forest. All around us the Germans are still in charge, and here we are in a trap."

"I got slapped around just like you, but I'm not cursing," I lecture Kari. "Believe me, the Nazis have had it," I say. "The Russians and the Partisans are going to chase them all the way to Berlin. Mark my words, the English or the Americans will capture Hitler; they will impale him and burn him to ashes after they've torn him to shreds."

Kari, the perennially mild-mannered painter, keeps on grumbling, "Bullshit, my brother. You don't know the Germans. They haven't pulled out their trump card yet. You'll see, they'll blast the whole of the U.S. and half of the world into pieces before they perish. They've got the smarts," Kari continues ranting, "they grabbed the Bor copper mines from the French because they cannot exist without copper. They felt sorry for their own kind, they wouldn't send them to do mine work in Bor, so whom did they force to do it? Slaves: Greek and Italian prisoners of war, Serbian peasants, Gypsies, Jehovah's Witnesses and filthy Jews. They wouldn't even spare sick people or invalids."

"And the Hungarians sold us for peanuts," I add.

Kari goes on, "I don't even trust that the members of the first contingent made it home. It's possible that they were driven on to Germany to build fortifications. I'm telling you, this whole world is all screwed up."

We've been immersed in conversation. We don't know where to look for our buddies, so we head to the Military Council building. We figure Kádár and company will have the same idea, since they don't know where we spent the night either. We cross a tiny, circular park. In the middle of it, there's a statue of a soldier. On a stone base, he strides heavily, holding a rifle and staring ahead into the distance. It's a monument from World War I. On the base, a copper plaque reads:

VI STE BILI HEROJ!
ČUVAMO VAS ZAUVEK U NAŠIM SRCIMA!

We try to make out the Serbian words written in Cyrillic: "You were heroes! We will keep your memory in our hearts forever!"

"You see, my brother?" says Kari. "Nothing has changed. When this killing is over, they will erect another statue. 'To the martyrs of World War II.' I don't even know why they need another statue. Another copper sign on the base would suffice: YOU WERE HEROES TOO!

"The war cost a lot, didn't it?" Kari continues. "They can at least save on the sign. The disabled servicemen with their gangrenous stumps will be begging on street corners in tattered jackets, sporting lots of medals. Incapacitated, injured soldiers will be hidden in alms-houses, and the ones blinded by shrapnel will be put in institutions for the blind."

This makes me think of what Hölderlin wrote in *Hyperion* about nothing being capable of rising so high and falling so low as man.

Kari Háy, usually a man of few words, is clearly depressed. His sketchbook turned into a soggy mess in the *šuma*, the forest. His drawings are all smudged, his pencil is worn to a nub.

"War has always existed," I tell Kari. "Peace just means a temporary pause. War is an ancient ritual. A soldier is not merely a slave who sells himself for a pittance, he is also a fool and a dreamer: he wants to be a hero and dreams about bloody battles and killing. You just don't get it…. What makes a soldier a soldier is that he wants to wage war."

We arrive at the Military Council building. Kádár is nowhere in sight, but there's an army of raggedy *muszos* men from Bor lurking around the entrance. They arrived early this morning from

Majdanpek. They came sporadically, in smaller and larger groups, in wet clothing and as filthy as roots torn from the soil. They are coughing, hacking, and shaking like leaves on an aspen. A few old men keep working their jaws idiotically, as if they're munching on raisin cake, and they keep licking their chapped lips, like pilgrims in the desert.

Smaller groups and their guides emerge from the building. They are being taken to people's homes for temporary shelter. Uncle Ede, Kádár and the rest of our group show up. For now, we don't see any other men from Heidenau.

We start strolling about aimlessly. Suddenly we don't know what to do with ourselves. There is no place to go; we don't have much money to buy food. However, we console ourselves that the small shops we saw in town were pretty empty — they hardly have anything to sell us even if we did have more money.

In front of the Military Council building, human wrecks are waiting to be assigned to homes. They are all suffering from various conditions: impetigo on their knees, festering lesions on their arms, burning cold sores, dry scabs, heads covered in blisters, foul-smelling rotten teeth.

A few days ago, behind the barbed wire, death lay in store for these men. Malevolent slave drivers herded them from their awful prisons to do hard labour, just waiting for them to croak.

Uncle Ede adjusts his glasses on his nose with dignity, then nods in our direction and says laconically, "Let's get away from here." And immediately we head to the town.

Before we reach the church square, we hear an excited cacophony. The former copper mine prisoners are surrounded by about a hundred locals, who are grilling them about their miserable ordeal with curiosity. We join the crowd and stand amid men, women, local farmers and artisans. Many are swearing, shaking their fists in anger, cursing the fascists. We catalogue our horrible vicissitudes, madly waving our arms and getting so worked up over the telling that perhaps we even exaggerate the atrocities.

The Serbs commiserate with us with such compassion that you'd think they understood every word we said. The women whisper among themselves, then one after the other they slip from the square, inconspicuously.

We are still talking when the women return with small bundles wrapped in coloured napkins containing hastily grabbed food — bread, sausage and whatever else they found in their larders. They offer us the food, trying to make sure that everyone gets a few bites. Moved, we thank them profusely. We stow the gifts in our knapsacks for a time of greater need. By now, our worn-out knapsacks have become part of our bodies.

But that's not all. Now the men are going through their wallets. Bills and change accumulate in our palms; they are almost forcing it on us, should we even think of refusing it, they'd be hurt.

Only persecuted, oppressed people can be so generous.

A pale man with broad shoulders and a thick neck is sitting on the church steps with his face averted; he is wracked with sobs.

Beside us, a young woman in a polka-dot kerchief says sympathetically, "Fašisti su ubili dva njegova sina." (The fascists killed two of his sons.) She adds quietly, "Both on the same day."

We hang around the church square for a while, and at noon we start roaming through the uneven streets. In a leisurely fashion, we have a look at the tiled-roof houses, the rotting fences, the rickety wooden bridge over the Pek River, the fancy signs above the workshops. We stroll along like young men of wealth and privilege. We climb to the top of a nearby hill, from where we can see the edge of the mysterious Kučevo forest. We take a roundabout route back to the more heavily trafficked main street. Squeaking peasant carts amble over ruts and bumps, and the young stallions strain against their heavy load.

A beautiful girl appears on the street. She's as white as a wall, as slender as a reed, her skin is translucent and her eyes are a violet blue; her exceptionally long golden blond hair flows over her shoulders like a silk shawl. Judging by her figure, she must be around sixteen or seventeen. Her clear, innocent gaze is simply dazzling. This is how I have always pictured Jeanne d'Arc, the French farm girl burnt at the stake by the British.

The worst thing is that I wouldn't be able to utter a word if I approached her — I'd just be stuttering like a kindergarten kid. I gaze longingly after the slim girl as she passes by. Uncle Ede casts a mischievous glance through his horn-rimmed glasses, then teases me, "You'd sell your soul to the devil for this girl, wouldn't you?" "You bet!" I answer overconfidently. I feel myself blush.

Bandi Reiner winks at me and gives a conspiratorial snicker. Oli Hollós eyes the peasant carts as they wobble drowsily past; he is annoyed to see how the driver is making his whip dance on the backs of the sweaty horses with foam on their lips.

We walk back down the main street. Diagonally across from the Military Council stands a building with badly cracked walls and a bright yellow sign that reads *kafana*.

We are already fifty metres past the building when Kádár has an idea. He turns around and rubs his hands as if he were washing them. "Come on boys, let's check out the kafana!" he says.

The last button has fallen off Reiner's raggedy shirt; he's trying to tie it around his waist with a piece of string.

"Let's go see what's inside!" Kádár urges the boys.

"Have you lost your mind? We look like beggars," Kari Háy grumbles.

But Reiner agrees with Kádár, "Yeah, let's just go in."

"What's all the fuss about?" Uncle Ede makes the decision. "Let's go!"

Kučevo's *kafana* has the ambience of a small country café. Arrayed on the counter are savoury cakes, fragrant pies, tea biscuits, plus Turkish-style coffee pots and cups by the dozen. Liquor bottles are lined up on the shelves behind the counter. At the round tables, locals wearing bluish-grey woollen stockings called *čarapa* are drinking *rakija* and smoking. They are deep in conversation and gesturing energetically; a graceful jug of brandy is being handed around. *Mahorka* smoke that irritates my nose covers the room with a pale-blue veil. The chipped ashtrays — cheap trinkets — are filled to the brim with cigarette butts burnt down to the ends.

In the inside room of the *kafana*, there are two long, oilcloth-covered tables by the window. *Muszos* men from Bor sit around one of the tables, smoking, drinking coffee and recalling the harsh memories of the recent past. The other table is free, and we sit down near the men from Bor.

The large window takes up almost the whole back wall. It affords a view of a weedy piece of flatland, with the outlines of a dense forest in the distance. On the right side of the room, about a metre away from the large window, is the rear exit. *Javni klozet* is written on a piece of cardboard tacked to the door, with an arrow indicating where the outhouse is.

Kádár points to the men from Bor: "You see? I'm not the only one who had the idea."

The two tables don't stay separate for long; we push them together, and right away the non-stop gabbing begins, as if we'd known each other for a thousand years. Six *muszos* men from Bor, from six different Lagers. They have already shed the submissiveness and paralysis of the Lager; their gazes reflect lively interest and eagerness to speak. They are glad that their audience has grown.

Right now the speaker is a forty-year-old man with red skin, red hair and large watery eyes; he leans forward near-sightedly. We arrived in the middle of his story: "In 1943, for almost half a year, the military commander of the Bor Lagers was Lieutenant Colonel András Balogh. You know what that scoundrel did? He ordered the guards to beat the *muszos* men with cudgels if the pace of work slowed down. One of our mates was in such bad shape that Dr. Kádár from Szeged prescribed one day of rest for him. What do you think happened? There were three doctors in the Lager, László Kádár, Böszörményi and Szilas. The lieutenant colonel had all three of them trussed up because, according to him, the patient was just faking it."

The waitress, a cheerful, charming brunette, comes over to our table. We all order coffee and pie to go with it. And pie is *pie* in Serbian, too, so there is no misunderstanding. It's frustrating that we can't speak Serbian. We mix up even the simplest words. Linguistic difficulties block us, we hem and haw, our speech is circuitous; we raise our voices and make hand gestures. Let's stick to pie and coffee. We have enough dinars to pay for it.

Now one of the men from the Vorarlberg Lager starts to enumerate his complaints: "We got a rough deal, too. Lieutenant Bruckner stole the parcels that were sent from home, we hardly got anything to eat, we had to pickaxe for sixteen hours a day no matter how bad the weather. Those guards kept beating us, kicking us in the kidneys, the liver, whatever they managed to hit.

"Private Schnitzer was the kicker and Ferenc Szokolits, a boxer from Pest, was the knock-out king of the Lager. Szokolits landed his walloping hooks so unexpectedly and so precisely on his chosen victim's jaw that the poor bastard would end up with a concussion. He'd be lying unconscious for long minutes in the filthy sand."

We are drinking our coffee, our pie long gone. It occurs to me that we have just finished with this hell, so why do we need to relive the horrors all the time? Our physical and psychological wounds are still fresh. Let's talk about something else, something beautiful, noble, something to cheer us up. But there is no way around it. We are far from our homes, and we haven't come to our senses yet either when fate brings us together with these wounded, broken down people in the *kafana* of Kučevo.

Their burning eyes have witnessed a million dramas.

We must listen to them, because they speak for the dead as well.

"Believe me, it wasn't a bed of roses in the Innsbruck Lager either," a new speaker, a lanky, stubble-faced man, joins in. A pink scar runs all the way from his forehead to his ear, and there are several stripes on his face, as if someone had used a pastry cutter on him.

"The guards, Sergeant Zbranke and Corporal Tusori, beat people to a bloody pulp with a cudgel that they'd previously soaked in piss. They'd do this for any old reason — because we broke a military rule, for example, or because our mess tin was dirty, because our hands were dirty from navvying, because we glanced to the left, because we accidentally touched them, whatever occurred to them. The Nazi beasts would pick someone, make him spread his legs, then keep flogging him until he collapsed. One time I happened to be standing beside Corporal Tusori when he was whipping a small, near-sighted slave. Inadvertently, the word 'Shame!' escaped my lips in a barely audible tone. Tusori heard it. He made me stand at attention. He even seemed to be smiling at me. Then right in front of my eyes, he pissed on the cudgel. The rest you can see on my face."

The man from Innsbruck shudders, as if he was having a shivering fit. "You know what the rotten bastard said after he carved up my face? 'Let this be a lesson to you. Dismissed.' But I still fared better than Tubi Gruber. I must tell you about him too."

The tall fellow stands up, straightens, and shivers as if shaking snowflakes from a fur coat, then continues his tale: "But I am alive. Tubi Gruber was our buyer; he looked like a rebel with stooped shoulders. We liked him, he was a good guy. At the beginning of July, the Germans took him on a military truck to buy provisions at the market in Bor. The vehicle overturned and Tubi Gruber died. The Nazis survived the accident with nary a scatch. We will never know the truth of what happened to Tubi Gruber. Tubi died. That's all."

Zoli Katz from Beregszász, a stumpy chap with freckles, keeps sighing as if he were carrying the weight of the world on his shoulders. "You'll see — nobody's going to believe these atrocities. If you tell people about them, they'll frown and a look of disbelief will cross their faces: 'Did all that really happen?' Then they'll get annoyed and brush it all aside: 'It's impossible that such things ever happened.'"

Zoli Katz reaffirms his claim in Yiddish: "Nit geshtoygn un nit gefloygn!" (It's preposterous!) "The slaughter, torture and trussing-up, the flogging, burying alive, mass executions, the burning down of barracks with people inside them — these are just the malicious creations of an overactive Jewish imagination. 'Such stupid lies!' the disbelievers and doubting Thomases will say. Posterity will smile reluctantly when it hears the hair-raising legends we leave behind."

"You are an awful pessimist, my esteemed friend Katz! Shame on you!" The fellow from Beregszász is hooted down by a chorus of men. Katz pays them no heed, as if he didn't hear a thing. He goes on: "I ended up in the Bregenz Lager, where Company Sergeant Major Császár was god. I don't think Mother Earth has ever spawned a more vicious creature than Császár. What a horrific sight he made: strong nose, jaw and cheekbones, fiery eyes and a constantly bobbing Adam's apple, a mouth that was always foaming like a hyena's. At times he would lay a *muszos* man flat with a single blow. Anyone who got in his way would be screamed at and slapped around. He was forever cursing, raging, swearing. I think it was Császár who invented the group trussing-up. In the winter of 1943, on a mercilessly cold day, he had prisoners stripped half naked then trussed up until they froze to death. He was assisted in this heinous crime by his boss, Second Lieutenant Rozsnyai. Császár had ninety-two slaves pulled up by ropes, and the unfortunate men dangled there like murderers on the gallows. They swung that way for hours. If they lost consciousness, they were hosed down. When the Lager doctors vainly protested at the sight of this cruelty, Császár barked at them: 'Damn your rotten hides, watch out or you'll end up changing places with these worthless pieces of shit!'"

Kádár, Uncle Ede and I exchange glances. We knew Császár from the Berlin Lager as Marányi's infamous henchman, whose hobby was killing.

"You remember the guard who was trussed up by the Partisans near Majdanpek? I'm sure that was Császár," Olivér Hollós informs us; he had been quietly listening to the stories up to now.

"Maybe it was him, or maybe someone else. One thing is for sure:

one of the guards was swinging on a rope, but we couldn't tell which one," states someone from the Brünn Lager.

Uncle Ede looked at Katz attentively and remarked wisely: "I don't think we should make generalizations. It's true that we've suffered extreme torture, but we mustn't hate the whole of humanity because of a few evil men."

There were also humane guards and even helpful officers in the Lagers, like Lieutenant Nagy and his deputy Ensign Jenö Halász from the Laznica Lager. Lieutenant László Schäffer, the commander of the Westfalen Lager, who was a high school teacher in civil life, would tell the *muszos* men in confidence: "Don't despair. The Germans have already lost the war."

In Majdanpek, fellows told us that Schäffer had made it known he'd turn a blind eye if someone fled to the Partisans. And at our place, in Heidenau, Lieutenant Száll wasn't one of the bloodthirsty sadists either.

"It's important to control our emotions with rationality," I venture.

"Those monsters beat me so that I can no longer walk!" one of the *muszos* men protests, waving his emaciated arm in the air. "You've got some nerve, talking about rationality. We are an amazing people! Our wounds have hardly closed, the mass graves haven't even been covered over yet, but in the holy name of rationality we are already engaged in whitewashing. Yes, I do insist that everyone knows that my flesh was torn out of my body strip by strip. We fell prey to evil, and wickedness was raging around us day and night!"

The proprietor of the *kafana*, a bald, moustached Serbian, approaches our table, wiping his hands on his apron. "Would you like another cup of coffee? Are you hungry?"

We are too shy to respond, even though we are indeed hungry. "Platiti molim," we'd like to pay, we say, almost in unison.

The proprietor won't accept the dinars we hold out to him.

"Put the money away, you'll make good use of it later," he says.

"As long as you're staying in Kučevo, feel free to come here for coffee. You'll be my guests."

The *vlasnik*, proprietor, pats the *muszos* men on the shoulder amiably; the pretty *kelnerica*, waitress, stands at his side, smiling. "Dobar prijatelj, dobar prijatelj," you are a good friend, good friend, we reiterate, and express our gratitude to them: *Puno hvala.*

Doviđenja! (Goodbye!) calls out the proprietor as we are leaving.

We step out onto the street. A storm is coming, and the first cold raindrops splatter the pavement. Every step of the way we come across people who greet us cordially, as if we were old acquaintances. In September, when the Partisans liberated the town from Nazi rule, fighting was fierce, and a lot of lives were lost. SS and Wehrmacht soldiers continue to lurk in the vicinity.

Although it's now October, danger still hangs over the town. In spite of this, life seems harmonious. Not even a trace of fear can be seen in people's faces. They are a smiling, self-confident and proud people — intrepid freedom fighters.

A wild wind sprang up and chased the storm away. Now twilight casts its mantle over the landscape. The company splits up in front of the *kafana*. Kari Háy and I head back to our lodging. We are hungry. It's not the kind of hunger you experience after missing a meal. It's a hunger that we feel is going to haunt us forever.

By the time we get to our place it's evening. The peaks of the Erzgebirge pierce the low-lying clouds. I am suddenly overwhelmed by a feeling of being defenceless and lost. I've become part of some helpless mass. I've been deprived not only of my human identity, but also of my culture and my country. I am a worthless nobody whose life is still at risk. It's not easy to shake this profound anxiety.

Starica, the sweet old woman with a thousand wrinkles, is waiting for us with hot soup — beans, potatoes and pork hocks cooked in a clay pot. When our plates are empty, she urges us to eat more. Such a large portion is beyond the capabilities of the dyspeptic Kari. I take a second helping.

I've been lying in bed for an hour, but sleep eludes me. "Are you asleep?" I say softly to Kari.

"What do you think, when will we be able to return home?" Kari sighs and turns over.

The words "return home" tear at my heart. I only answer after a long pause. "Tell me, Kari, do we have a home, a country?"

For eight years, I was a student at the downtown high school in Budapest. For eight long years, we students were united in good times and bad. We played tricks on our teachers together; we played billiards in the Göbel tavern off Kazinczy Street. We memorized Cicero and "der, die, das," we teased the girls from Veres Pálné High School. Catholics, Protestants, Jews, we all fretted together before exams. We all had our class graduation photos taken by a photographer on Rákóczi Street, who mounted them on a large sheet of cardboard. Each graduating student sported the same kind of white shirt, dark jacket and tie. When the board was finished, wonder of wonders, the photos of the Jews were all grouped together at the right, as if to inform the whole world that these people don't belong here.

This happened in 1943. I learned from Gyuri Gara in Heidenau that by that time *muszos* men were being burnt alive in the Ukraine. There we sat on our high school benches, with no idea what was going on. Less than a year later, we too were sold as slaves for Judas money. "Kari! Do you honestly think that we've got a country?"

"Little brother, you're very young. From the moment of birth, we are all prisoners. We fall in love with the soil, the landscape, the gentle hills, our streets, our acacia trees. Our relatives and friends, lovemaking, embraces — these things keep us in captivity. So does the language that we've consumed with our mother's milk. Our language with its thousand enchantments. I'm fond of Mozart, Verdi, Beethoven, Bach, but my heart beats rapidly only when I listen to the music of Bartók and Kodály. You heard Miklós's poem too, where he expresses more eloquently what I feel:

I cannot tell what this land means for others. For me,
This little country ringed by fire's the mother-land —
The far-off world of childhood rocking in the distance.
I have grown from it like a frail branch from a tree
And my hope is that my body will sink into earth here.[1]

Kari continues, "Do you know what Krylov, the Russian writer of fables, once wrote? Someone who isn't able to be useful is better off going to live in a foreign land. Because, little brother, if you leave your homeland, you will forever be a foreigner in the eyes of other people. Let's try to sleep. Good night."

I did fall asleep and had an improbable dream. In it, I am in a pale-blue tiled bathroom, splashing about in the steaming bathtub, with bubbles from pine-scented bath tablets fizzing to the surface of the water. On the stool, there are snow-white terrycloth towels and a stack of clean underwear. From the radio on the shelf comes Gigli's bel canto, enchanting me with the sentimental tune "Torna a Surriento."

I wake up with a start. I am lying with my face pushed up against the wooden bunk. My raggedy pants, torn shirt and threadbare blanket are all soaked with sweat. My teeth are chattering. I feel as tired as if I had been pickaxing all night long. The pale, weak light of dawn is filtering through the window.

Kari is sitting motionless on the bunk bed, staring off into the far distance through the open window. "I find it hard to accept food from these poor people, they must be doing without so that we can eat," Kari worries aloud. "This bothers me more than our aimless wandering in this mountainous region."

Early in the morning we head to the *kafana*. What else can we do? The Military Council advises us to wait patiently. We've got a good

---

1   "I Cannot Tell." January 17, 1944.

place here. If we venture any further, we might come across German-friendly Chetniks or SS units.

The fellows from Bor have been hanging around outside the *kafana* for quite a while. Soon it'll open and we'll be able to sit down, get warm and shoot the breeze. Jovanka, the vivacious waitress with the thick brown hair, is the proprietor's daughter. We throng into the back room through the wide entrance and settle down at our regular tables in front of the large window. In no time, Jovanka brings us coffee, placing three steaming pots on each table and enough cups for everyone.

This morning, Laci Stollenbau, an old-hand from the Berlin Lager, takes a seat at our table. He's a small guy with an egg-shaped head and messy hair. He talks a blue streak, wheezing like a tropical parrot with a hooked beak. This young guy from Novi Sad can't be more than thirty. Laci's one of those oddities who gets to know everyone within seconds, gets informed about everything, makes acquaintances, jots down names and addresses, and in no time starts dishing out advice to everyone. Our new-found friend also speaks Serbian well, which helps him to gather a lot of information.

Laci's surname was originally Bartos. How did it become Stollenbau? As the story goes, three brigades from the Berlin Lager were digging a mine tunnel for Tilva Mika at the base of the mountain. The swastika-wearing slave drivers from Todt referred to the construction work as *Stollenbau*. And so the other Lager inmates took to calling the tunnel diggers the Stollenbauers. As a joke, or maybe out of laziness, they called each other Laci, Gyuszi, Kálmán, Béla, Sándor and so on Stollenbau — and the name stuck.

Laci is an affable fellow, but he speaks so fast that we have trouble following him. We've been in Kučevo for two days, and he's been talking non-stop the whole time.

"We are lucky," starts off Stollenbau from Novi Sad, "that we didn't come to Kučevo earlier. The quislings were terrorizing the whole surrounding area, including Majdanpek. Had we been caught by those

Nazi-sympathizing Chetniks, rest assured we wouldn't be here drinking coffee. On September 20 and 21, in Majdanpek and in around Kučevo, Tito Partisans engaged in fierce fighting against an enemy who put up stout resistance. Ferocious battles took place, leaving wounded people and corpses all over the place, but finally they managed to rout the quislings."

Laci takes a few leisurely sips of coffee then rattles on: "Over at the Military Council, they said that a bunch of guys who managed to escape from the Bor Lagers were fighting for the Partisans in Kučevo. When I heard this, I asked the Partisan girl working in the office if she could tell me who these Hungarian boys were. Without a word, she got the list of members of the Partisan brigade out of her desk drawer and handed it to me to see if I recognized any of the names on it. Well, I didn't see anyone I knew, but I wrote down the names."

Impatiently, Laci starts searching through the dirty pockets of his worn jacket and then produces a scrap of cross-ruled paper full of names: "Zoli Bihari, Péter Rubin, Ervin Pataki, Béla Kurucz, Ferenc Leitner, Márton Seres…. These boys have been fighting against the Chetniks here for weeks. I wonder where they might be now."

Laci turns over the crumpled paper. "Here are a few more names, see if any of them rings a bell: György Román, László Erdélyi, both physicians. If I can make it out right, one is attached to the brigade's mobile medical unit, and the other is working in the Partisan military hospital. There are two more names here: László Kockás and László Kulcsár. They were also here in Kučevo fighting on the side of the Partisans."

The *muszos* man from Novi Sad has been talking for a long time. He seems to foresee a much rosier future for us than is likely in reality. "How much longer will we have to cool our heels here?" Bandi Reiner asks anxiously. "The strangers will become a burden for the hosts sooner or later."

"True! But how long can this slaughter last? Two, maybe three months? Then there will be peace again, I give you my word. Marshal Tolbukhin is already in Serbia with the Ukrainian forces, and the first stage of the Belgrade offensive has begun. Most likely the Nazis will be smoked out of this region in a week or two."

"Small consolation," says Reiner. From his sour expression it's evident that Laci's theory doesn't satisfy him at all.

"What's important is not to despair, my friend, because if you give in to despair, it will sap all your strength. As the Chinese poet Tu Fu wrote: 'Oh, if only like birds we had wings, / to throw ourselves into the white clouds and return home!' I for one am happy every evening to have a roof over my head."

With her usual warm smile, Jovanka puts three plates on the table, which are piled high with fragrant, freshly baked savoury pastries with cracklings. Her little sister, Stefica, assists her, and they fill up our empty pots with hot coffee.

The boss, Aleksandar, a cheerful guy, gives us a friendly wave. The snacks are rapidly disappearing. It's terrible that we can't control our instincts. One's primal nature is most evident when it comes to food; on such occasions, a person becomes a beast.

Uncle Ede is wiping his bifocals. He is clearly elated at the imminent arrival of the Soviet comrades. The usually reticent Kari Háy starts rummaging around in his knapsack for his worn-out sketchbook. He examines the torn pages and then passes the book around the table. Large roosters with lacy combs appear on the banks of the Mlava River, proud cocks with fancy feathers strut among the ancient stones of unassailable citadels. Roosters feature in every drawing on the curled-up and rain-soaked pages. Medieval castles are encircled by an army of knights whose faces are etched with fear. On one of the loose pages a noble chevalier, helmetless and clad in armour, points his crooked spear toward the east. His arm is bare and blood streaks criss-cross his white skin, as he clutches the fabled thrusting weapon.

The knight's features bear a marked resemblance to Jóska Junger from Heidenau.

Kádár eyes the picture in amazement. "Kari," he says, "I could swear that you modelled the man with the spear on Junger."

Being a modest artist, Kari lets the remark pass without comment.

Inscribed in beautiful calligraphic script alongside the drawing are the words of the prophet from Radnóti's "Eighth Eclogue":

> So you suppose. Your latest verses I know. Their venom
> preserves you. Kindred the prophet's and the poet's rage,
> as meat and drink to folk. Who would live may live on this
> till Kingdom come, so promised that keen disciple, that rabbi
> who fulfilled the Law and all our words. Come, proclaim
> with me that the hour approaches, the Kingdom's being born.
> I ask: what's the Lord's aim? that Kingdom, behold! Come,
> let us set forth, summon all the people: bring your wife,
> prepare a staff, the wanderer's good companion,
> see here! pass me that staff, I would have it,
> for I prefer gnarled things.[2]

My thoughts wander off. I remember so well when Miklós wrote the "Eighth Eclogue" at the end of August in our barracks: we were the poem's first audience. Kari Háy copied the last verses of the poem from the *Avala* into his sketchbook, saying he liked them so much he was going to illustrate them.

By the end of the summer we were more comfortable and open with each other than when we first arrived in the Lager. We didn't stand on ceremony, we learned to read each other's body language, we began to think like brothers and we banded together against anyone who treated us with disdain.

------

2   "Eighth Eclogue." Heidenau Lager: in the mountains above Žagubica, August 23, 1944.

I recall how after lights out my bunkmate, the annoyingly pedantic painter–art teacher, and I would long for the return of the cloudless days of our former life. In the pitch-dark, stinking barracks, we were trying to figure out how to arrange the future world to make sure that it would be gentle and good.

One night I pulled the cover over my head to fend off the bedbug invasion; I was half asleep when Kari nudged me because he couldn't get to sleep. We started talking about the "Eighth Eclogue" and about Miklós, whom we both found very depressed.

Kari set out his theory: "In the poem, the poet and the prophet Nahum converse just like Virgil's shepherds. Do you know what idea keeps running through my head? That the prophet Nahum with his crooked staff is none other than Junger. What do I base this on? On Sundays, Miklós often leafed through Junger's Bible for hours, and then there was the evening that he called Jóska Junger's hand-carved walking stick a knotty crooked weapon."

"You're fantasizing, you're making up legends, creating a myth around Jóska," I countered.

"That's entirely possible. The eclogue had an immense effect on me. I was trying to record the tune of the hexameters. Don't you think that one day Miklós will be the great poet of the nation, like Petőfi, Arany and Ady?"

Here in the *kafana*, the *muszos* men from Bor are looking at the sketchbook. Kari asks them, if at all possible, to handle with care the torn sheets, the stained and washed-out pencil sketches, to avoid smudging the graphite further. A few of the fellows give it only a perfunctory glance, but most of them pore over the drawings with interest and praise Kari's art.

Laci from Novi Sad is reading the lines of the eclogue. He likes it and asks who the author is.

"Miklós Radnóti," replies Kari. "He was with us in Heidenau."

"I remember him from the Berlin Lager!" says Laci. "If I'm not mistaken, he was the man in knee breeches who was always smoking a pipe. He was usually surrounded by a bunch of young guys near the fence. Once I walked over to them, but they were philosophizing and talking about things that held absolutely no interest for me."

Around the pushed-together tables, most of the men had never heard of Radnóti. It was only us fellows from the Heidenau Lager who knew his poetry.

One of the older men, wearing a worn-out burgundy vest, gives us a toothless smile, scratches his greying whiskers and claims that he also saw Radnóti among the young men. In his recollection, Radnóti wore a grey jacket, was slightly stooped, gesticulated a lot and had a habit of chewing on an English pipe. "I don't know him, had never heard of him, but now that you mention it, I recognize him. When I passed by the group, I overheard them talking about writers."

The majority of the men don't know Radnóti, but at the tables they start tossing around the names of other Lager comrades. Károly Nóti from Transylvania, who wrote the screenplay for *Hyppolit, the Butler,* also suffered in Bor. The men used to joke around with him about his popular comedy sketch "Lepsény."

Warming up to the subject, we are enjoying a lively chat. One short, rather nondescript *muszos* man mentions László Lukács, the socialist poet, but all he remembers is that the guards beat him until he spat up blood. They mention the composer Béla Tardos, the conductor György Lehel, the funnyman Laci Keleti, who played the clown Szamóca on the radio show *Csinn-bumm Cirkusz* (Clang-bang Circus), and Pali Justus, who occasionally recited his poems after lights out.

"Do you remember Csillag, the graphic artist who was murdered in cold blood by Marányi?" Kádár says quietly.

"They threw him in the potato pit, and he was at the mercy of the guards, who could cudgel him whenever they felt like it."

They bring up the names of artists, scientists, journalists, surgeons, teachers, engineers. Olivér Hollós lists the names of lawyers and government legal experts he met in the Berlin Lager.

"We can keep on talking about who was in the Lagers with us, but who knows where the men of the first contingent are?" interrupts Gyuri Kádár. "They must be home by now; in fact, it's possible that the whole group has been discharged from service."

"How unlucky we are not to have been included in the first transport," moans Reiner. "We were a hair's breadth from having all the men from Heidenau included. We are being treated worse than criminals. Even a murderer is protected by the law in some ways. And now we've been driven out and made homeless."

"Stop your constant bellyaching," the others gang up on Reiner. "Can't you get it into your thick head that we are free at last?"

Wanderings

About three days and nights had passed when we noticed some sort of a commotion in the town. By the farmlands, on the paths and along the country roads, farmers, women and others were standing around, peasant carts were creating a log jam, and people were rushing back and forth.

We were heading to the *kafana*. Suddenly Kari shuddered, his lips trembling so he could hardly utter a word, until he finally managed to say, "I'm feeling so strange, nothing makes any sense. I don't know what this could be. I have a premonition of some sort of imminent danger."

"No matter where we are, there is always some danger around us, Kari. A few days or a few years sooner or later, what does it matter? Whatever is written in the big book is what will happen to us."

In the *kafana*, all the tables are occupied. Those who couldn't find a place at the tables sit on the benches by the window that faces the street or around the hot stove. Their eyes are alight as they discuss the extraordinary events. Cigarette smoke mixes with brandy fumes in the air. The jugs of *rakija* are being passed around, amid much joyful toasting.

As is their custom, the boys from Bor are sitting at the tables in the back. A burly farmer approaches us from one of the Serbian tables with a full bottle of *rakija* in his hand. The man appears to be chewing tobacco, he is staggering a little, and he plunks the bottle on our table ceremoniously. "Drink up, my friends! We lived to see this day at last!"

We spring to our feet to go see what the Serbs can tell us, because we have no idea why the mood is so festive. However, we suspect that there's a direct connection between the commotion on the street and the unusual atmosphere in the café.

"Šta se dešava?" (What is going on?) I ask them.

Delirious with joy, the locals can't contain their high spirits. "Haven't you heard? The Nazis are in headlong flight. At dawn, the Military Council received the news that our boys have chased the fascists out of the whole of Bor County. The Wehrmacht men are tossing the loot they stole in Serbia off their trucks onto the highway. They are in a mad rush. They just want to save their own hides!"

Aleksandar, with his sleeves rolled up, swiftly replaces the empty jugs of *rakija* with full ones. Two additional jugs of brandy land on our table. Jovanka and her little sister bustle and buzz among the happy guests. They bring us sweet and savoury pastries, whether we ordered them or not — today everyone is the *kafana*'s guest.

Only people with really sharp hearing can make out the sound of horses' hooves on the street over the din. Through the window, we see a Partisan jumping off a panting grey stallion. He ties his horse to the wooden railing in front of the *kafana* and enters straight away. On his cap is the five-pointed red star insignia of the Tito Partisans. His boots are dusty, and he has a revolver holstered on his side. He can't be more than forty.

He is Duško Milić, the president of the National Liberation Council of Kučevo. There's a cheerful gleam in his small black eyes. He takes a quick bow, and while everyone is quieting down, he mops his sweaty forehead. Duško, as everyone calls him, has been fighting in the mountains since 1941. He has suffered one serious and three minor injuries.

"Men, I'm bringing you good news! Soviet and Yugoslav divisions,

with the support of the Danube Military Flotilla, occupied Donji Milanovac and gave chase to the enemy. The Partisans and the Soviet
soldiers have already liberated Bor and recaptured Štubik, Popovica
and Sikola."

Duško Milić steps up on the bench by the window so that everyone can have a good view of him when he announces the great
news: "My friends! Less than half an hour ago, a report arrived at the
Military Council: the Soviet troops and our Partisan brothers have
broken the resistance of the fascist enemy. The soldiers of the Soviet
army will march through Kučevo in two hours, or before sundown at
the latest."

Duško delivered these words almost in a shout. He can't manage
to keep his cool any longer: "There are still a thousand tasks to be ac-
complished, but the first and most sacred of them is the fight itself, to
drive Hitler's forces from our country once and for all."

"Hooray! Hooray!" In the smoky café, a cheer goes up at the incredibly good news. The men embrace Duško, the messenger of good
tidings, and pat him on the back. People are hugging each other, kiss-
ing each other on the cheek, some are crying from joy, five or six old
men start singing in a chorus.

We refugees from Bor also belong to this big family. The Serbs put
an arm around us, sit down at our table, and have Jovanka bring more
jugs of *rakija*. The bottle doesn't stop going around. We pretend to be
drinking, taking tiny sips, so as not to insult our hosts. Who cares if
we start getting a little tipsy?

We didn't even notice that Duško is no longer in the café. Amid
the happy hubbub, he slipped away unnoticed and rode off on his
grey horse. The council president–Partisan fighter is now carrying
the good news to the four corners of the town.

The Soviet troops are going to arrive in two hours. Before sundown at the latest. The men who were liberated from the Bor forced
labour camps are on cloud nine, just like the locals. All around us,
the Serbian men rejoice, singing raucously in their hoarse bass voices:

"Killing, killing, we'll drive the Nazis to the brink, we'll impale those bastards in a wink."

Our worn-out human shells — you can hardly call them bodies — are trembling at the well-founded hope that we'll soon be able to leave for home. We can't remember the last time we were in such a great mood. We demolish the savoury pastries, drink *rakija*. Glasses clink as we plan our future.

Soon it will be two hours since Duško triumphantly announced the imminent arrival of the Soviet troops.

"The soldiers are as punctual as a stopwatch," announces Uncle Ede. "You'll see, they'll be here in a matter of minutes. From the kafana we'll be able to hear clearly when they march through."

Like someone in the know, he adds officiously, "I'm sure they will leave a patrol behind for protection."

It is early afternoon, maybe three o'clock, when we first hear the rumble of engines in the distance, as though heavy vehicles are approaching. The sound is quite close when all of a sudden the whistle of machine gun fire slices the air.

"Vivat! Vivat!" we start cheering at the top of our lungs.

Machine gun fire strikes almost next door to us — the victorious weapons are ratatatting. Hurrah, hurrah, our liberators have arrived!

The armoured cars have turned onto the main street.

Shockingly sharp machine gun fire blasts the front window of the *kafana* to smithereens. A few seconds later, the back window shatters with an ear-splitting crash. Artillery shells make notches in the walls.

Blood spatters on the *rakija* jugs and wounded men lie moaning on the floor. The furniture is all helter skelter. Behind the tables that are being used for cover, men are frozen in panic.

"Vreme je isteklo!" (The time is up!) Aleksandar shouts as loud as he can. His face is flushed beet red. "The Nazis have returned! The Nazis are here again!" he yells, his eyes blazing.

The owner jumps over toppled chairs and writhing bodies to reach his daughters, who have become pillars of salt. He grabs them and pulls them down onto the wood floor, and before the Nazis crash into the room he gives forceful commands: "Everybody down on the floor! Radi što i ja!" (Do as I do!) Aleksandar throws himself on the floor beside the girls.

The whirring engines of military trucks brimful of plundered goods seem to be moving away from the *kafana*. But only seconds later, more heavy vehicles rumble by. From the street: rough German shouts, rattle of machine guns, piercing screams, loud shelling, whiz of dumdum bullets.

Out on the street, a voice madly barks, *Stinkjude!* There's a second of deathly silence, then a gunshot is heard. We all know in an instant: death has caught up with one of our Bor comrades.

In unexpected dramatic situations, a person sometimes loses his head, or is totally paralyzed. At times, a secret force seems to propel a person's blood and they instinctively find a means of dealing with the calamity. As if we had agreed in advance on a course of action, the men from Bor don't heed the proprietor's advice. Instead of throwing ourselves on the floor, we jump through the empty frame of the rear window into the field behind the café. A few men escape by way of the door leading to the outhouse.

This all happens so fast. There is no time to think it over. We act solely on reflex, taking risks like gamblers.

Directly outside the back window of the *kafana* there is a deep, freshly dug trench, where they were likely planning to lay pipes. The shards of glass gave us bloody scratches when the window frame was splintered by the shower of bullets, but it doesn't faze us. In a flash we jump into the wet, head-height ditch. There might be fifteen or sixteen of us; confused and scared to death, we huddle together in silence.

It seemed that the weapons quieted down for a few seconds, but then the rattle of machine guns starts up again out in the main street. Shivering, shaking uncontrollably, we confer in whispers. There is no way out. Those bloodthirsty brigands will kill us all any minute now.

We gasp for breath as we discuss our options. The older men press together in fright.

We hear the drone of airplanes in the dull grey sky. Two fighter planes circle overhead. Gyuri Kádár orders us in an ominous whisper, "Don't move!" The airplanes fly off in a westerly direction.

Distances can often be deceiving, but it seems that we are at most three hundred metres away from the dense dark forest. If we manage to run there, perhaps we will escape.

Bandi Reiner has the same idea: "On an agreed signal, let's run toward the forest. It shouldn't take more than two minutes, but we have to give it all we've got. Once we reach the edge of the forest, we will be safe."

The fighter planes have returned; they are circling again, scanning the landscape. We wait, motionless. The planes will most likely fly over us a few more times, so that doesn't leave much time for action between passes.

The older men decide to stay in the ditch. They'll take shelter there, hoping that the Nazis won't look through the rear window of the café. Many fear that the fighter planes will spot the running people on the ground and kill them from above.

We can't hesitate any longer — every moment is critical. Laci Stollenbau, Kádár, Reiner and two other guys from Bor and I decide to count to ten then make a dash together for the forest, fanning out as we go.

We are almost out of breath and we haven't covered half the distance yet when the planes come back. In abject terror, we run across the bumpy ground, not daring to look up. It's only from the drone of the engines that we know the planes are returning. Since we have fanned out far apart, we are each alone when from above, like a thunderbolt, the machine guns start rattling.

The first shots land in the loose earth twenty metres from me. Luckily, I keep my wits about me: I fling myself down and play dead.

During the next carpet bombing, the shells zoom right past my head. Like hawks starving for prey, the fighter planes strike again and again. The cries of the injured and of men in mortal agony split the air. There are dead bodies lying on the field.

I jump to my feet and resume running toward the woods as fast as my lungs and legs can take me. When the planes reappear this time, I only have about fifty metres left to cover. I run in a zigzag. I am so close to the edge of the forest that the planes cannot pursue me.

I don't stop at the edge of the forest. Like a hunted animal, I crash through the bushes and evergreens at breakneck speed. We have split up. I realize that I am all alone in the wilderness.

I have left the town far behind me. Evening approaches fast, and the trodden mountain trails are barely visible anymore. Suddenly, complete darkness descends on the land. It's a mysterious, starless night. The howl of a dog can be heard from a distance, ghostlike.

Where could the others be? Who managed to escape? Who bled to death in the fields?

I don't dare shout out to them. I don't even dare move. The Nazis know that several people fled into the forest and will probably want to retaliate for our escape. I take refuge beneath the thick shrubbery. I'm so exhausted that I instantly succumb to sleep.

I can't have been sleeping for long when I'm roused by dogs barking and a sharp gunshot. The Nazis, most likely SS units, have followed us and are combing the forest. After a few minutes, from a bit further away, a dull handgun shot resounds. The dogs are whimpering plaintively.

This is the night when my dreadful wanderings began.

Awake in the pitch-black night, with every nerve on edge, I stare into the inky blackness, like a panther sensing a trap. I crawl on my belly from bush to bush, alarmed even by the sound of a twig snapping somewhere around me.

I hardly believe that I will ever escape from here unscathed. I hear shouts; it's my impression that they made a surprise attack on a group of people. Next there's the terrible sound of a fusillade, then dumb, deathly silence. I tense my muscles to the utmost to simulate rigor mortis, in case they discover me.

Nothing matters anymore. I have taken stock of my short life and given up on it. I am done caring about danger. I'm just waiting for the inevitable. Can I really be so impotent? What is this insanity? Who understands it? Do I really have to offer up my head without a word, and even show them, here's where you shoot, damn you?

No, I mustn't be afraid! Fear just incites the enemy to even more cruel carnage.

It starts raining, coming down in buckets. It rains for one hour non-stop. I'm drenched right through, but a sense of calm overtakes me because the weapons have gone silent and the howling of the dogs has also ceased. It appears that the Nazi bloodhounds have stopped their pursuit and returned to Kučevo. Without a watch, I have no idea of the time, but it seems like dawn is breaking.

Anxiety is suffocating me. You can't imagine what an oppressive experience this is, if you haven't lived through it. All around me, the vast forest. Yesterday afternoon I ran into the deep woods with my lungs heaving like a man running amok. I spent the night soaking wet, in a panic. I crawled silently through the undergrowth like a scared caterpillar. Now I don't dare to move. The Nazis might come after me again, or the Chetnik collaborators might show up nearby.

Where should I head? It dawns on me that I haven't a clue where I am. Wherever I look there are century-old trees. Where could Kučevo be, the place where we fled from the Nazi slaughter? Where are the boys from Bor hiding now? Bandi Reiner, Laci Stollenbau and the others, I wonder if they are alive. A nameless fear grabs hold of me.

I'm moving unsteadily to and fro, aimlessly. I am suffering from thirst and hunger. For days I'd been subsisting on savoury cakes, which was bearable, but right now I have no food. The air is thick and muggy, there's a pervasive smell of rotting mushrooms and swamp. I'm gnawing on dried-up leaves and the kind of unidentified weeds you find everywhere.

If I wasn't ashamed to, I would cry. My God, why has fate dealt me such a hand? Warily, I start off. I'd like to come upon some companions. Where should I look for them? It's a stupid, senseless undertaking. I crawl between two thick bushes and stare into the void, hopeless and bewildered.

I don't remain idle long. As quietly as I can, I gather brushwood and twigs to build a hideout among the bushes. If only I had a gun, I'd make those raging, murderous fascists pay a high price for my life. Failure stokes the bloodlust of the retreating Nazis.

Loneliness is a terrible, throat-tightening feeling. This is the first time that I've been all on my own since I was called up in Vác. The Ukraine veteran Kádár or the omniscient Stollenbau could show me where to go. Where might they be in this wilderness? Perhaps they are no longer alive. Maybe the bastard Germans slaughtered them last night. Happy are the dead, they don't need to figure things out anymore!

During last night's downpour, I collected some rainwater in my cupped hands and slurped it to ease my thirst. At dawn it was still drizzling, then it abated. A strong wind has come up and is drying my rags. I begin gathering branches with the utmost precaution. As I am crawling about noiselessly, a barely audible sound reaches my ear. Motionless, holding my breath, I wait for it to repeat. It could be a rabbit searching for food in the undergrowth, or a badger, mole, raccoon or marmot making the rustling noise.

There is a long silence, broken from time to time by the whistle of the wind as it picks up. A shaggy man emerges from the towering trees very cautiously. His haggard face is covered by a bushy beard, his clothes hang in shreds, and his blistered feet can hardly drag his spent body forward. Madness seems to burn in his wildly darting eyes. He must have been watching me for a long time.

I recognize him. Why, it's Italo, the Italian prisoner of war who joined us briefly on the forest trail between Majdanpek and Kučevo! Gyuri Kádár gave him some bread and then he vanished like smoke.

I ask Italo where he came from, where he has been. Did he see any Hungarians from Bor? Are the Nazis still around here? "What do you know, Italo? What do you know? For the love of God, tell me!"

Like a madman, Italo keeps poking his filthy, bloody paws into his gaping mouth; he croaks something like, "I want to eat!"

I say, or gesture, to the Italian that I haven't got any food either, that I am also starving, that I've been chewing on bark and leaves. Italo rolls his confused bug eyes in alarm. A peculiar whine escapes through his clenched teeth. "I'm starving! Can't you understand?!" he almost screams. Then abruptly he slumps down and starts sobbing.

Shaking badly, I try to soothe him, worried that this insane Italian will wake up the whole forest. I ask if we can join forces, maybe together we can come up with a plan, and perhaps our luck will take a turn for the better. Italo is no longer wailing and sobbing, but crouching quietly. Then he struggles to his feet, shrugs his shoulders, and all alone he wanders deep into the forest.

~

Before evening, I scramble out of my nook. Hunger was tormenting me to the point that I didn't feel any more fear; I couldn't care less about the dangers lurking out there. If my fate dictates that I must die, so be it.

My muddled senses had me believing that when we trudged through the forest toward Kučevo, it lay northwest of Majdanpek. On the way back from our first stroll along the main street, we spotted the fatal *kafana* on the left side. Since we fled through the back window, we distanced ourselves from the site of the slaughter by heading in a westerly direction. The Pek River crosses the village from east to west, so in all probability I have to keep moving west to get as far away from Kučevo as possible.

All my life I've had a poor sense of direction. What will happen if I'm wrong again? It's quite possible that in my addled state I've miscalculated and I'm heading the wrong way. I decided that as soon as evening comes, under cover of darkness, I will take off into the unknown. In reality, this was infinite audacity on my part, but I could no longer distinguish reality from fantasy. I had become the victim of my numbed senses. I was reeling from hunger and thirst, seeing spots before my eyes. Exhausted, summoning up all my strength, I started off into the night, lost and lonely, in an eerie, completely unknown region.

I've been forging ahead cautiously for perhaps an hour by the pale glow of the crescent moon when I catch sight of a flickering light in the far distance. I slow down my pace in the dark. I slither on my belly like a lizard, then creep stealthily ahead on my hands and knees, avoid the crevices in the rocks, shuddering at the rustling of each leaf. With bated breath, I inch ahead over clods of earth and through the thicket.

Unexpectedly, deep in the forest, several shots ring out. Then it becomes quiet. Whether it was a revolver or a rifle I couldn't tell. I heard the shots from behind me, so I assume I am getting farther away from Kučevo. This all seems perfectly probable to me.

Taking no chances, I stay pressed to the ground and crawl onward. Approaching the dim light, I'm at the mercy of the universe. The forest is thinning out and the landscape becoming more barren, when the dark outline of a farmhouse becomes visible in the narrow strip of moonlight.

I wonder what I should do. If I leave the cover of the forest, I could land in Chetnik territory; either they will kill me right away or hand me over to the Nazis.

I sneak around near the house, then suddenly turn and bolt back toward the forest. An inner voice stops me: "You made the wrong decision: you have no business in the forest. Come on, get going! Go back to the house!" I've got nothing to lose, so I turn back and knock on the door. I hear a dog barking in the backyard. A burly man with a dour expression stands at the door, leaning on a crudely fashioned crutch. A slight young woman peeks out from behind him with anxious eyes. The man and the woman whisper something to each other and then open the door wider.

I must have looked disgusting in my worn-out tatters, stubble-faced and incredibly filthy, worse than a scarecrow in a field.

"Veoma gladan…veoma žedan" (Very hungry…very thirsty), I moan.

The heat that rushed from the room hit me so hard I got dizzy. The man's sullen expression became friendly and reassuring. I tried to recount how I got here, the slaughter, the flight, the wandering. I got so confused by my muddled speech that even I didn't know what I was talking about.

The lined face of the Serbian mountain man went ashen. Leaning on his crutch, he stood before me solid as a rock. He immediately saw that I was a refugee and went straight to the point: "Veruj nam, mi ćemo vas sakriti!" (Trust us, we are going to hide you!)

A kerosene lamp is burning inside the warm but scantly furnished room. On the floor there is a narrow homespun rug, which is as shabby as the walls. Against the wall in the kitchen stands a wood-burning stove with a steaming pot on it. A large table with a flowered tablecloth and four solid chairs are in the middle of the kitchen.

The little woman in her old brown knit vest puts pottery plates on the table and gestures to me to sit down. The man also seats himself at the table. My dirty, tattered clothing bothers me. My hands and feet are filthy, my fingernails are black, my hair is a tangled mess. I am fretting about my appearance like a high school kid showing up for a date. Actually, it's almost funny how vain, how self-conscious, I have suddenly become.

The farmer seems to have an inkling of what's going on in my head: "We are going through extraordinary times! It won't be long until we're able to return to our normal lives." Then he continues, "You seem very tired, my friend."

"No, I'm not tired," I parry, even though I feel utterly exhausted.

The woman darts a quick glance at me: "You must endure it! You will get home soon."

"Home…I don't know," is all I answer.

The woman returns to the glowing stove and portions out hot corn porridge into the deep dishes, adding a salad and some *bryndza* on the side. Rye bread and a jug of goat milk also land on the table. The smell of the corn porridge nearly knocks me over. I wolf it down, even as I try to restrain my voraciousness.

Under his arm, my brawny host has a single crutch, which is more of a strong stick that has a crosspiece of wood with a rag wrapped around it. He springs nimbly to his feet, signalling that dinner is finished. He motions with his head for me to follow him. He's walking just as fast as men with two good legs. Two stallions whinny as we arrive in the long stable at the end of the sandy backyard. Past the stable there's a kitchen garden in full autumn glory and a pit for storing grain, which at this time of year is filled to the brim with tasselled corn cobs in their husks.

"Here's where you'll spend the night. You'll be safe here," says the farmer reassuringly. I eye the cellar-like pit dubiously. The farmer senses my misgivings: "If you're afraid, you can stay up on top. It might be better for you." His words touch my heart. Though my knees are shaking, I force a smile and thank him for everything. I'm going to stay in the pit for the night.

～

These past months, everything in my life has gone terribly wrong. I was driven out of my hometown, Budapest. I was auctioned off as a slave for a few crumbs of copper because I had become a burden on my nation. We were shackled together and thrown to the frenzied murderers, like the gladiators to the tigers in the Roman arena.

When is the bubble going to burst? When is this nightmarish vision going to disappear?

Our family was cruelly torn apart; our fathers and friends were exiled to the snowy fields of the Ukraine. Simple people were so poisoned by shameless propaganda that when we passed them on the street we were met with reproachful glances, with cold disdainful looks, and at times with *schadenfreude*.

I tell myself that I have to stay strong for just a little while longer, that the ground is burning like the fires of hell under the soles of the *Übermensch* Nazis. This painful, horrible reality will soon come to an end, and we will be rid of our shackles. How nice it would be to believe that afterwards everything will be fine, that it will all go smoothly, that decency and the honest constitutional state will be restored — the storm will subside and peace will prevail once more.

The farmer hobbles back to the pit carrying a thick wool blanket, which he throws down to me. Then, *dobro veče*, he bids me good evening.

One day followed the next in the farmer's home. On the first morning, I drew water from the well and using a rusty tin basin I found lying around, scrubbed my skin red with a tiny piece of soap that I got from the woman. She also gave me a rough broadcloth shirt, a huge pair of pants and a well-worn pair of peasant shoes.

"Most of the corn is still standing in the field, we need to hoe it and weed it," explains the broad-shouldered farmer. Then he adds, "If you happen to see any Germans, don't say a word, just keep working diligently. You will be safer here than near the house."

He is a husky, youngish man of about forty. I learned that his name was Koča Zujović. He could move with a devilish agility on his makeshift crutch, and in a short while I didn't even notice that I was working in the field alongside a man with a disability. When we stopped for a half-hour break around noon, Koča related that he'd been an "amphibious" Partisan since 1942, like many others here in the mountain region of Bor. By day he'd be ploughing, hoeing and harrowing the land, and by night he'd be blowing up German military depots and Wehrmacht vehicles or he and his buddies would be wedging razor-sharp iron plates between the cobblestones of the roads.

He got injured four times; twice he took a bullet in the left arm and once in the shoulder. At the end of September, during a night foray, a Partisan friend of his stepped on a landmine and died on the spot. Koča, who was right beside him, was hit by shrapnel — that was the fourth time he was injured — and the explosion shattered his right leg. In the Partisan hospital at Negotin, where first aid was administered, a Hungarian doctor operated on him. The orderlies called him Rubányi, if memory served him correctly. There was another Hungarian doctor in Negotin, a young, brown-haired man, whom everyone called Bella or Béla, but he only has a faint recollection of his name.

"Great changes will be taking place in the world, you'll see," says Koča. "Those who were subjugated, dispossessed, defiled, will be compensated. There will be no discrimination based on religion or race, poverty will be eliminated, and everyone will have the opportunity to succeed according to their abilities."

The veteran Partisan is surprisingly well informed. He tells me that the Bor Lagers were liberated on October 3 by the Partisans, and all of the forced labourers from Bor who were left behind survived. I find out from Koča that Soviet troops, with the collaboration of Partisan units and the support of the Danube Military Flotilla, recaptured Donji Milanovac in fierce fighting and drove off the enemy toward Požarevac.

"The president of the Military Council happily informed us in the *kafana* that within hours the Soviet liberators would be arriving in Kučevo," I tell Koča. "And what happened? He had the time right, except it wasn't the Soviets who arrived, it was the Nazis."

"That was a major gaffe, indeed," comments Koča. "The war is full of surprises. A Partisan brigade was fighting near Rudna Glava; they were exhausted from previous battles and no relief was arriving from central command. So these Partisans couldn't prevent the breakthrough to Kučevo of the German division. That's what led to the massacre and bloodbath."

At first we don't even notice that his wife is waving her out-stretched arm at us. She comes running toward us in the cornfield and then stops, gasping for air. "Oh!" she exclaims joyfully. As fast as he can, Koča gets to his feet, leaning on his crutch. The woman's sudden appearance in the field seems to be an exceptional event. The farmer's wife is still trying to catch her breath, but in rapid bursts of speech she tells us that Mitra, their neighbour, rushed over with the news: the Nazis beat a hasty retreat from Kučevo at dawn. Mitra also informed her that the Soviet soldiers arrived an hour later.

The woman is excited and speaking so fast that I can only catch the gist of her remarks. Noticing my uncertainty, Koča says with a calm, reassuring smile, "Nacisti su otišli. Možeš se vratiti bezbedno u Kučevo." (The Nazis have left already, you may safely return to Kučevo.)

The woman is still happily telling the story to her husband, but by now my thoughts are wandering off to faraway places. Koča's wife goes back to the farmhouse, and we continue hoeing in the cornfield. It's only a little bit after noon, and although we usually stop work at four o'clock, Koča lifts his crutch in the air and signals that we are finished for the day.

When we are plodding back to the farm, Koča says, as though talking to himself, "I hope our son makes it home soon."

My host has never mentioned his child before. Even now, he only talks about him briefly: his son is a Partisan, currently taking part in the liberation of Plavna and Klokočevac over by Rudna Glava. He is nineteen, the same age as I am. As Koča tells me this, he looks at me with piercing eyes that still hold a trace of a smile: "You could easily be my son…."

By the time we get back to the farm, Koča's wife has my raggedy things all ready, including my worn-out boots, and she has put the boot rags that were dried stiff into my sack. They know I'm not going to hang around much longer; I'll be on my way soon. I am about to take off the broadcloth shirt, but she indicates that I should keep it. The weather is turning cool, and I'll be in need of warm clothes.

I don't want to accept the present, as I know how precious it is to them. It's practically irreplaceable in these hard times, with such dire poverty here in the mountains. In a tone that brooks no opposition, they both insist that I leave the shirt on. I kiss the woman on the cheek, give Koča a hug and bid the couple farewell. I owe these two people my life to some extent.

My arrival was frightening; my departure is painful.

An Unpredictable Path

I throw my bundle over my shoulder and set off toward the dark forest. Turning back, I see Koča leaning on his wife and waving his crutch. As loudly as possible I shout, "Hvala! Puno hvala!" (Thanks! Many thanks!)

It is Sunday, October 15, an unusually mild autumn day when I say goodbye to Koča's home, where they courageously hid me, even risking their own lives for my sake. To get to Kučevo, I have to cut through the forest again. According to Koča, when I reach the trees, I should keep walking straight ahead until I come to a hunter's hut.

"Once you see the hut, you'll be close to Voluja, where you must make a sharp turn to the right, and then you'll be in Kučevo in an hour," he said. He added that ten minutes after entering the forest, I'd see a ditch on the right. I was to go around it then continue straight ahead.

I am striding through the dense forest at a comfortable pace. Sometimes I turn over on my ankle on the narrow pebbled trail. My ears are attuned to the myriad sounds of the forest: the rustling of leaves, the cracking of dried-out tree trunks, the plopping of pine cones. I keep my eyes on the winding path; whenever I come to a fork, I anxiously look around, because if I miss the hunter's cabin, I could wander endlessly like a lost soul in the Minotaur's labyrinth.

It's almost a week since October 9, the day the Nazis launched their surprise attack on the *kafana*, where we were merrily revelling and drinking *rakija* while awaiting the arrival of the Soviets. I'd been walking for about another quarter of an hour when, through the thick trees, the ash-grey hunter's cabin appeared. It looked kind of like a guard hut with a flat roof. I recalled Koča's instructions — I have to take a right turn here and I'll reach the village in an hour.

Most likely I will see Soviet soldiers in Kučevo. Until now I'd only known one Russian, Fedor, a cobbler, who married my mother's sister. When they came from Szatmár for a visit, he brought me presents, some fritters and a tumbler toy he'd made himself. Fedor immigrated to the United States in the early years of the Depression, where he and his family now live. He was a good, warm-hearted man, and that's how I've pictured Russians ever since.

In the newsreels made by the UFA, the German film and television production company that made Nazi propaganda, I saw cowardly Soviet soldiers, scared and running from the heroic German fighters. When the Red Army was captured and its frightened soldiers appeared on the screen with their hands up in surrender, the audience broke out in enthusiastic applause.

Whatever else I know about the Russians I learned only from reading, although on Sundays in Heidenau, Miklós used to talk about Russian literature and authors. Once he remarked, looking amused, that the Nazis would have turned Pushkin into a slave because he had some African blood running through his veins, but he added that Pushkin was always proud of this fact. He also talked about Krylov who, like La Fontaine, wrote fables.

In my student days, I devoured books. When I read Gogol's *Taras Bulba*, I would feel as fiery as a reckless Cossack, or I would race through Russia in a troika. And when I leafed through the pages of Gogol's *Dead Souls* late at night by the light of my reading lamp, I was shocked but also amused by the incredible fraud that went on.

As I press on toward Kučevo, I dredge my memory for everything

I know about the Soviets and Russian culture. I think of *Anna Karenina*, Tolstoy's novel about a great love. I saw the movie at the Apollo Cinema, with Fredric March as the blameworthy Count Vronsky and Greta Garbo as the unfaithful wife. I also read *The Idiot* by Dostoevsky. There's a memorable scene in the novel where everyone must recount the story of the worst thing they have ever done.

As I move forlornly through the woods, I am anxious to know what happened to Kari Háy and the others who were cowering in the ditch when we jumped out and ran to the forest. I wonder where Kádár, Reiner and Laci Stollenbau are.

We've been persecuted for centuries and we are always fleeing.

Lessing wrote: "If there is to be trust and honesty between two peoples, then both have to contribute to it equally. But how, if for one of them it's a point of religion and almost a sacred duty to persecute the other?"

At last our liberators, the Soviets, have arrived. We've been praying for this great moment for years. But will we ever be able to forget about the people who became the rulers of our fate?

The forest is thinning out. I hear some ducks quacking nearby where the forest ends, and just then I catch sight of the first Soviet soldier. He is sitting on a log and wearing creased boots and a quilted jacket. There's a weapon on his lap. He is rolling a cigarette in rough paper. Another Soviet private emerges from the trees; he must have been doing his business, because he is still buttoning up. His belt is taut, and so are his lips.

I greet the soldiers amiably. I walk toward them, but the stout Soviet sitting on the log springs to his feet in a hostile manner and screams *Stoj!* (Stop!) He points his gun at me. Then they make me get on the ground while they search me and examine my almost empty bundle. The one with the belt is looking at my wrist.

They ask for my papers.

"My papers? I was in captivity. I was liberated by the Partisans. I'm on my way home."

The first Soviet has an old-fashioned hairstyle, and he scratches his head in a coarse way. Then slyly, like someone who doesn't believe a word I say, he asks, "Haven't you got any papers?"

"None," I answer. "Everything was taken away from me."

"Then what is this?" He takes my prayer book, which was a gift from my Hebrew teacher in Grade 8, and shoves it in my face.

"Here is my name in this little book, look." I am perfectly calm at this point.

"I've had enough of you!" the stout guy shouts at me rudely, and he turns his weapon on me. The sour stench of brandy is heavy on his breath. Now the Soviet soldier and I are staring each other down, and I'm well aware that my life is at stake. It crosses my mind that they must take me for a Chetnik or perhaps a spy. "The Nazis took me to do forced labour. They enslaved me because they hate my religion," I explain in order to save my hide. Perhaps it was exhaustion, or maybe my trials and tribulations that compelled me to spread my arms and implore, "Tovarish [Comrade], I am a friend. Let me go on my way, enough is enough."

The stout Soviet flies into a temper. He puffs himself up like an angry turkey and waves his fist in my face: "You call yourself a tovarish, you stinking Jew? I dare you to say it one more time, you despicable cur."

The Soviet is shaking with rage: "Gryaznyy zhid, ya ub'yu tebya!" (Dirty Jew, I'm gonna kill you!)

The lanky soldier with the belt tries to calm his buddy. He looks at me then eyes his agitated comrade. They appear to be arguing. My heart is beating a mile a minute. I'm trying not to let my anxiety show, because I know that would aid my enemy's cause.

The irascible boor starts shaking his head and tapping his rifle against his boot, then abruptly he turns to me. "You are free. Reluctantly, we are letting you go. And you can go to hell! Come on, get a move on! Get out of my sight!"

Like a beaten dog, I slink away. Shakespeare's thoughts on overcoming adversity spring to mind: "In the reproof of chance lies the true proof of men." My God, the Soviets are strange!

Now I've left the forest behind me and can see some plump ducks waddling near the edge of the town. On this Sunday, Kučevo is grey and deserted. The narrow and capricious Pek River and the road leading to Golubac look like they've been painted onto the scene.

Among many similar dwellings, I'm searching for the pleasant little home where we spent our first night in Kučevo. I find it and rap on the gate. The spindly, stooped old Serbian mountain dweller comes toward me, chewing tobacco; he unbolts the door, looking surprised to see me again.

The old woman is puttering around in the kitchen. She recognizes me and motions me to put my belongings in the same little room as before. Shuffling like old people do, she lays out cornmeal cake, milk and dark plum butter on the oilcloth-covered kitchen table and kindly invites me to partake. Without waiting for an answer, she puts a large portion of cornmeal cake on my plate.

I set my knapsack on the bench beside the boards in the closet-like room. The woollen blankets are cuddling up to the straw on the boards as if they'd been waiting for me.

I ask the old man if he has seen my companion, the one who shared the room with me at their place. I hope that Kari Háy will show up very soon. I have difficulty making myself understood. The old man just keeps nodding and shoving the tobacco from left to right with his yellow teeth. The old woman comes to our rescue. She tells me that the Hungarian man who was my roommate spent the previous night there. This morning he said goodbye and left. I ask the woman if he told her where he was heading. She shakes her head, and then remembers that he might have mentioned he was intending to go to a faraway place.

So Kari left. By himself? With others?

I spread the woollen blanket on the straw and drop off to sleep. In my mind, I too am wandering far away.

For the first time in a long time, the sun rises in a cloudless sky over a hilly horizon. My first waking thought is: Kari is alive!

~

In the morning I bid farewell to the lovable old couple. I embrace the woman and gently squeeze the man's arthritic hand. I say, "See you again," although I ought to know that I'll never see them again. I resume wandering along my bumpy, unpredictable path.

On the main street I head for the building of the Provisional Military Council. I hope that the fellows from Bor who were hiding in the vicinity dared to come out of the forest and return to the town, because this is the route to the Romanian border. On this Monday morning, all the people of Kučevo are up and about. Peasant carts piled with straw make way for carriages coming from the opposite direction on the rough road; the horses are soaked in sweat. I feel the early morning Serbian sunshine warming my body through my ragged clothing. I look around the lively, bustling settlement, and by the time I get to the council office the sun is high in the clear sky.

The sign in Cyrillic for the Provisional Military Council has been removed, and they have affixed a larger wooden board bearing red letters: NATIONAL LIBERATION COUNCIL.

Inside the large hall-like room, Partisans — young men and women — are linking hands in a circle and singing one of their endless songs, while tapping out the beat with their feet.

I pay no attention to the dancers. A few people are busying themselves with files and reports; transmitting and receiving military reports on the radio mounted on a huge table; pasting messages, commands and news on a notice board on the wall. I'm trying to figure out whom to approach for advice about what I should do. What will happen tomorrow and the day after?

There's a clerk wearing a Titovka hat sitting at a small table, shifting files around. I decide to ask him for advice. I mustn't keep standing here forever, like a ninny. Life is short and can pass you by. I'm going to join the Partisans. I'm standing just beside the table when the young man looks up from behind the mountain of files and raises his finger benevolently: "The road is clear for your return home."

Then I turn around and right behind me stand Kádár, Bandi Reiner and a whole bunch of guys from Bor! What a racket as they all begin speaking at once. Everyone had a horror story to tell: how frightening the forest was, how the leaves were whooshing and sighing, how it felt like being clawed by monsters. The SS patrols that were sweeping through the forest with their German shepherds found Laci Stollenbau and shot him on the spot. The guys heard that after the carnage in Kučevo, the farmers took in the wounded, and then in the dark of night, managed to take them to the Partisan hospital in Negotin. Several fellows from Bor were among the wounded.

The singing fades. The door opens and Duško Milić, the president of the Liberation Council, arrives, accompanied by Partisan officers in bluish-grey uniforms and a Soviet colonel with gold braid on his uniform. The officers, along with the highly decorated Soviet colonel, are hurrying toward the office of the council president when the burly, square-shouldered Duško notices the boys from Bor. He turns back from the door and heads our way. His beetle eyes shine happily, his tone is emotional. "My friends, what you were hoping for has happened. I've got good news for you: yesterday at noon, Hungarian radio interrupted its broadcast to say that Miklós Horthy had asked the Allies for an armistice and that he had announced it to the representatives of the German Reich. Horthy instructed the commanders of the Hungarian army to obey his orders immediately."

We are overwhelmed by Duško's announcement. The wonderful moment we've been waiting for since our rescue has arrived at last, the one we could hardly believe in any longer but were always hoping would come true — that we can return to our homes in Hungary. After Duško's news, we experience a rush of patriotic idealism. To feel such immense brotherly love after all that has happened is rather vexing; it's just not right. There is a lot we have to process.

But the extraordinary news raises the spirits of the group from Bor. Gyuri Kádár is ready to organize things: "There is no point in waiting any longer. In the afternoon we'll take off toward Golubac. That'll put us close to the Danube, and we'll somehow make our way home from there. Who wants to join me?" The initial response is lukewarm, so Kádár adds details to the picture: "Golubac is about the same distance from Kučevo as Kučevo is from Majdanpek; it can't be more than forty kilometres."

I'm thinking of Sanyi Szalai, wondering where he is. Had we listened to him, we could have avoided the slaughter in Kučevo. It's hard to decide where to go next. We all long to go home, but there is still a lot of danger around us. The marauding Chetniks haven't given up the fight yet. Even though the Wehrmacht units are scattered and surrounded, stubborn hatred drives them to keep on murdering — to avenge the death of one of their own, they shoot five, ten, a hundred people.

The minutes crawl by at a snail's pace as we discuss our best course of action. Finally, six of us decide to go with Kádár. Gyuri rushes over to the commander's office and in a short while returns waving a sheet of paper:

TRAVEL PERMIT
Issued to Gyuri Kádár and a further six persons to allow them to go to Golubac on their way home. We kindly ask the authorities to assist the above-mentioned persons and refrain from impeding their progress.
16 — X — 1944
The President of the National Liberation Council
Duško Milić

The slaves of the second contingent have dispersed. After the more than two thousand forced labourers from Bor were liberated by the Partisans, they took off in all directions. Some headed for Jasenovo with the Partisan commanders, many returned to Bor, which was liberated on October 3, and continued their trek to Romania from there. Some of the men who chose the route to Belgrade were caught in the fighting with German troops fleeing in panic from the Balkans. The weary men from Bor who headed north from Majdanpek reached the Danube in a short while. The local fishermen carried them in broad boats to the other side of the river for a few dinars, smuggling them into Romanian territory.

An unfortunate group of *muszos* men found themselves right in the middle of the bloody battles taking place around Klokočevac. They were caught in the Soviet-German crossfire, and the German armoured troops mowed them down mercilessly. Some of them were mistaken for spies and were shot in the head; a few were taken prisoner along with the Nazis by the Soviet liberators, a few days after their liberation from Bor.

We take leave of our comrades from Bor, several of whom are still wavering about what direction to take. Led by Kádár and armed with a travel permit, Bandi Reiner, four other *muszos* men and I set out for Golubac, which is to say we follow the road that leads north. Gyuri, Bandi and I represent Heidenau. The two younger *muszos* lads were prisoners at the Laznica Lager, and the other two joined us from Westfalen Lager. We are sorry that Uncle Ede is not with us, and Kari Háy has also disappeared. Olivér Hollós is not with us either. Who knows where they are? We all scattered during the calamity at Kučevo.

The sun has hidden behind a veil of fog. Only pausing for a short break on the banks of the Pek River, we reach Rabrovo before dark, exhausted from the hard six-hour march.

Rabrovo is a small village of maybe a thousand inhabitants. The locals don't seem to be surprised by our arrival. It's as if they've been expecting us. That's because larger or smaller groups of refugees have been passing through the village for days, most of them heading for Golubac. The villagers themselves have scant supplies, but bread and corn, if nothing else, will always be offered to the stateless.

We were trying to get to the village before dark because we didn't feel like knocking on the door of some Serbian home at night. Before we can ask for directions, an old woman loitering at a gate points and says, "Go straight ahead to the church square, that's where the women are baking pies."

In the twilight there is a lot of hustle and bustle in front of the Eastern Orthodox church. A colourful crowd: Partisans in transit, locals, farmers, tradesmen and refugees. We arrived at the right time. The women are cooking soup outdoors in a giant cauldron and baking round cornmeal pies in some sort of an oven they've rigged up.

As though they'd known us for a hundred years, they offer us food. There is no need to explain anything, as they know we are wanderers. We eat with ravenous appetites. After a while, a friendly, muscular man of average height joins us. "I suspect you are from Bor," he begins, "and I think you're on your way home like the others who've passed through the village." Then he adds, "I'm the mayor of the village."

"Yes, we are going home," Kádár eagerly answers on our behalf. "Hungary has withdrawn from the war, we heard it this morning in Kučevo."

The mayor keeps silent for a long time. His eyes cloud over and his face looks pained, as if he'd been stabbed in the heart. For a while he deliberates whether he should tell us or not, then he continues, "I have sad news for you. May Jesus Christ help you. Your hopes are in vain, you can't go home. The Germans have occupied the strategic centres of the capital. Miklós Horthy ordered the army to continue fighting. He handed power over to Ferenc Szálasi and resigned his post as regent."

One of the *muszos* men from Laznica lets out a groan of despair as if he'd been hit by shrapnel. "I knew it would turn out like this!"

"What we feared has actually happened," says a dejected Reiner.

"Don't be distressed and above all don't do anything crazy," the mayor makes an attempt to soothe our agitated spirits. "Panic, chaos and wailing only exacerbate an already difficult situation."

"So the putsch is kaput," sighs Kádár miserably.

The mayor of Rabrovo, who understands our sorrow and sympathizes with us, clears his throat then purses his lips like he's about to whisper. It seems he has more to tell us, and it's clear that he's hesitating. He's apologetic, his information could be wrong, or perhaps inaccurate. "I received a radio communication from the central military command that last week more than five hundred forced labourers from Bor were massacred by the SS in Cservenka [Crvenka]. I don't know any details of the terrible slaughter except that the prisoners were killed by machine guns."

The horrendous news paralyzes us. Apathy and helplessness take hold of us. I am stricken to the depths of my soul. How many appalling tragedies do we have to find out about? And all that in a single day.

Like images on a movie screen, the faces of our Heidenau comrades who left with the first contingent appear before my eyes: Gyuri Gara, the physician Bárdos, Pista Horn, Ákos Grósz from Jászberény, my friends from the Radnóti circle: Miklós, Peti Szüsz, Zoli Budai, Jóska Junger and the rest.

I wonder what happened to the cook, Szabados, whom we teasingly called Gravedigger? And Zoli Heller? Pista Löwy from Lónyay Street? Jóska Weisz, Dr. Vajda and Lorsi the fiddler? Who was cut down by Death's sickle? Who stayed alive, and who perished?

I get a lump in my throat: to think that I could have left with the first contingent. Junger offered to change places with me. Was it higher powers that decided our fate?

~

In July, during a Sunday afternoon rest, Miklós recited one of his earlier poems in the blazing sun on the banks of the brook, Lipa. The lines of the poem, like a prophetic vision, reverberate in my head.

I can see Radnóti's rather long, animated face, his darkly furrowed brow on my imaginary movie screen.

> I lived on this earth in an age
> When man fell so low he killed with pleasure
> And willingly, not merely under orders.
> His life entangled, trapped, in wild obsession,
> He trusted false gods, raving in delusion.[1]

No, it can't be true!, I think to myself. The mayor said it happened last week. This must be some colossal mistake. After all, the men in the first contingent left on September 17. They set out for Požarevac on a Sunday morning, and they were told they'd be taking a train from there to Hungarian territory. Let's estimate that the march to Požarevac took three, maybe four days, and the trip to Hungary another two days, throw in an extra day or two for good measure. By this calculation, the *muszos* men from Bor must have been on Hungarian soil before the end of September.

Tomorrow it will be a month since the members of the first contingent left Bor. How could they have ended up in Cservenka? There must be some disastrous misunderstanding behind all this! And that news about home: the reign of Szálasi, young men with Arrow Cross insignia. It's conceivable that the Arrow Cross men will try to outdo the Nazis in brutality. All hell has broken loose back home.

When Miklós sat across from me that day, I could almost feel his breath as he read aloud the third stanza with the measured cadence of a professor:

> I lived on this earth in an age
> When any who spoke out would have to flee —
> Forced to lie low and gnaw their fists in shame.
> The folk went mad and, drunk on blood, filth, hate,
> Could only grin at their own hideous fate.

---

1 "Fragment." May 19, 1944.

We spend the night on makeshift bunks covered with straw in the wood-panelled basement of the cultural centre, behind the church. We are aghast that all of a sudden our motherland has become a single scream for blood. Who is responsible for this whole filthy and despicable story?

I'm tossing and turning on my bunk, not used to having a comfortable bed. I'm awake but dreaming, seeing scenes from my life in bygone days. Grandma Eszti's house in Szatmár. On a big table set up on the velvety grass of the garden, there's white bread, raisin cake and hot cocoa steaming in a red polka-dot mug. A small wicker basket is heaped with apples that have been freshly picked from the trees of the valley. Another small basket contains sweet-fleshed apricots, plums and glossy black carob pods. There are jars of acacia honey and rosehip jam.

I am lost in reverie. The faces of the members of the first contingent from Heidenau are consumed by flickering, nightmarish flames. They vanish into the mist. Then I sink into a deep sleep.

We are ready to leave at dawn. The first half of the trek seems to go quickly. If we keep moving at a good pace, we should reach Golubac by noon. We march in twos without talking. Kádár plods along either in the lead or at our side. We make our way in silence. None of us has the nerve to mention the atrocities we heard about last night. We stop for a short rest every hour and adjust our boot rags or nibble at the pie saved from yesterday.

The trip took longer than we planned even though we were trying to move at a brisk pace. It is two o'clock in the afternoon when we reach the centre of the village of Golubac. Intending to ask for advice on which direction to take, we inquire of passersby where we can find the mayor, the *gradonačelnik*. Two of the locals tell us we are better off turning to the Military Council, the *Vojni Savet*, for information. Keep going straight ahead and we'll see the office of the Military Council on the left side of the street, *Kancelarija* (office) is written on a large sign.

We find the building easily. Above the rundown entrance, a Partisan flag flaps in the wind; the stones are crumbling, the paint is peeling. For a while we hang around in the spacious foyer, reading the notices posted on the wall — some we understand, others we only think we understand. After a short wait, a young Partisan woman with an air of self-importance leads all seven of us to the room of the commanding officer. The elderly, moustached soldier sitting at the table casts a friendly look our way and asks us to be patient for a moment. He is flipping through files and making a phone call.

As soon as he finishes the conversation, he turns to us. "How can I be of assistance? You are in a foreign country and it's our duty to help you. I know you want to go home, but for the time being it is not possible."

"What do you advise us to do, Commander, sir," asks Gyuri Kádár.

The commander lights up a cigarette, fishes a piece of paper out of the drawer, grabs a pen and starts writing: "The above-named persons reported to me in Golubac. I am sending them to Vinci so that they can go on to Moldova from there." Signature: Commander M. Dušjanić.

The officer stands up. Although he's trying to conceal his limp, we can tell there's something wrong with his right leg. After shaking hands with all of us, he says, "Have a good trip, my friends. Everything will be fine. Believe me the war will not last much longer." Then he adds with sorrowful irony, "At least not for those who lived to see the end."

The commander hands us the document and informs us that Vinci is only ten kilometres away, so we should be able to make it in two to three hours. He politely wishes us "Srećno" (Good luck), and then heads back to his seat at the table, dragging his foot as he goes. The hearing has finished.

We gather strategic bits of information from the infrequent passersby on the deserted streets: they tell us that the Danube narrows at Vinci, and it's possible to cross over to Romania there. They assure us that the road is safe to that point.

We march along the wet road enveloped in the gloom of the fall afternoon. Our progress is slow. A drizzling rain that's been falling since early afternoon has soaked the road thoroughly. The mud sticks to our worn-out boots like tar, and we are slipping and sliding as if on ice. We exchange very few words. Occasionally, we stop to adjust our sodden knapsacks and wring out our boot rags. Slowly, but steadily, we trudge onward.

We arrive at the village of Vinci before dusk. By now we're so used to marching that we don't even feel tired, here under the vast foreign sky. We go straight to the bank of the Danube. We pick up meaningless fragments of words, then suddenly we see tall fishermen with deeply lined faces undoing their nets, scuffing around their boats in patched jackets. They glance over at us; they have a pretty good idea what we are after.

One of the fishermen, a young guy with a face like a gopher, gives us a wink: "Zdravo, druže!" (Hello, comrade!) "You're at the right place." He wears a broad smile and starts singing when we are close: "Over the ripples the boat makes its way, the guard isn't watching the Danube this day."

The bargaining doesn't take long. We scrape together our dinars from Majdanpek and quickly strike a deal with the resourceful young fisherman: as soon as evening falls he will row us over to the other side, to the river port of Moldova Veche.

That very night, we squat in the boat, all squeezed together. With its unusually heavy load, the boat creeps slowly across the river. The young man's arms are straining, sweat streams down his forehead.

When we reach the Romanian side, we scramble out of the boat and take our leave of the fisherman. He calls out directions from his boat: "Go straight to the centre of the village, don't spend the night on the shore." At which point he turns back, and we can soon hear the splashing of the oars.

We heave a sigh, as if a giant weight has been lifted off our shoulders. We have left the storms of war behind us. We have entered a free country. Happiness floods us. Feeling relieved, we are following the track when all of a sudden a sharp voice rings out: "Attention!" Then comes the order to stop, and two armed guards block our path.

The higher ranking one, standing with legs apart and hands on his hips, shouts, "Come over here! Your papers!" We hand him the papers from Kučevo and Golubac. The hulking officer with a walrus moustache arrogantly eyes the Cyrillic handwriting, then crumples the papers into his pocket with angry impatience. His clumsy, broad-shouldered companion is following the proceedings out of the corner of his eye.

"The rotten scoundrel," mutters Reiner.

"What have you got brains for if you don't know how to control yourself?" one of the guys from Westfalen jabs Bandi in the side.

Kádár tries to make himself understood by the Romanian border guards: "We are Hungarian refugees…we are on our way home. Give us back our papers."

The soldier frowns maliciously and signals us to walk in front of them. Reiner starts whispering that we should try to escape; we could disappear in no time in the dark. It's an insane idea. Kádár overhears what Reiner is up to and yells at him, "Don't be crazy, the guards have guns and rifles and if we make a move they'll just shoot us. They'll make mincemeat out of us. Take it easy."

Anger makes me clench my fists. How naive we were to think that we were free.

We've become prisoners again. Flanked by armed guards, we are being led who knows where. We are still dancing on top of a volcano.

We arrive at the border guards' station. They lead us down a spiral staircase to a short corridor with three empty cells opening onto it. Three of our buddies are shoved into one cell, four of us are squeezed behind the iron bars of another. We start rattling the bars, demanding a hearing and cursing — all in vain.

"Louder! Louder!" our young cellmate from Laznica keeps repeating. He's so angry that the veins in his neck stand out and dark red blotches appear on his ochre yellow skin.

We run out of steam and stop the useless racket. From above, quiet music filters down to our cell. This is insane! A Rachmaninoff prelude squawks away on some sort of a scratchy gramophone. In Moldova Veche, at night, in a filthy cell, far from any concert hall, we are listening to classical music. Someone winds up the record player again, and we hear a pianist playing one of Chopin's mazurkas.

"Sheer lunacy," groans Reiner. Then he lets out a yell and starts banging again.

"They are the odious Iron Guard," shouts Kádár from the next cell, "the infamous, antisemitic, nationalist scoundrels of the Garda de Fier. They hate our guts."[2]

"They're messing with us. I hope they all rot in hell!" fumes the *muszos* man from Laznica.

The stocky guy from Westfalen is livid: "These fascist skunks are pretending to be asleep. Here at the border they don't give a damn that Romania turned its back on the Nazis two months ago. Traitors, mongrels!" He is raging like a madman.

We come to the realization that the shouting, banging and swearing are getting us nowhere. Exhausted, we quiet down. Stubble-faced, hungry, lice-ridden, now listening to Scriabin's études, we drift off to sleep on the bumpy cement floor of the Moldovan cell.

"Do you believe the massacre in Cservenka really happened?" someone whispers.

There is no answer. And the gramophone has finished playing as well.

I can't sleep. I keep darting glances to the left and right like a frightened animal. Free, imprisoned…free, imprisoned…then free again, and imprisoned again. What a mess we've got ourselves into. I

---

2   Although the Iron Guard had been overthrown earlier in the war and these were likely Romanian police officers, Andai and his friends are associating them with the notorious Romanian militia.

recall something I once read: "Don't count on tomorrow before it arrives, because you never know what bad news tomorrow will bring."

Early the next morning the stamping of boots echoes on the spiral
staircase. Beside the guard with the walrus moustache there's another
one with a bull neck. They open our cells with keys that dangle from a
rusty chain. Without a word of explanation, they herd us up the winding stairs like sheep. Probably they're taking us to be interrogated.

In the office upstairs, a bespectacled soldier who looks like a student doesn't even glance our way. He is busy changing the needle in
the gramophone. We anxiously wonder where the hearing will take
place.

The two border guards walk ahead of us. They open the door and
herd us out into the misty grey morning.

"Where are you taking us?" we ask the one with the walrus moustache, worriedly. The guards pretend to be dumb and don't deign to
answer. We try to engage them several times, to no avail.

We notice that we are leaving the village and getting closer to the
Danube again, along the same track we followed yesterday. We have
a good idea what fate awaits us. Our aggressive slave drivers gesture
roughly to us to get into the patrol boat. The bull-necked guy is about
to start rowing, while the one with the walrus moustache stays on
the shore. He digs the confiscated papers from his pocket and throws
them in the boat before the oars even hit the water. In less than half
an hour we are back in Serbia.

None of our plans ever seem to work out. We feel a growing sense
of disappointment, a strange lethargy. And we thought from now on
everything would be easy. We are rid of our shackles, we are no longer
chained together like prisoners, all stupidity and tyranny has ceased,
and we can live according to the rule of law again.

We look at each other listlessly, disappointed. Not saying a word,
we sit by the bank of the Danube, kicking pebbles and staring straight
ahead — angry and overcome by the unfairness of it all.

Gyuri Kádár struggles to his feet with a sigh. He rubs his stubbly face, scratches his tousled head, then grins. "We just had bad luck, that's all. We walked right into their arms. Had we left later, after midnight, the guards would have been sound asleep in their huts."

"How do you know that, mister wise guy?" the man from Laznica challenges Kádár.

"Many people before us managed to cross over to Moldova, otherwise we wouldn't have been given those papers," reasons Kádár. "We'll ask the fisherman to take us over again. I still have dinars, and you must have a few left, too. You'll see, we'll be able to get to the village and there we'll figure it all out."

"I'm not going back," says Reiner with determination.

"Why not?" asks Kádár in surprise.

"I'm scared. I'm scared that we'll be caught again, and this time we won't get off so easily."

"In my life I had to start all over again seven times. I was thrown out, I was fired, and I started again. Don't be such a coward."

"What are you trying to say?" Reiner reacts angrily. He is clearly upset.

Before the fight can get out of hand, the stocky guy from Westfalen starts clucking his tongue. "Tut-tut-tut…don't be childish. There's no need to quarrel. Listen to this: those who want to try again go ahead with Kádár, those who don't should find a better solution for themselves, how to proceed. Unfortunately, either way it's a game of chance. You're right, one shouldn't always pay attention to what another person is doing. After all, none of us is smart enough to figure out what the right step is. Damn the men who invented war! You see, being dragged to a foreign country has made us all sick."

The man from Westfalen didn't elaborate on what he meant by that remark.

Kádár tries to boost the boys' morale: "At night we'll make another attempt. What kind of people are we to put up with all this abuse? Listen to me! I'm absolutely sure that we'll be able to get across."

The *muszos* men from Laznica and Westfalen are nodding in

agreement: they are all going along with Kádár. It occurs to me that it was Kádár who suggested Kučevo. Maybe we would have fared better if we had gone with Sanyi Szalai. After this Moldovan fiasco, heaven knows which way to go to avoid another bad outcome.

"I'm staying with Bandi," I say decisively.

Kádár and the *muszos* boys gaze at me in surprise and disappointment.

"Listen!" Kádár tries again. "We'll take off tonight. Come with us! Believe me, it's not risky."

"I find it hard to leave you guys, but my mind's made up. Maybe it's stupid, but I'm not going with you."

Kádár looks at us through narrowed eyes. He is concerned that the two young men from Heidenau will stay without a guardian. "You're being bad boys…I'll have to box your ears." Kádár is joking but we can tell he's affected. Then he gives both of us a long embrace.

We shake hands with the *muszos* guys two times. "See you boys in Budapest."

Scattered Lives

As soon as we depart from Kádár's group, we start marching at a military pace along a narrow trail that leads to Braničevo. We then head north on Serbian soil. From time to time we hear the distant roar of cannons. We are so used to it, we hardly notice it.

Bandi Reiner is a squat, moon-faced fellow. We are the same age. Our bodies ache all over from fatigue, but we know there is no room for self-pity.

We quit the trail along the Danube and turn onto the main road. It is littered with junk discarded by the fleeing Nazis, stuff they'd been pillaging for years: musty odds and ends, remnants of fabric, empty boxes, pillows, wooden dummies from a country fair shooting gallery, rock-hard rinds of cheese, a spool of iron chain, horseshoes by the sackful, framed holy pictures, a tub of lard, coloured candy in cellophane bags, stinking sacks.

The cannon blasts are growing stronger. We grab a few bags of candy from the orgy of trash and return to the safer trail. Eventually, at Kostolac, the landscape becomes gentler. We have put the barren mountain country behind us and managed to cross over the Danube River, though due to the river's path, crossing here means staying within Serbia. Bandi starts humming a mournful tune:

I am slowly walking homeward,
defeated armies are running homeward —
never before did I have a wife,
at home, for me, now waits a wife.

After finally passing through Pančevo and Jabuka, we spend a night in Opovo. Wherever we go the locals can tell by our scruffy appearance that we are refugees. They provide us with food, shelter for the night and good advice. The family we stay with in Opovo recommends that we go to Petrovgrad (Zrenjanin), where we should be safe. We have walked more than a hundred kilometres since Vinci, which means we have covered a considerable portion of the distance to Petrovgrad.

Our host in Opovo is a Hungarian from Bácska, and his wife is Serbian; they are farmers. In the morning, before we set out, he gives us some sad news: the Arrow Cross rule of terror is raging in Hungary. They are planning ghettos and looting Jewish apartments. We ask the man if he knows anything about the first contingent of prisoners from Bor. Has he heard about the slaughter in Cservenka? He doesn't know anything about the Cservenka atrocities, but he does know a lot about the men from Bor. Not needing to be coaxed, he launches right into the tale:

"I heard this from a man named Katz. He and three of his buddies escaped from the first contingent near Smederevo. He told me that they didn't get real railway cars in Požarevac the way they'd hoped. The Nazis kept all the wagons for themselves; they couldn't have cared less about giving a ride to Jewish forced labourers.

"Katz also said that they spent the first night near the Heidenau Lager, the second in Žagubica and the next in Krepoljin. Then came Petrovac. By the time they marched through Požarevac they were dead tired, thirsty and hungry, but if the local people tried to give some food to the pitiful group, the guards would drive the Serbian women off with their rifle butts. He also said that one of the *muszos* men was shot to death near Smederevo because he picked a corn cob from a field beside the road."

When the farmer from Opovo notices that Reiner's eyes are welling up with tears he stops talking and looks at the boy with compassion. "I'm sorry…." His wife puts her head down on the kitchen table and sobs.

~

It is now the second half of October. The hours, the days, the weeks are dragging on. When we arrive in Petrovgrad, Soviet soldiers are marching down the main street, people are standing about on the sidewalk, cyclists are whizzing by and women are doing their shopping in the stores.

By this date the Soviet army had fought its major tank battle at Debrecen, the Red Army had forged as far south as the Tisza River, then pushed on to Baja and established a massive bridgehead on the Danube south of Baja. Our enduring hope is to be able to return home soon. We are callow lads, forever longing for home.

Petrovgrad is an orderly little town, a haven of calm after the storm. It was once called Nagybecskerek, or Becskerek. As soon as we reach the main street, Bandi starts singing, in his rich baritone, an impromptu ditty that features silly rhymes on the name of the town. He's in high spirits and another song quickly follows: "Two friends set out from Bor to Petrovgrad hoping for a better fate…."

In the refugee section of the town hall, a clerk with sleeve protectors and a bowtie gives each of us an address for accommodations and vouchers for the Disinfection Institute. Tactfully, he advises us to go to the disinfecting place first. He points out the direction, and from the window of the town hall we can see that it's only three hundred metres away.

Our bodies are crawling with lice, and I even have fleas. One night in that Moldovan cell was all it took for me to pick up some fleas that

I could not get rid of afterward. The fleas are fighting the lice for my blood.

It has been almost half a year since we've had a hot bath in a bathtub. Using industrial strength soap and a well-worn brush, I scrub my grimy skin in the sudsy water. I lie back in the pleasant warmth. I am in a state of rapture in the steam-filled bathroom, as if I were in paradise.

There is a short but forceful rap on the door. A hoarse woman's voice shouts something in Serbian; I assume she's telling me my time is up. My tattered clothing, now spanking clean, is in a neat pile in front of the door. While I was daydreaming in the bathtub, my ragtag belongings were disinfected in scorching hot ovens.

Soon Bandi shows up, refreshed and grinning, and starts singing another nutty verse about Becskerek. We head to our separate lodgings after agreeing to meet in front of the Disinfection Institute the next morning at ten o'clock. It takes me less than ten minutes to find the slate-roofed house of my prospective host. I quickly verify the address, then knock three times on the door.

I am received by a buxom, jovial woman wearing a wide, pleated skirt. Holding a jar of preserves in her left hand, she dries her right hand by running it through her piled-up hair, so that she can shake hands with me. The town hall informed her I'd be coming. She leads me into a freshly swept room that contains an iron bed frame with a burlap covered mattress. There's a shelf above the bed with postcards on it, a small table, a chair, a holy picture on the wall and a wash basin with some soap on a stool.

My hostess is a Hungarian widow from the southern land. She lives here with her teenage daughter and her son, who attend high school in the little town. It is evening before the shy girl dares to put in an appearance. I also meet Lali, the lanky student and gangly teenager. This stiff, awkward, yet somehow genuine kid is only three years younger than me, but I seem like a Methuselah beside him.

I keep tossing and turning on the iron bedstead. My forehead is covered in sweat, and I can't fall asleep. I find the cleanliness, the comfort of a peaceful home, the temporary sense of security, overwhelming. When I finally drift off, I'm in my Sunday best sitting at a table covered with a linen tablecloth, raising small bites to my mouth with a fork. Then with a sudden crash, Corporal Sisák barges into the room and locks me up in the stocks laughing crazily, "You can't escape me!" He comes closer and a yellow flash shoots from his gun.

In the morning, the widow, Auntie Sári, tells me that the neighbours across the road have invited me for dinner. She assures me that they are decent Hungarian people. Through a mouthful of bread, Lali asks me if I know how to play basketball, but he doesn't wait for an answer. Still gnawing on a heel of bread, he grabs his satchel and rushes off to school with his sister, her blond hair flying in the wind.

We spend two weeks in Petrovgrad. Every day we walk past the heavily guarded headquarters of Marshal Tolbukhin, the commander of the 3rd Ukrainian Front. The troops of the Red Army had begun the final push of the Belgrade Offensive on October 14, and on October 20, the capital was liberated from the hands of the Nazis.

As soon as we learn that Szeged has been liberated we bid farewell to our benefactors and embark on the more than one-hundred-kilometre journey. We're in better shape now. Not only did Auntie Sári's neighbour treat me to dinner and supper, but she also made me a present of a jacket of her husband's and a pair of his boots. My trench coat with the Star of David and my disintegrated boots are a thing of the past. Bandi was also outfitted by his hosts, so that in only two weeks we have regained our human form.

Halfway to Szeged, as we trudge along the main road, cars, farm wagons and carts pass by us. One of the Soviet trucks slows down, and in its open wagon there are about half a dozen cheerful soldiers in jackboots. We notice that they are waiting for us, signalling us to get on board. At first we are reluctant, but the soldiers seem genial. They tell us that we're in luck because they are heading to Szeged.

When the big truck starts off again, they unleash their curiosity:

"Have you got anything to drink? Šljivovica? Vino?" they inquire, asking about Serbian plum brandy or wine. We shake our heads and hold out our upturned palms to show them we haven't got anything. Their faces fall, but one of the guys in a quilted jacket reassures me, "Nitchevo." (No matter.)

We've been lurching along for half an hour when the rickety truck makes a grinding noise and breaks down at the right side of the road. The soldiers jump off the vehicle carrying their rifles and motion us to join them. The gesture looks aggressive; it could be interpreted as an order.

Barely a hundred metres from the main road a well-trodden track leads to a farmhouse. One of the Soviets, a cigarette butt in the corner of his mouth, pushes his solid shoulder against the door, which opens easily. It wasn't even locked. The occupants of the small house are away. Perhaps they fled in haste leaving all their goods and chattels behind — who knows what exigency turned them into displaced people?

The Soviet soldiers search the house at will: rummaging, nosing around, opening cupboards and chests, sniffing at bottles and generally bustling about. One of the soldiers with almond eyes and a flat nose shows up grinning proudly and holding two hefty demijohns, large jugs probably full of wine, he found in the musty cellar.

The party is starting. Bandi and I are ill at ease. Our brand-new buddies keep embracing us, patting us on the shoulder, forcing the sour red wine on us, making us clink glasses with them. They've already put back quite a few mugfuls of wine when a soused soldier with a waxed moustache comes roaring at us: "Shpion!" (You are spies!) "Your mothers are dirty whores!" A stream of obscenity spews out of him. He shoves us against the wall, cocks his rifle with an audible click. He is going to kill us.

His pal sprints over to him and tries to calm him down. He hugs him, whispers something in his ear, caresses his pockmarked face, then kisses him on the mouth. The angry bull is mollified; he lays his weapon on the floor. From an executioner devil he turns into an angel in the blink of an eye. As if nothing at all had happened, he lifts the demijohn and fills glasses to the brim, both for himself and for us.

Woohoo! We are friends again.

We are searching for a way to get rid of these unpredictable booze-hounds. The previous tragic circus is repeated two more times with minor variations: we're lined up against the wall to be executed, then pardoned magnanimously. If only we could escape!

The demijohns have been drained to the dregs. Now our soldiers are staggering back to the truck singing. We fall behind on the track without anyone noticing. It seems as though they've completely forgotten about us. We hear the engine being started up, and amid rattles, wheezes and backfiring, the truck full of partying Soviets drives off trailing a cloud of smoke.

Bandi and I look at one another. "Drunken pigs!" we shout after them.

"We are free again," I add.

"But for how long?" Bandi ripostes with his usual gallows humour. And he flashes a grin.

Every two or three minutes, military convoys zoom past us with an ear-splitting noise, acting as if they own the road. When they slow down, we move over to the side, to avoid being invited on board their rattletrap. The soldiers wave, shout and hurl beer bottles onto the highway.

～

On November 8, early in the afternoon, after an interminable tramp, we find ourselves in downtown Szeged. We keep asking how to get to the mayor's office. The people here are strange, rough, clearly reluctant to help. There's a pervasive sense of violence, misery and fear in the city. Armband-wearing Soviet soldiers patrol in pairs, with rifles on their shoulders, asking everyone they see for their papers. People go by carrying bundles in wheelbarrows and on tricycles. They move about like sleepwalkers.

The secretary at the mayor's office eventually condescends to give us an address where we can find shelter for the night. On our way from the office, we see that Soviet soldiers are picking out young and middle-aged men from among the passersby and adding them to a growing group on the other side of the street. The shivering band is guarded by four armed Soviets. We gape in surprise at the strange gathering.

An elderly man in a grey hat shuffles by and warns us in passing, "You'd better disappear, boys, otherwise you'll be added to the transport as well."

"What type of transport is it?" we inquire, amazed.

"Siberia, sonny, Siberia... These poor souls are all bound for Siberia."

We start moving cautiously, making a large detour to get out of the way of the Soviet patrols. Finally, we locate the address we were given. Inside the apartment building we hand our paper to the superintendent, who, without a word, unlocks the downstairs apartment of an Arrow Cross man who had fled.

The next morning, I tell Bandi that I don't want to stay in Szeged any longer. I don't feel like playing a cat and mouse game with the Soviets, only to eventually end up freezing into an ice statue in the snowfields of Siberia. Bandi regards me intently; he looks flabbergasted. "Fine, buddy. And where do you intend to go?"

"I haven't got the foggiest," I answer. "All I know is that we live in such crazy times when Marxism, antisemitism or Nazism can cast a spell on people. One wrong step and you become an innocent victim."

"There are situations when it's worth your while to stop and think," philosophizes Bandi. "I am already home in Hungary. I will somehow sit it out until I can make my way to Pest."

We are afraid of going out on the street, where people are being seized or recruited for *málenkij robot*.[1] Someone is being picked up on

---

1   Term used by Hungarians from the Russian *malen'kaya rabota*, meaning "little work," to refer to forced labour in the Soviet Union.

almost every street corner. As warily as possible, we sneak over to the mayor's office, taking the long way, frequently checking all around. I think it was in one of Tolstoy's books where I read that Russians like feeling sad. They haven't even liberated the country and have already caused so much sadness.

There is a long lineup in the office. We receive meal tickets to the eatery nearby. I inquire at the secretariat how one might get to Romania. "Where exactly in Romania?" asks a dignified, white-faced elderly woman, as she twirls a fountain pen with purple ink between her fingers. To my surprise I say, "It doesn't matter." She answers, "There is a train leaving for Timişoara, Romania, at two o'clock in the afternoon. Will that suit you?" Then she adds, "I can give you both travel permits."

I look at Bandi. "Are you coming? Think about it…. Do come."

"It's all right. You go ahead — if I get home before you, I will let your mum know that you are alive."

The secretary writes my name in both Latin and Cyrillic script in the blank space in the Hungarian-Soviet permit, along with the following: "I authorize his travel to Timişoara. Szeged, 10.XI.1944." On one side of the paper there's a round Soviet stamp in red ink; on the other, there's a "Szeged Free Royal City" stamp and the signature of the mayor.

When we leave the office, the sun is still hiding behind a veil of fog, and a harsh November wind is blowing from the north. Bandi and I discuss where we should go now, but we don't have any bright ideas. It's too early for lunch. So we walk along the side streets quietly, exercising caution for fear of running into Soviet patrols.

Only now do we realize how incredibly difficult it is to part. Neither of us has a watch but we are aware that time is ticking by. Our stomachs are rumbling from hunger, so we set off for the eatery, scanning the road with eagle eyes as we go. There, they serve us hot soup and potato and egg casserole. We consume our food in silence, even though I feel that I have a lot of urgent things to say about the world, about people, and the hope for freedom. However, I feel tired and burnt out. The war is not over yet; we are still living in a state of eternal war and fear. The sad-eyed cook motions to us to bring our plates over. She piles more potatoes and eggs on them and cuts a large slice of bread for each of us. "Have seconds, boys. I can see that the regular portion wasn't enough for you."

The clock on the wall shows noon. I'd like to leave for the railway station, but I'm trying to figure out how to say goodbye to Bandi. As if sensing my thoughts, Bandi attempts a cynical nonchalance: "So, what are you waiting for? See you, and hurry back home!"

The beat-up train is twice as long as the soccer field in Üllői Street. The steam engine is puffing away. The carriages are already chock full of families with small kids, women in boots, greenhorn Soviet soldiers with accordions and firearms slung over their shoulders. Armband-wearing NKVD patrols scour the platforms, scrutinizing people's papers and rummaging through their bundles. I give them a wide berth.

Inside the crowded, drafty cars, two large women make room for me. We warm each other up, and even before the train starts moving, they offer me bread and sausages.

There are soldiers with bayonets in the station; the sounds of tearful farewells can be heard in the cars. Additional grey throngs of people surge toward the tracks. Miraculously, everyone manages to settle in the corridors, perched on top of trunks, boxes, baskets.

At last the engine is attached to the front. There's a lot of chuffing, wheezing and snorting, then we take off with a clanking sound. The train crawls along at a speed of thirty to forty kilometres per hour.

It is late afternoon when we pull into the north railway station in Timişoara. The refugee committee is located on the premises. They promptly give me directions, handing me a photocopied map and the address of the Timişoara emigration office. They assure me that the office stays open until 10:00 p.m. every day of the week.

Soon I am walking down Lloyd Row, now known as Piaţa Victoriei, or Victory Square, the main street of Timişoara, in the gleam of the well-stocked shop windows. With my weather-beaten face, frayed, shabby pants and shrunken knapsack, thanks to the Petrovgrad Disinfection Institute, I feel like an intruder, a pariah skulking in a sanctuary, expecting at any moment to be yelled at: "For shame! What business do you have here?"

On the sidewalk, fancy women with fur collars and stylish walking shoes chat as they mince along, and men in suits tip their hats every now and then to the people they pass. In front of the opera house, elegant Soviet officers exchange pleasantries in French with blond soubrettes. In the window of a pastry shop, there is a decadent array of mille feuilles, chocolate mousse cake and whipped cream–filled pastries. I am transfixed by the bewitching sight. I have never been to Switzerland, but I picture its towns to be as peaceful and clean as this one.

There's a Jewish subcommittee operating inside the emigration office. A lot of refugees have already arrived, including some from Bor. The way the subcommittee handles things is quick, professional and equitable: I receive a *dovada*, a refugee document, with the number 1486, a pair of socks, underwear and two thousand Romanian lei. In one corner of the roomy office, well-groomed, nicely dressed men and women are sitting in armchairs, conversing. A fine-featured older woman seems to be watching me attentively. She gets up from the armchair and heads my way. "I see you have just arrived. Are you from Bor as well?"

"Yes," I answer, somewhat surprised. I am no longer accustomed to being addressed in such a polite, refined manner.

"From what place were you taken, my son? I hope you don't mind if I address you as my son — age has its privileges, after all."

"I'm from Budapest, that's where I lived with my mother." Then, I don't know why I add this, maybe I feel the need to boast: "I was about to start university...."

"I'm Mrs. Gartner. My dear son, if you haven't got any accommodations yet, we'll be pleased to have you."

Auntie Gartner knows very well that I don't have a place to stay. It's obvious that she, like the others, came to the office intending to take a refugee back to her home.

During the trip to 6 Pestalozzi Street, the Gartner residence, in a genteel neighbourhood, the woman relates that her son and daughter-in-law are physicians, and that she keeps house for them and pampers her precious granddaughter. I find out from her that the Jewish community of Timişoara has remained relatively intact; then she goes on to say, "The Romanians didn't stab us in the back the way you were stabbed by...." She doesn't finish the sentence, perhaps because we have arrived at the gate, or out of tact.

Auntie Gartner leads me to the nursery, and the little girl moves over to her grandmother's room. I hardly ever encounter the physician couple. They work from morning till night, either in their office or at the hospital. Auntie Gartner informs me that I may stay in their house until I am able to return home. They will give me breakfast, but I should ask for lunch and dinner at the kitchen run by the Joint, the American Jewish Joint Distribution Committee. Then she adds that it won't take me long to learn the ropes, that there are a lot of refugees from Bor in Timişoara, and I will surely meet people I know.

In 1944, Timişoara has about one hundred thousand inhabitants. Half of them are Romanian, one quarter are German and the other quarter, Hungarian. It is a city of culture and peace, home to many Hungarian language institutions, including theatres, an opera, coffee houses, hotels, an elementary school, four grades of junior high school and a newspaper.

The spacious hall of the Joint is a favourite meeting place of the *muszos* men from Bor who flocked to Timişoara. Every day more refugees arrive, and every day there are some who leave, having grown tired of waiting. The refugees regale us with horrible stories about the world of the Lagers. They follow the daily news intently, and they are all worried about their loved ones.

The first acquaintance I run into is Gyuri Horváth, the cellist. I can discern both sadness and calm in his blinking, rather tired eyes; there's a faint smile on his lips. Gyuri gathers that I have arrived recently, and the news starts spilling out of him like out of the *New York Times*: "The situation in Hungary is terrible. The Arrow Cross has set up a National Calling to Account Bench. These 'Hungarists' haul Jews out of the ghettos[2] and murder them on the banks of the Danube, they reduced cities to rubble by gunfire. Air raids are taking their toll as well. Eichmann is in Budapest again, and he is organizing the deportation of the remaining Jews."

Where has Gyuri's calm look gone? His chest is heaving, he is getting more and more worked up as he speaks, but I interrupt him to quiet him down: "You are exaggerating."

"You think my view of things is too dark? The Arrow Cross men tear up people's protection documents and they drag our women to the west by the thousands. Just recently I heard on the radio that the victims are herded into cattle cars at the Józsefváros station in Budapest to be taken to Germany to build fortifications. Hand-in-hand with the SS, Arrow Cross men continue to murder people. They killed hundreds in Hidegség, eight hundred in Nagycenk. Unruly teenagers are massacring people in Ilkamajor, Mosonszentmiklós, Sopronbánfalva, and God knows where else. Do you still maintain that I'm exaggerating? Then listen to this: do you know what happened to our people in Cservenka? Do you know about the slaughter there?"

I nod my head without a word. I mention that in Serbia I heard something about it from the mayor of Rabrovo, but with no precise details.

─────────────

2 The Budapest ghetto was not established until November 29, 1944. Andai is likely referring here to other buildings in Budapest where Jews were forced to live at this time.

"Let's have lunch together," suggests Gyuri. "In the afternoon, I'll take you to the market square. There's a coffee house where the men from Bor have set up camp, and you'll learn a lot more there."

In the Joint's eatery, the food — potato soup and noodles with sautéed cabbage — leaves a bitter taste in my mouth. Everything tastes bitter, even though I'm terribly hungry.

I enter the smoke-filled coffee house uncertainly, even timidly. Three tables have been pushed together, and around them the men from Bor are poring over newspapers and magazines in wooden holders, exchanging news, looking at creased and worn photographs, drinking espresso, playing chess, arguing with each other and reminiscing.

I recognize some of the boys right away. There's Sanyi Szalai pushing up his tortoise shell eyeglasses. From the way he jumps up to greet me it's clear that he's sincerely happy to see me. "Have you heard anything about Miklós?" he asks me, hopefully.

I shake my head and say, "Nothing, not a single word!"

"And about Cservenka?" Sanyi inquires. "There was carnage, hundreds were murdered by the Nazis…at night I wake up in fear that Miklós perished, too. It's awful, awful. I submitted Miklós's Bor poems to the *Szabad Szó* newspaper, and they've already been published. I'll give you a copy. Do you remember when he copied them from his Avala?"

With tobacco-stained fingers, Szalai lights one cigarette after another. He keeps squeezing my arm; his hot breath seems to singe my face. He stares into space for a long time, then his gaze becomes questioning: "Tell me! Explain it to me! Why did Miklós make a copy of his poems? Tell me why! Do you think he had a premonition? His poems are like burning embers in my pocket." Sanyi rakes a trembling hand through his wavy hair and lights up again. "The shadow of the men of the first contingent haunts me day and night."

That evening, before returning to my lodging, I cannot resist the temptation: in the pastry shop I eat two mille feuilles generously sprinkled with icing sugar. Out on the street, shopkeepers are attaching padlocks to the roll-down shutters, while shop clerks and assistants are hastening home.

From the entrance hall at Dr. Gartner's, I can see a flickering fire burning in the oak-trimmed living room. Just as I am about to go to my room, the door on the right opens and a well-groomed young woman enters the living room. At that point the physician couple notices me, and the husband cordially beckons me to join them. Dr. Gartner is a dynamic young man with pleasant manners. Holding his glasses in his hand, he invites me to sit on a chair with a Gobelin covered seat. The other Dr. Gartner, his wife, is very pretty and is simply and stylishly dressed.

He tells me that his mother has informed them they have a guest; they are glad to be able to help me, and if I need anything I shouldn't hesitate to ask. They strike me as refined, cultured, courteous people; their manner is sincere and natural.

The likeable doctor tells me that he has met a lot of refugees from Bor in his clinic and at the hospital. He turns to his wife: "That reminds me; this morning my colleague Dr. Brück requested a consultation, promising to show me a medical miracle." Then Dr. Gartner asks me, "Have you heard of Cservenka?"

I nod, thinking, good God, this is the third time today I've been kicked in the gut by that infamous, hellish place.

"In the presence of eight other colleagues of mine," Dr. Gartner continues, "Dr. Brück brought in a twenty-five-year-old man from Carpatho-Ukraine wearing a yarmulke who was executed by the Nazis in Cservenka — excuse me, who thought he'd been executed. The bullet entered his neck, three centimetres below his right ear, severing the artery. The shot shattered his jaw, but fortunately the bullet exited near his nose. Zalman Teichman, that's the Orthodox man's name, plummeted into the corpse-filled pit as though struck by lightning. Blood was gushing from his wounds. More corpses were heaved on top of him, until finally everything quieted down. But only for a moment. Before the Nazis left, they threw hand grenades on top of the mountain of corpses. That's when a lot of shrapnel ended up in his leg. We all examined Teichman. I don't want to go into the medical details, but we all agreed that we have never witnessed such an amazing miracle of survival. In the medical literature it's without precedent."

Dr. Gartner's wife doesn't comment on the case. She gets up and, with a polite glance in my direction, tells her husband, "I think our guest must be very tired. Let's let him go to bed."

"Yes," I say. "I am tired and I have a bit of a headache too."

In the nursery I start sobbing. I'm wracked with emotion. I can feel the sickeningly sweet mass of the two mille feuilles in my throat, and I start throwing up. I recall that not so very long ago I had been dreaming about becoming a brain surgeon, Olivecrona's assistant or I would beat Jesse Owens's world record for the hundred-metre dash; I would speed along a Roman highway at two hundred kilometres per hour with Nuvolari, the famous racecar driver, and I would confess my love to Aliz in the sport swimming pool; I would bring Grand-mother from Transylvania to Budapest; I would be the next winner of the Nobel Prize in Literature after Eemil Sillanpää; I would be a champion of the downtrodden like Robin Hood.

And now, here I am in this nursery in Timişoara, staring at the azure blue ceiling and feeling utterly hopeless. I am weighed down by an intangible feeling of guilt because I survived.

⁓

New refugees arrive at the Timişoara train station daily. The latest ap-palling, heart-rending news is broadcast daily on the radio.

In the market square, with its many second-hand stalls, in the smoky coffee house, around the green-felt covered billiard table in the Szarvas café, beside the railway tracks and in the Joint office, you

can find the motley crew of *muszos* men from Bor with their haggard faces. They exchange shocking rumours, and every day they dish
up incredible and outrageous stories: "Szálasi and his cronies have
handed over an additional fifty thousand forced labourers to the Germans…in the Arrow Cross headquarters at 60 Andrássy Street, medieval torture devices are being used to make Zionists talk…killing is
going on in the ghettos of Pest…the Jews of the countryside are being
incinerated in crematoria." From morning until night, we plague one
another with this type of unsubstantiated news.

No matter how much we'd love to be reunited with our families,
for the time being there is no prospect of returning home. I'm impatient. Everywhere I turn, I run into refugees who keep parroting the
same refrain: the Allied armies are heaping victory upon victory; the
Nazis and the Arrow Cross are continuing their murderous rampage
all over the country. Newspapers are publishing special editions, and
sensational articles about the war can be seen in cafés and on kiosks.
People seem almost intoxicated when they read reports of the latest battles. The outcome of the war depends on blind chance. Each
power considers itself the strongest, and meanwhile millions perish.
According to cynical nihilists, wars — like epidemics — guard the
world against overpopulation.

I say goodbye to the boys from Bor: Szalai, Justus, Horváth and
the other homeless fellows who deserved a better fate.

After having enjoyed three weeks of warm hospitality, I bid
farewell to kindly Auntie Gartner and the physician couple. Auntie
Gartner's daughter-in-law gives me a hug and tells me that she is sorry to see me leave. Her husband, though, frowns, as I've taken him
by surprise: "Where do you intend to go in these turbulent times?"

"I don't know," I reply with a shrug. I realize right away what an
awkward, stupid answer this is. Quickly I add, "I don't know. I'm just
going…I think maybe to Bucharest."

The doctor shows that he's a tactful psychologist. He ponders for a
while, as if deliberating on a diagnosis, then fishes a prescription pad

out of his shirt pocket, writes something, and hands me the piece of paper. "If you run into any difficulties, look up this old family friend. Tell him that Dr. Gartner sent you."

With a faint smile and a polite incline of his head, the doctor gives me a brief handshake and leaves me alone in the spacious entrance hall. I look at the prescription slip he gave me, but have trouble deciphering his messy scrawl: Gheorghe Fesus, Str. Spătarului 7, Bucureşti.

I stuff the paper in my pocket, cram the copies of *Szabad Szó* that Szalai gave me into my meagre bundle and close the door of the house on Pestalozzi Street behind me. I am setting off in the middle of December, in freezing weather, under bare trees. In my light jacket, I quicken my pace along Lloyd Row, as I head toward the railway station. The sun has tinted the horizon with a pinkish hue. The fragrant, fluffy snow crunches underfoot.

After two days of jostling in a crowded, ramshackle and unheated train, travelling via Braşov and Ploieşti, I arrive frozen and shivering at the central railway station of the Romanian capital. Like a lonely exile, I wander around the streets of Bucharest for weeks. On December 27, Mr. Lache, the head of the Disinfection Institute, rids me of my parasites and gives me a stamped certificate to attest to it. Hooray! I am free of lice again.

Equipped with refugee papers, I traverse the country: Brăila, Galaţi, Constanţa on the Black Sea. Recruiting for Palestine. "Come with us! You will have a good life!" The aliyah steamship lies at anchor in the harbour.

I keep reading the issues of *Szabad Szó* from Timişoara. These lines from one of Miklós's Heidenau poems, resonate with me: "…on coals like Hell's, / if I must, amid toppling flames, and casting spells, / I'll make my way through; somehow I will break free; / if I must, I'll cling on as tight as bark to a tree…"[3]

---

3   "Letter to His Wife." Heidenau Lager: in the mountains above Žagubica, August– September 1944.

The October 11 issue of the magazine discloses details of the massacre at Cservenka. The article informs us that Béla Deszkal and seven other wounded men managed to clamber out of the pit of corpses after the Nazis had left.

I tear the paper into shreds and throw the pieces in the sea — let them float away.

No, I won't go to Palestine. I'll cling on as tight as bark to a tree and I'll make my way through.

Epilogue

I find out much later that for the men of the first contingent, who left on September 17, the journey home was brutal. I learned this from the professional accounts of several historians, the memoirs of a few survivors, as well as from the valuable research of Ábel Kőszegi and Gábor Tolnai.

Lajos Wintergrün, the first slave to die out of the thirty-two hundred, was buried by his comrades beside the road in Smederevo. Who killed him? Was it the soldier Szalai? Was it Ensign Pál? A shot rang out like a thunderclap. Wintergrün had picked an ear of corn. He paid the price.

On September 28 the true death march began. In Vojvodina province, the black-jacketed henchmen of the Deutsche Miliz, German militia, ruthlessly cut down the men from Bor. At this point, Radnóti and his pals had passed through Mala Krsna and Smederevo, followed by Belgrade. Near Szenttamás (Srbobran), twenty prisoners were murdered because they wanted a drink of water; ten more near Újverbász (Vrbas) because they were limping. The murderers slaughtered the lice-ridden army on any pretext: because they picked blackberries beside the road, because they pulled down their pants to relieve themselves.

Three kilometres before Jabuka, a hundred and thirty-three boys from Bor, reeling with exhaustion, were shot in the head by the Germans, put down like rabid cattle. Around Novi Sad, ten determined *muszos* men tried to escape. Their reward: an immediate shot to the head.

Sunday, October 8, during Sukkot, on Hoshana Rabbah, "the last day of judgement," the SS men used machine guns to shoot nearly seven hundred prisoners from Bor in groups of twenty. They fell directly into the forty-metre-long pit of the Gläser Welker Rauch brickworks in Cservenka. The deep pit had been dug by the Jehovah's Witnesses, whose religion forbids them to bear arms. Hungarian officers and guards assisted the fascists; those with more self-respect turned away. The prisoners took refuge in the kilns and drying sheds. They resorted to drinking from the slop in nearby pigsties and from the stinking swill of fermented barley.

When the machine guns fell silent, the SS men tromped off with the satisfaction of a job well done. Only then did the village folk dare to come out: in the mass grave five or six people were still moving. One of the *muszos* men managed to climb out by himself. The villagers rescued the wounded men and tended to them. I heard that Péter Szüsz was hidden by the Gyulai family in the attic of a farm near Kula and that György Laufer, who was wounded in the forehead, was also concealed by a Bosnian family in the Kula district.

In Sivac the slaughter continued. That's where Miklós Lorsi, the sad violinist from the Liliom restaurant, met his death. Our Heidenau comrade's treasured instrument was smashed to pieces by the guards. On October 31, in Szentkirályszabadja, a village in Hungary, Radnóti writes these lines in his final poem:

I fell beside him. His body — which was taut
As a cord is, when it snaps — spun as I fell.
Shot in the neck. 'This is how you will end,'
I whispered to myself. 'Keep lying still.

Now patience is flowering into death.'
'Der springt noch auf,' said someone over me.
Blood on my ears was drying, caked with earth.[1]

"Blood on my ears was drying, caked with earth." A simple little report on death. A cry of pain in iambic verse.

In September, Marányi and his thugs had hacked down a huge number of prisoners in Bor. After the relentless killing had gone on for more than a month, only half of the men of the first contingent from Bor were still alive when the group arrived at Szentkirályszabadja. Lieutenant Colonel Marányi, who hadn't been seen for some time, reappeared and issued his murderous commands. Uttering vile curses, Marányi called for the execution of a dozen prisoners in order to restore discipline.

Given the go-ahead by their boss, the guards began battering the pathetic wretches with clubs and rifle butts. Like the others, Miklós was very weak, his feet were swollen, his boots had disintegrated. Some men — exhausted, starving and barefoot — dragged their broken bodies along like sleepwalkers.

In the morning hours of November 3, they set off in a rainstorm for Győr by way of Bakony. Gyulafirátót, Olaszfalu, Zirc, Kardosrét are some of the villages the appalling bone brigade passed through. Sobbing and wailing, the local women covered their faces with their aprons and kept crossing themselves. The irate soldiers chased the women away.

Radnóti could barely manage to keep going. He fell behind and limped after the column. Near Győr, twenty-two helpless prisoners, Radnóti among them, were loaded onto two farm wagons. Then, on November 11 at Hegyeshalom, the rest of the staggering slaves from Bor were handed over to the Germans.

---

1 "Postcard IV." October 31, 1944. The comment "Der springt noch auf," spoken by one of the guards, can be understood as: "That one is still moving."

The unenthusiastic conscripts accompanying the wagons didn't know what to do with the miserable *muszos* men; the drivers were also fed up with all the fuss. The senior non-commissioned officer was trying to come up with a solution. The hospitals in Győr were overcrowded, and they refused to accept the extra load.

On the outskirts of Abda, the officer ordered the half-dead men off the wagon. He made them dig a ditch beside the pebble-covered road, next to the weeping willows. The helpless slaves were shoved to the edge of the wide ditch two at a time. The officer and one of the guards then shot the twenty-two forced labourers from Bor — including Miklós Radnóti, the Hungarian poet — in the back of the head.

Those prisoners with a flicker of life left in them would be swallowed up by the Nazi camps of Flossenbürg, Sachsenhausen and others.

∼

More than half a century has passed since these atrocities occurred. There are even people who don't believe that these horrible events ever took place, especially since the majority of witnesses are no longer alive.

My stored-up memories have become hazy with the passage of time. They have become distorted and there are probably some inaccuracies as well.

The Bor Lagers were burned down by the SS right after they were evacuated: burned to the ground. The veil of oblivion has covered these horrendous events. On gloomy fall evenings, I often think of the three thousand souls from Bor, especially of my comrades from Heidenau, who died a cruel death, and also of those who are still alive somewhere in this world, I don't know where. At times I still hear their sighs and screams.

Gyuri Gara, Ákos Grósz, Jóska Junger, Miklós Radnóti, Pista Hajdú — my friends' voices died off one by one. I stare into the void bewildered and at a loss.

I suspect that the few of us who survived could fit in the shade of a plum tree. The rusty wheel of time keeps turning monotonously. In the whirlwind of life, memories break up and are scattered around, like the yellowing leaves of the old plum trees.

Afterword

After surviving the Bor forced labour camp, my father reached Budapest in April 1945 and was reunited with his widowed mother and older married sister. He attended university in Budapest and completed a degree in history. He enrolled in night classes to complete this degree, since he had to work at various jobs during the day to support his mother, who had no income. After receiving his degree, he was offered a position as a journalist with a Hungarian newspaper. That's where he met my mother, who was working as a photographer for the same newspaper. He was also a freelance writer, and his stories were published in magazines and journals and serialized on Hungarian radio. My parents lived and worked alongside many writers, artists and journalists during a turbulent time in Hungary, when conditions under the Communist government were difficult and dangerous.

In 1956, during the Hungarian Revolution, my parents, who had only been married for a few months, left Budapest in search of a safer and potentially more fulfilling life for themselves and their future family. They reached freedom here in Canada in 1957, but at a very high initial price. Risking their lives to cross the Hungarian border, leaving their careers and beloved families behind, and not speaking a word of English, they experienced a life full of difficulties and homesickness in their first few years in Canada. They were no longer in danger, however, and slowly began to establish a new life here in Canada. My parents embraced the freedom and safety in Canada and enjoyed being able to travel, read and communicate without the frightening restrictions and danger they had left behind.

Within months of arriving in Canada, my parents took advantage of being able to freely cross Canada's border and were able to see places they had only heard about. One of their first trips by car was to Miami Beach and New York City. My father became a history teacher at a high school in a small town called Shawville in Quebec, and my mother started a photography business from inside our home. Over the course of many summers, my father travelled to Montreal so that he could complete his master's degree at the Université de Montréal and then eventually his PhD from Eötvös Loránd University in Budapest. My father was always drawn to the profession of teaching, and it turned out to be a career he was passionate about.

My father would usually teach his history courses without using a textbook, which is what made him an extraordinarily engaging high school teacher. One of my father's greatest joys was his ability to share his life experiences and wisdom with others, and he passed on his insight to thousands of students over a teaching career that covered more than thirty years. After his death, many former students wrote to our family, and the general tone to the tributes was the appreciation for his storytelling and how he was able to offer a unique perspective to the history classes he taught. Several individuals wrote that it was my dad who opened their eyes to the world, teaching them to never take freedom and democracy for granted.

Through poetry, journalism, public speaking and lecturing, my father educated not only high school students but young children, university audiences, members of various clubs and organizations, academics and friends. He never turned down an opportunity to pass on knowledge to others and answer questions about his personal experiences. It is also why it was so important to him to have his story translated into English so that it could reach a larger audience. For this, our family wishes to express our deepest gratitude to the Azrieli Foundation, who made this possible.

My father was an educator and also a student throughout his adult life. Although his teaching focused on history and the past, he believed that life is a wheel that turns and moves forward and that it was just as important to learn from others. Learning was a lifelong pastime for my father. He would spend time learning about not only academic topics but areas of language, technology, culture, religion and current affairs. He was extremely interested in the trends of the younger generation and went to considerable efforts not to judge but to understand and encourage young people he encountered.

Along with a passion for teaching and learning, family was of utmost importance to my father, and our family of four was always tight-knit. We had no relatives in Canada, and our little family was just my parents, me and my brother. We took several trips to Hungary together so that we could be exposed to our Hungarian heritage and relatives. I have no childhood memories of my father reading to me the typical children's stories that most parents read to their children. Instead, my father entertained my brother and me with stories about his boyhood and young adult years in Hungary. My mother would come into our room at night when my father was telling his stories and would tell him that it was late and time for us to go to sleep, but we would beg my father to continue, which he always did. Considering what my father lived through, one might expect that the stories would have been dark and terrifying to a child, but they were fascinating and full of twists of fate and even hope. I know now that these stories were his way of educating us about history. They are stories that I can continue to tell my children as well.

My parents lived a busy, happy and peaceful life in Montreal, Shawville and, after their retirement, in Ottawa. My father enjoyed spending time at their cottage outside of Shawville, where he could swim in a beautiful clean lake and read undisturbed for hours on end. My father read and wrote mainly in Hungarian, since this was the language with which he felt most comfortable. He used to tell me about the rhythm he could hear in the Hungarian language and he especially loved to translate and read poetry. In the room where my father kept his treasured books and did most of his writing, including the writing of this book, was a framed eight-by-ten portrait of Miklós Radnóti, the poet, along with faded black-and-white photos of his parents. Honestly, I didn't realize the significance of who Radnóti was until I read this story of his time in Bor.

My father remained very connected to Budapest, where he was born and to where he returned almost every year to visit family and friends. While growing up, we only spoke Hungarian at home and ate traditional Hungarian dishes. Many Hungarians and Holocaust survivors whom I have met have not shared the same desire to retain their roots, and of course I respect their decisions. However, I am grateful that my father passed on to me his love for his birthplace. On our trips back together, he showed me and my family places in Budapest and throughout Hungary where he experienced both joy and sorrow. There were stories about streets that instilled terror and places where people "disappeared." But I also swam in the pools and lakes that my father swam in and ate pastries in the same coffee houses where he ate as a boy. This was his way of teaching us that even through darkness and terror, life continues and lessons are learned.

In 2005, when my father was already eighty years old, he was contacted by an American film producer, Hugo Perez, who was working on a documentary about Miklós Radnóti and the poet's legacy. The documentary, entitled *Neither Memory nor Magic*, was released in 2007. The producers asked my father if he would accompany them and travel back to Bor in Serbia, to the site of the particular labour camp, Heidenau, where my father and Radnóti were taken. There is not much known about Bor and the satellite camps around Bor or of the horrifying events that took place there. My father did not hesitate to go back there and to participate in the documentary over the course of several months. I recently viewed the film and paused it when I came to the part where my father is standing at the site of Heidenau, where as a nineteen-year-old he must have experienced indescribable terror and suffering. I studied my father's face and wondered how he was able to return sixty years later and confront this site of former horror so calmly. I wondered what emotions he felt as he knelt down to pick wildflowers growing where there was once a slave labour camp, which he later placed on a memorial statue of Radnóti. I have no doubt my father would have said that this is history and our story to tell if we and future generations are to keep learning.

Diana Andai
2020

Glossary

aliyah (Hebrew; pl. *aliyot*, ascent) A term used by Jews and modern Israelis to refer to Jewish immigration to Israel; the term is also used to refer to "going up" to the altar in a synagogue to read from the Torah.

Allies The coalition of countries that fought against the Axis powers (Germany, Italy and Japan, and later others). At the beginning of World War II in September 1939, the coalition included France, Poland and Britain. After Germany invaded the USSR in June 1941 and the United States entered the war following the bombing of Pearl Harbor by Japan on December 7, 1941, the main leaders of the Allied powers became Britain, the USSR and the United States. Other Allies included Canada, Australia, India, Greece, Mexico, Brazil, South Africa and China.

American Jewish Joint Distribution Committee (JDC) Colloquially known as the Joint, the JDC was a charitable organization founded in 1914 to provide humanitarian assistance and relief to Jews all over the world in times of crisis. It provided material support for persecuted Jews in Germany and other Nazi-occupied territories and facilitated their immigration to neutral countries such as Portugal, Turkey and China. Between 1939 and 1944, Joint officials helped close to 81,000 European Jews find asylum in various parts of the world. Between 1944 and 1947, the JDC assisted

more than 100,000 refugees living in DP camps by offering re-
training programs, cultural activities and financial assistance for
emigration.

Antonescu, Ion (1882–1946) The prime minister of Romania from
September 1940 to August 1944 and marshal of Romania from
1941. Antonescu allied his country with Nazi Germany, aim-
ing to expand the territory of Romania, and was directly responsible for the deaths of approximately 300,000 Jews from
Romanian-occupied territories and at least 12,000 Roma. Under
his antisemitic, nationalistic and dictatorial regime, anti-Jewish
measures were implemented and tens of thousands of Jews were
murdered in mass killings. Antonescu did not deport the approximately 375,000 Jews living within Romania proper, yet he sanc-
tioned the deportation of hundreds of thousands of Jewish civilians living outside Romania proper to the Romanian-controlled
territory of Transnistria, where many either died in captivity or
were murdered. Ion Antonescu was executed for war crimes in
1946. *See also* Iron Guard.

Arrow Cross Party (in Hungarian, Nyilaskeresztes Párt – Hungarista
Mozgalom; abbreviation: Nyilas) A Hungarian right-wing ex-
tremist and antisemitic party founded by Ferenc Szálasi in 1935
as the Party of National Will. The newly renamed Arrow Cross
Party ran in Hungary's 1939 election and won 15 per cent of the
vote. The party was fought and largely suppressed by the regime
in the coming years, but re-emerged as a major force in March
1944, when Germany occupied Hungary; in August 1944, the party was temporarily banned. Under Nazi approval, the party, led
by Szálasi, assumed control of Hungary from October 15, 1944, to
March 28, 1945. The Arrow Cross regime instigated the murder
of tens of thousands of Hungarian Jews. Starting on November 6,
with the last group leaving on December 11, 1944, approximately
70,000 Jews were rounded up and sent on death marches towards
Greater Germany. Tens of thousands died or were murdered

along the way, and some 50,000 survivors were handed over to the Germans. Between October 1944 and January 1945, the Arrow Cross murdered thousands of Jews in Budapest. *See also* Budapest ghetto; Szálasi, Ferenc.

Aryan A nineteenth-century anthropological term originally used to refer to the Indo-European family of languages and, by extension, the peoples who spoke them. It became a synonym for people of Nordic or Germanic descent in the theories that inspired Nazi racial ideology. "Aryan" was an official classification in Nazi racial laws to denote someone of pure Germanic blood, as opposed to "non-Aryans," such as Slavs, Jews, part-Jews, Roma and Sinti, Black people and others of supposedly inferior racial stock.

Badoglio, Pietro (1871–1956) An Italian general in both World War I and World War II who succeeded Benito Mussolini as the prime minister of Italy in July 1943. In September 1943, Badoglio signed an armistice with the Allies, and under Badoglio's leadership Italy officially declared war on Germany on October 13, 1943. Badoglio was replaced as prime minister of Italy in June 1944.

Berlin A forced labour subcamp of Bor. Berlin was the largest of the Bor subcamps and housed the Organisation Todt headquarters. *See also* Bor; Organisation Todt.

Bor A forced labour camp complex in the mines (Bor Copper Mine and Metallurgy Company) near the town of Bor, Serbia, run by the Siemens Construction Union and the Organisation Todt. The complex included twenty subcamps, most named after places in Germany, Austria and Serbia, including the Berlin, Bregenz, Dresden, Graz, Heidenau, Innsbruck, Laznica and Westfalen Lagers. An agreement with the Hungarian government for 3,000 workers to be sent to Serbia had been signed on July 2, 1943, as per a request from the vice-president of the Organisation Todt, Gerhard Fränk. The first Hungarian labourers arrived at Bor by July 15, 1943, and a second convoy of forced labourers arrived in the summer of 1944; from 1943–1944, more than 6,200 Hungarian forced labourers were sent to work at Bor and its subcamps, which included Jews, Jews who had converted to Christianity, Jehovah's Witnesses and Szekler Sabbatarians. The labourers in the camps endured torture, filth and hunger. The Germans and Hungarians evacuated the camps in September 1944. While 200 of the most weakened workers were left behind and liberated later by local Serbs, thousands of labourers were forced to march in two convoys; the first 3,200 labourers left on September 17 and became victims of several massacres on their forced march, with those who survived eventually ending up in Nazi concentration camps; a second 2,600 workers left Bor on September 29 and were liberated three days later when their convoy was ambushed by Partisans. *See also* Labour Service; Organisation Todt; Partisans; Szekler Sabbatarians.

Bregenz A forced labour subcamp of Bor. *See* Bor.

Buchwald chairs Chairs made of light-coloured wood and wrought-iron frames on the promenade along the Danube River in Budapest. They were named after Sándor (Alexander) Buchwald (1837–1919), who furbished parks with these chairs and rented them out.

Buda The western part of Budapest, situated west of the Danube River. The area comprises about one-third of Budapest and is mostly hilly and wooded. *See also* Pest.

Budapest ghetto The area of Budapest in which Jews were confined, established by Hungary's Arrow Cross government on November 29, 1944. On December 10, the ghetto was sealed off from the rest of the city. Jews who had held "protected" status first moved into the separate ghetto known as the international ghetto, which was merged into the main one in early January 1945. By that point, the population of the overcrowded ghetto reached close to 70,000, and people lacked sufficient food, water and sanitation. Supplies dwindled and conditions worsened during the Soviet siege of Budapest, which began in late December 1944. Thousands died of starvation and disease. The ghetto was also vulnerable to Arrow

Cross raids, and thousands of Jews were taken from the ghetto and murdered on the banks of the Danube. Soviet forces liberated the short-lived ghetto on January 17, 1945. *See also* Arrow Cross Party; Danube River.

cattle car Freight cars used to deport Jews by rail to Nazi camps. The train cars were usually ten metres long and often crammed with more than a hundred people in abhorrent conditions with no water, food or sanitation.

Chetnik (in Serbo-Croatian, Četnik; also known as the Yugoslav Home Army or the Chetnik Detachments of the Yugoslav Army) First used to describe armed fighters in Serbian-inhabited areas of Yugoslavia opposing the Turks from 1912–1918, the name Chetnik was taken up again after the Nazi invasion of Yugoslavia in 1941 by various factions of resistance fighters all over Yugoslavia, but especially by those led by Colonel Dragoljub (Draža) Mihailović. The Chetniks, as a Yugoslav royalist and Serbian nationalist movement, aligned themselves with the government-in-exile and King Peter, who had left the country after the Axis invasion, and the Allies. Early in the war, the Chetniks fought against the Germans alongside the other major Serbian resistance movement, Tito's Partisans, but avoided large-scale battles against the Germans. However, these two groups were eventually in conflict with each other, as Chetnik factions collaborated with Fascist Italy, Croatia and even Nazi Germany, and the communist Partisans aligned with the Soviets. By October 1944, when the Germans were withdrawing from Serbia, the Chetniks had become a deflated mix of different armed groups engaged in diverse resistance activities. In April 1945, the Chetniks, with Mihailović as leader, intended to start a resistance movement against the new communist order in Serbia, but they were ambushed by well-equipped Partisans. The few thousand Chetniks who reached Serbia were eventually defeated when Mihailović was captured by Partisans in March 1946. *See also* Mihailović, Draža; Partisans; Tito.

Danube River The second-longest river in Europe, running through ten European countries, including Hungary. It is an important source of drinking water and mode of transportation for millions of Europeans. During the winter of 1944–1945, members of the Arrow Cross rounded up Jews from the streets and the nearby Budapest ghetto, marched them to the shore of the Danube and shot them so that their bodies would fall into the river to be carried away. A memorial consisting of sixty pairs of rusted cast-iron shoes was erected on the site in 2005. *See also* Arrow Cross Party.

Dresden A forced labour subcamp of Bor. *See* Bor.

Eichmann, Adolf (1906–1962) The head of the Gestapo's Jewish Affairs department, which was responsible for the implementation of the Nazis' policy of mass murder of Jews. After escaping US custody and fleeing to Argentina after the war, Eichmann was captured in 1960 by Israeli intelligence operatives and was eventually sentenced to death after a public trial and hanged in 1962.

Einsatzkommando (German; task unit) Sub-units of the Einsatzgruppen, units of Nazi SS and police that were charged with securing the territories occupied by Nazi Germany after the invasion of the Soviet Union in 1941. These mobile death squads, with the support of local collaborators, were responsible for rounding up and murdering over a million Jews and many others in mass shooting operations. They were a key component in the implementation of the Nazis' so-called Final Solution in Eastern Europe.

ghetto A confined residential area for Jews. The term originated in Venice, Italy, in 1516 with a law requiring all Jews to live on a segregated, gated island known as Ghetto Nuovo. Throughout the Middle Ages in Europe, Jews were often forcibly confined to gated Jewish neighbourhoods. Beginning in 1939, the Nazis forced Jews to live in crowded and unsanitary conditions in designated areas — usually the poorest ones — of cities and towns in Eastern Europe. Ghettos were often enclosed by walls and gates, and entry and exit from the ghettos were strictly controlled. Family and community life continued to some degree, but starvation and disease were rampant. Starting in 1941, the ghettos were liquidated, and Jews were deported to camps and killing centres.

Graz A forced labour subcamp of Bor. *See* Bor.

Heidenau A forced labour subcamp of Bor. *See* Bor.

Horthy, Miklós (1868–1957) The regent of Hungary during the interwar period and for much of World War II. Horthy presided over numerous governments that were aligned with the Axis powers and pursued antisemitic politics. After the German army occupied Hungary in March 1944, Horthy served primarily as a figurehead to the pro-Nazi government led by Döme Sztójay; nevertheless, he was able to order the suspension of the deportation of Hungarian Jews to death camps in the beginning of July 1944. Horthy planned to withdraw his country from the war on October 15, 1944, but the Nazis supported an Arrow Cross coup that same day and forced Horthy to abdicate. *See also* Arrow Cross Party.

Hungarian Revolution A spontaneous uprising against the Soviet-backed Communist government of Hungary in October 1956, the Hungarian Revolution led to the brief establishment of a reformist government under Prime Minister Imre Nagy. The revolution was swiftly crushed by the Soviet invasion of November 1956, during which thousands of civilians were killed.

Innsbruck A forced labour subcamp of Bor. *See* Bor.

Iron Guard A fascist movement founded in Romania in 1927, characterized by nationalism and extreme antisemitism. Between September 1940 and January 1941, Romania was ruled by both the Iron Guard and Ion Antonescu, a period during which Jewish property was seized, Jews were deported and anti-Jewish terror escalated. In January 1941, the Iron Guard movement was crushed when it attempted to overthrow Ion Antonescu's dictatorial regime. *See also* Antonescu, Ion.

Kaddish (Aramaic; holy. Also known as the Mourner's Kaddish or Mourner's Prayer.) The prayer recited by mourners at funerals and memorials and during Jewish prayer services. Kaddish is traditionally said by a relative of the deceased for eleven months after the death of a parent and for thirty days after the death of a spouse or sibling, as well as each year on the anniversary of the death.

Labour Service (Also referred to as Auxiliary Labour Service or forced labour service) Units of Hungary's military-related labour service system (in Hungarian, *Munkaszolgálat*), which was first established in 1919 for those considered too "politically unreliable" for regular military service. After the labour service was made compulsory in 1939, Jewish men of military age were recruited to serve; however, having been deemed "unfit" to bear arms, they were equipped with tools and employed in mining, road and rail construction and maintenance work. Though the men were treated relatively well at first, the system became increasingly punitive. By 1941, Jews in forced labour battalions were required to wear an armband and civilian clothes; they had no formal rank and were unarmed; they were often mistreated by extremely antisemitic supervisors; and the work they had to do, such as clearing minefields, was often fatal. By 1942, 100,000 Jewish men had been drafted into labour battalions, and by the time the Germans occupied Hungary in March 1944, between 25,000 and 40,000 Hungarian Jewish men had died during their forced labour service. *See also* Bor.

Lager (German) Camp.

Laznica A forced labour subcamp of Bor. *See* Bor.

Mihailović, Draža (Dragoljub "Draža" Mihailović; 1893–1946) The most well-known member of the Chetnik movement and generally considered its leader. The Yugoslav government-in-exile in London named Mihailović minister of the army, navy and air force in 1941, promoting him to chief of Supreme Command of the Yugoslav Army in the Homeland in 1942. By 1944, Mihailović had lost these titles from the government-in-exile and all support of the Allies, who had switched to supporting the Partisans. After retreating at the end of the war, Mihailović was captured by the Partisans, found guilty of treason and collaboration with the Nazis, and was executed in Belgrade on July 17, 1946. *See also* Chetnik.

minyan (Hebrew; count, number) The quorum of ten adult Jews required for certain religious rites. The term can also designate a congregation.

Mussolini, Benito (1883–1945) Prime minister of Italy from 1922 to 1943 and founder of the National Fascist Party. Under Mussolini, Italy entered into an alliance with Germany in May 1939, officially becoming part of the Axis powers in September 1940. Mussolini was ousted from government in July 1943 and executed in April 1945.

muszos (Hungarian; from *munkaszolgálat*) Colloquial Hungarian term for men in the labour service. *See also* Labour Service.

NKVD (Russian) The acronym of the Narodnyi Komissariat Vnutrennikh Del, meaning People's Commissariat for Internal Affairs. The NKVD functioned as the Soviet Union's security agency, secret police and intelligence agency from 1934 to 1954.

Organisation Todt A construction and civil engineering group named for its founder, engineer and architect Fritz Todt (1892–1942), that undertook major civilian and military projects under the Nazis. Organisation Todt began in the Nazi period as a quasi-governmental agency, but in 1942 it was absorbed by the German government, becoming part of the Ministry of Armaments and War Production under Albert Speer after Todt's death. The Organisation Todt made extensive use of forced labour during World War II.

Partisans The Yugoslav Partisans (officially the National Liberation Army and Partisan Detachments of Yugoslavia) were a resistance force in Yugoslavia during World War II that grew directly out of

204 IN THE HOUR OF FATE AND DANGER

the Yugoslav Communist Party following the 1941 Axis invasion of Yugoslavia. The Partisans, led by Josip "Tito" Broz, sought to appeal to all Yugoslavians instead of recruiting on an ethnic basis and fought to create a new communist state through unremitting war on the Axis. By the end of 1943, the Partisans claimed to have a force of more than 200,000 fighting men and women, and by late 1944 the Partisans had become the most effective resistance movement of World War II, able to force the Germans out of their country almost on their own. *See also* Tito.

Pest The mostly flat, commercial eastern part of Budapest divided from Buda by the Danube River. It comprises about two-thirds of the city.

quisling A person who collaborates with occupiers, a traitor. The term comes from Vidkun Quisling (1887–1945), a Norwegian army officer and diplomat who collaborated with the Nazis. Quisling was executed after the war.

Radnóti, Miklós (born Miklós Glatter; May 5, 1909–November 1944) Considered one of the greatest Hungarian poets of the twentieth century, Radnóti published nine collections of poetry during his lifetime, as well as a memoir; he also completed a doctorate on the Hungarian poet Margit Kaffka at the University of Szeged, translated poetry and wrote fiction. His early work was inspired by avant-garde techniques, and he was involved with Hungarian literary magazines and was friends with Budapest's prominent artists and intellectuals. Although he and his wife converted to Catholicism in May 1943 amid rising antisemitism in Hungary, because he was born to Jewish parents Radnóti was called up to the forced labour service, eventually being sent to do forced labour in Bor, Serbia, in May 1944. Radnóti was murdered on a forced march, and when his body was exhumed from a mass grave a year later, a small notebook of poems written during the march and at the labour camp was discovered. His collected poetry, including poems found in the notebook, was first published in 1946, and his poetry has since been translated into numerous languages.

Roma (singular male, Rom; singular female, Romni) A traditionally itinerant ethnic group originally from northern India and primarily located in Central and Eastern Europe. The Roma, who have been referred to pejoratively as Gypsies, have often lived on the fringes of society and been subject to persecution. During the Holocaust, which the Roma refer to as the Porajmos — the destruction or devouring — Roma were stripped of their citizenship under the Nuremberg Laws and were targeted for death under Hitler's race policies. It is estimated that between 220,000 and 500,000 Roma were murdered in the Holocaust. Roma Holocaust Memorial Day is commemorated on August 2.

Rosh Hashanah (Hebrew; New Year) The two-day autumn holiday that marks the beginning of the Jewish year and ushers in the High Holy Days. It is celebrated with a prayer service and the blowing of the shofar (ram's horn), as well as festive meals that include symbolic foods such as an apple dipped in honey, which symbolizes the desire for a sweet new year.

Serbian State Guard (in Serbian, Srpska državna straža; abbreviation: SDS) The Serbian military force for German-occupied Serbia from 1942–1945. The force collaborated in implementing the German occupation of Serbia, including running German concentration camps in Serbia. General Milan Nedić was the leader of the SDS, though the force was ultimately under the control of the German SS. When the Serbian puppet government was dissolved, after which Nedić fled from Belgrade on October 6, 1944, SDS units were also forced to flee and ultimately placed themselves under Chetnik command. *See also* Chetnik.

shamashim (plural of *shamash*; Hebrew; also *gabbaim*) Synagogue caretakers who assist with the running of synagogue services.

SS (abbreviation of Schutzstaffel; Defence Corps) The elite police force of the Nazi regime that was responsible for security and for the enforcement of Nazi racial policies, including the implementation of the "Final Solution" — a euphemistic term referring to the Nazis' plan to systematically murder Europe's Jewish population.

The SS was established in 1925 as Adolf Hitler's elite bodyguard unit, and under the direction of Heinrich Himmler, its membership grew from 280 in 1929 to 52,000 when the Nazis came to power in 1933, and to nearly a quarter of a million on the eve of World War II. SS recruits were screened for their racial purity and had to prove their "Aryan" lineage. The SS ran the concentration and death camps and also established the Waffen-SS, its own military division that was independent of the German army.

Star of David (in Hebrew, *Magen David*) The six-pointed star that is the most recognizable symbol of Judaism. During World War II, Jews in Nazi-occupied areas were frequently forced to wear a badge or armband with the Star of David on it as an identifying mark of their lesser status and to single them out as targets for persecution.

St. Stephen's Day A Hungarian national holiday on August 20 celebrating the founding of the state and the first king of Hungary, Stephen I.

Sukkot (also Sukkoth; Hebrew; Feast of Tabernacles) An autumn harvest festival that recalls the forty years during which the ancient Israelites wandered the desert after their exodus from slavery in Egypt. The holiday lasts for seven days, during which Jews traditionally eat meals in a *sukkah*, a small structure covered with a roof made from leaves or branches. The seventh day of Sukkot is called Hoshana Rabbah.

Szálasi, Ferenc (1897–1946) The founder and leader of the Hungarian fascist Arrow Cross Party, which actively collaborated with the Nazis in Hungary, notably in the persecution and deportation of Jews. Following the Nazi-orchestrated coup in Hungary on October 15, 1944, Szálasi was the leader of Hungary until March 1945 and continued Hungary's war on the side of the Axis. Szálasi had fled Budapest by the time the Soviet and Romanian forces had completely surrounded the capital city on December 26, 1944, and continued to rule over a shrinking territory in western Hungary.

He was convicted of war crimes and executed in 1946 in Budapest. *See also* Arrow Cross Party.

Szekler Sabbatarians A religious group dating back to late-sixteenth-century Transylvania, who were a small minority group in Hungary and elsewhere in Europe at the time of World War II. Sabbatarians were non-Jewish people with a Christian background who tended towards Jewish beliefs and traditions. Seen as non-Jewish according to initial anti-Jewish laws and persecution in Hungary, after the Nazi invasion of Hungary in 1944 Hungarian Sabbatarians faced much of the same persecution as the Jews of Hungary, with estimates that a few hundred were murdered in Auschwitz-Birkenau. Many Sabbatarians who were exempted from the antisemitic laws were nevertheless sympathetic to the situation of the Jews in Hungary and were sent to forced labour camps after refusing to serve in the army or take part in anti-Jewish actions. Along with other prisoners, these Sabbatarians were marched to Nazi concentration camps when the forced labour camps were evacuated.

Teichman, Zalman (1919–?) One of the few survivors of an SS massacre of 700 Jewish forced labourers at Cservenka (Crvenka), Serbia, in October 1944. Teichman's early postwar testimony of his survival was given to Yad Vashem in Yiddish and first published in English by Nathan Eck in "The March of Death from Serbia to Hungary (September 1944) and the Slaughter of Cservenka" (*Yad Vashem Studies*, Jerusalem, vol. 2, 1958, 255–294). According to Eck, Teichman told part of his account in conversation at the end of 1944 in Temesvár (Timişoara), which is where Ferenc Andai relates hearing his account.

Tito (Josip "Tito" Broz; 1892–1980) A communist revolutionary and the leader of the Yugoslav Partisans during World War II. Politically active since 1920, Tito became the leader of the Yugoslav Communist Party in the late 1930s. After the Axis invasion of Yugoslavia, Tito transformed the Yugoslav Communist Party into a guerrilla resistance force, referring to themselves as the Yugoslav Partisans. Tito was an exceptionally effective leader of this wartime resistance movement and was able to transform this force into a revolutionary political movement as the war ended. From 1945 to 1953, Tito was the prime minister and minister of defence in the newly created communist Federal Republic of Yugoslavia, and then become its first president in 1953 when he refused to fully integrate the country with the Soviet Union, remaining president until his death in 1980. *See also* Partisans.

trussing-up (Also strappado) A form of torture in which a victim's hands are tied behind their back before being suspended from a bar by a rope attached to the wrists.

ukase (Russian; imposition) Originally, a decree made by a Russian emperor or government, but *ukase* can also refer to any command, especially an arbitrary order.

Ustaša (Croatian; pl. Ustaše; insurrectionary) A Croatian nationalist fascist movement led by Ante Pavelić (1889–1959) that developed in the 1930s. The Ustaša was granted by the Axis the power to create and lead an Axis-satellite state, the Independent State of Croatia, in April 1941 after the Axis invasion and partition of Yugoslavia. Upon creation of the new state, the Ustaša declared war on the Allies and started a campaign of terror and mass murder against Jews, Orthodox Serbs and other non-Croats in the region; they also erected and operated concentration camps, including the large Jasenovac camp complex. Following Germany's gradual withdrawal from the region in late 1944, the Ustaše were eventually pushed out by Tito's Partisans in May 1945.

Waffen-SS Military division of the Nazi SS. *See also* SS.

Wehrmacht (German) The German army during the Nazi period.

Westfalen A forced labour subcamp of Bor. *See* Bor.

yarmulke (Yiddish; in Hebrew, *kippah*, plural *kippot*) Small head covering worn by Jewish men as a sign of reverence for God.

Yom Kippur (Hebrew; Day of Atonement) A solemn day of fasting and repentance that comes eight days after Rosh Hashanah, the Jewish New Year, and marks the end of the High Holidays.

Zionism A movement promoted by the Viennese Jewish journalist Theodor Herzl, who argued in his 1896 book *Der Judenstaat* (The Jewish State) that the best way to resolve the problem of antisemitism and persecution of Jews in Europe was to create an independent Jewish state in the historic Jewish homeland of biblical Israel. Zionists also promoted the revival of Hebrew as a Jewish national language.

Postcards and Photographs

Kedves Dezsőkém,

Nagyon megkérlek benne-
teket, hogy amint megkap-
játok lapomat, jöjjetek
el s hozzatok csomagot.
Bakkancs!! ~~két~~ télő be-
kecs kapca. Ennivaló
nem kell, még egy pár
napig vagyok itt, a többit
majd Erdélyben.

Csókollak,
Tegi

... az Erdély átköl-
töztünk más ü-
... Szeretető
... A batár ...
életbevágóan fontos,
hogy jöjjetek!
...

Feladó:
Kovách Les T.

Bonczi Dezső
vrnal
Budapest,
Mária-Valéria u.
7.

Postmarked: Budapest, May 27, 1944
To: Mr. Dezső Bonczi
Budapest
7 Mária Valéria Street

My dear Dezsőke

I implore you, as soon as you receive my card, to come here and bring me a parcel. Sturdy boots!! Winter duffle coat, foot rags. I don't need food. We will be here for a few more days. The rest we'll discuss in person.

Kisses

Feri

[Back, on left]
If by any chance we move to another street make sure to find me.
Unit IV
It is a matter of life and death that you come.
Sender: Vác
4 Kossuth Square
[written slantwise] Don't say a word to Mum.

Drága, aranyos Putyikám!

Nagyon búsúlódom, hogy annyi lapomra, nem jöttetek le meglátogatni s még egy lapot sem kaptam tőletek. Hogy vagy? Mit csináltok Pesten? Én hál' Istennek nagyon nagyon jól érzem magam, már mint egészségileg. Remélem társaság van együtt, csupa frontot járt fiú.

Nagyszerű az ellátás. Háromszor naponta étkezés, ki mennyit akar. Ma pl. marhafőzött volt burgonyával. Mindennap fehér kenyeret kapunk. Csudajó fekvőhelyünk van. Mindennap mehetünk fürdeni. Forró zuhanyozó és kád is van. Egy díjmentes üdülés az egész. Mindamellett, mióta itt vagyunk össze-vissza két órát sem dolgoz-

tunk. Egész nap pihenünk, alszunk, szórakozunk, játszunk és napozunk.

Drága aranyos Putyikám! Sajnálkozom ez volt az utolsó nap, amit itt töltünk. Valószínűleg messze megyünk utazni. Így ne aggódj, ha majd egy pár napig esetleg nem írok. Azért mindennap írok majd, hátha megkapom. Csókollak. Tibi

1944. máj. 26.

Feladó: Goldberger Ferenc
õm. Curia-szálló.
IV. szakasz.

Ngs.
Goldberger F-né
úrhölgynek
Budapest,
W. k. Ráday-u. 7.
f. 13/a

Dated: May 26, 1944
Postmarked: 1944, May [?]
To: Mrs. I. Goldberger
Budapest
IX district, 56 Ráday Street 12/a

My dear sweet Putyika! [term of endearment]

I am saddened that after sending you all those cards you didn't come and visit me. Moreover, I didn't even get a card from you. How are you? What are you up to in Pest? Thank God I'm really fine, as far as my health goes. I am in excellent company, [with] boys who have been to the front.

The food is top notch. We have three meals a day, and as much as we want. Today for example we had beef goulash with potatoes. We get half a kilo of bread every day. Our sleeping accommodations are really good. We can bathe every day. There are showers and bathtubs with hot water. It's like a free holiday. And to top it all we have not worked more than two hours since we arrived.

[continued]

All day long we eat, sleep, play chess, and sunbathe. My dear sweet Putyika! I think today was our last day here. We'll probably be moving to a more distant location, so don't worry if I don't write for a few days. But in any case, you should still write to me, maybe I will receive it. Kisses: Feri

Sender: Ferenc Goldberger, Vác Curia Hostel, Unit IV

1 & 2 Ferenc's father, Izidor Goldberger. Budapest, Hungary, circa 1916.

3 Ferenc's mother, Blanka Goldberger (née Grunbaum), and his father, Izidor Goldberger. Budapest, circa 1920.

1

2

3

1   Ferenc after liberation, wearing the Titovka cap given to him by Duško Milić, the president of the Kučevo National Liberation Council, and boots and a jacket that were a present from Auntie Sári's neighbour in Petrovgrad (Zrenjanin), Serbia. Bucharest, Romania, 1944.

2   Ferenc after the war, on his birthday. Budapest, April 15, 1945.

3   Ferenc (right) at an event for the sports club M T K (Magyar Testgyakorlók Köre) Budapest as part of a volleyball team. Budapest, circa 1950.

1 Ferenc with his mother, Blanka, and his sister, Rozsi. Budapest, 1946.
2 Ferenc's sister, Rozsi Bonczi, and his niece, Judit. Budapest, circa 1948.
3 Ferenc's brother-in-law, Dezső Bonczi. Galyatető, Hungary. 1950.

1

2

3

1 Ferenc and his fiancée, Eva. Budapest, circa 1955.
2 Ferenc and Eva. Budapest, 1955.
3 Ferenc and family after they moved to Canada, during one of his mother's visits
   from Hungary. From left to right (in back): Ferenc's wife, Eva; Ferenc; and his
   mother, Blanka. In front, Ferenc and Eva's children, Diana (left) and Tom (right).
   Shawville, Quebec, 1962.

1 Ferenc (far left) at a party with colleagues from his first workplace, Ciba pharma-
ceuticals. Montreal, circa 1958.

2 Ferenc (fourth from the left) with fellow teachers at Pontiac Protestant High
School. Shawville, Quebec, 1982.

1   Ferenc visiting Miklós Radnóti's wife, Fanni, at her home in Budapest. Circa 2000.
2   Ferenc receiving the Radnóti Miklós National Prize for the publication of his memoir in Hungarian. Budapest, 2004.

1 Ferenc at a National Day concert and reception to commemorate the 1956 Hungarian Revolution with then Canadian ambassador to Hungary, Dr. Pál Vastagh, and then Governor General of Canada Michaëlle Jean. Ottawa, October 19, 2008.
2 Ferenc in his personal library. Ottawa, circa 2005.
3 Ferenc Andai, circa 2007.

Index

Credits and Permissions

Lines from Johann Wolfgang von Goethe's *Faust* (1829) translated by George Madison Priest. New York: A.A. Knopf, 1963. Part 1, lines 410–411.

Lines from Miguel de Cervantes's *The History of Don Quixote* (1605) translated by John Ormsby. Project Gutenberg, 2004. Ch xxxiv.

Line by Blaise Pascal from *Pascal's Pensées* (1670) translated by W. F. Trotter, originally published by E. P. Dutton, 1958. Project Gutenberg, 2006.

Line from Gotthold Ephraim Lessing's *The Jews* (1749) translated by Coby Lubliner, 1999. http://faculty.ce.berkeley.edu/coby/jews.htm.

Line by Dante Alighieri from *The Divine Comedy of Dante Alighieri, Inferno* (1472) translated by H. W. Longfellow, 1867. Project Gutenberg, 1997. Canto 1, line 7.

Line from Virgil's *The Æneids of Virgil: Done into English Verse* translated by William Morris, 1900. Project Gutenberg, 2009.

Lines from "Mégis elveszem" ("I Shall Take Her") by Attila József translated by John Bátki. Thanks to John Bátki for allowing us to use his unpublished translation of the poem.

"Letter to His Wife" by Miklós Radnóti is translated by John M. Ridland and Peter V. Czipott in *Selected Poems of Miklós Radnóti*. © 2013 by John M. Ridland and Peter V. Czipott. Used by permission of New American Press.

The Azrieli Foundation was established in 1989 to realize and extend the philanthropic vision of David J. Azrieli, C.M., C.Q., M.Arch. The Foundation's mission is to support a wide spectrum of initiatives in education and research. The Azrieli Foundation is an active supporter of programs in the fields of education, the education of architects, scientific and medical research, and the arts. The Azrieli Foundation's many initiatives include: the Holocaust Survivor Memoirs Program, which collects, preserves, publishes and distributes the written memoirs of survivors in Canada; the Azrieli Institute for Educational Empowerment, an innovative program successfully working to keep at-risk youth in school; the Azrieli Fellows Program, which promotes academic excellence and leadership on the graduate level at Israeli universities; the Azrieli Music Project, which celebrates and fosters the creation of high-quality new Jewish orchestral music; and the Azrieli Neuro-developmental Research Program, which supports advanced research on neurodevelopmental disorders, particularly Fragile X and Autism Spectrum Disorders.